Hollywood and the
Military Bureaucracy

ALSO BY BOB HERZBERG
AND FROM McFARLAND

The Third Reich on Screen, 1929–2015 (2017)

*Savages and Saints: The Changing Image
of American Indians in Westerns* (2008; paperback 2015)

*Revolutionary Mexico on Film:
A Critical History, 1914–2014* (2015)

*Hang 'Em High: Law and Disorder
in Western Films and Literature* (2013)

*The Left Side of the Screen: Communist and Left-Wing Ideology
in Hollywood, 1929–2009* (2011)

*The FBI and the Movies: A History of the Bureau
on Screen and Behind the Scenes in Hollywood* (2007)

Shooting Scripts: From Pulp Western to Film (2005)

Hollywood and the Military Bureaucracy

Depicting America's Fighting Forces at Their Best and Worst

BOB HERZBERG

McFarland & Company, Inc., Publishers
Jefferson, North Carolina

LIBRARY OF CONGRESS CATALOGUING-IN-PUBLICATION DATA

Names: Herzberg, Bob, 1956– author.
Title: Hollywood and the military bureaucracy :
depicting America's fighting forces at their best and worst / Bob Herzberg.
Description: Jefferson, North Carolina : McFarland & Company, Inc.,
Publishers, 2021. | Includes bibliographical references and index.
Identifiers: LCCN 2021012479 | ISBN 9781476678481
(paperback : acid free paper) ∞
ISBN 9781476641881 (ebook)
Subjects: LCSH: War films—United States—History and criticism. |
Motion pictures—Production and direction—United States—History. |
United States—Armed Forces—In motion pictures. | BISAC: PERFORMING ARTS /
Film / Guides & Reviews | HISTORY / Military / General
Classification: LCC PN1995.9.W3 H49 2021 | DDC 791.43/658—dc23
LC record available at https://lccn.loc.gov/2021012479

BRITISH LIBRARY CATALOGUING DATA ARE AVAILABLE

**ISBN (print) 978-1-4766-7848-1
ISBN (ebook) 978-1-4766-4188-1**

© 2021 Bob Herzberg. All rights reserved

*No part of this book may be reproduced or transmitted in any form
or by any means, electronic or mechanical, including photocopying
or recording, or by any information storage and retrieval system,
without permission in writing from the publisher.*

Front cover image: *Sands of Iwo Jima*, 1949
(Republic Pictures/Photofest)

Printed in the United States of America

*McFarland & Company, Inc., Publishers
Box 611, Jefferson, North Carolina 28640
www.mcfarlandpub.com*

To the men and women of the
United States Armed Forces

Acknowledgments

Here's the part where I give credit to the various individuals and organizations without whom this book would be but a fervent dream—or at least a pilot for an unsold cable series; either/or.

First of all, I'd like to thank the wonderful staff of the Special Collections Desk at the Margaret Herrick Library in Beverly Hills for providing studio files for my research; these included Breen Office correspondence, production memos, budget sheets, scripts, synopses, newspaper clippings, pressbooks and ad copy for the various films I discuss. And even though I didn't see them this year, I'd also like to thank the folks at the University of Southern California's Warner Brothers Archives at their School of Cinematic Arts. In years past they have always been helpful; and though the archives were closed at the time we flew out to Los Angeles, I was able to consult the copies of production memos, letters and other studio correspondence I got from them in previous years for other books. (Never get rid of files, Pilgrim, it's a sign of literary weakness….)

I was able to obtain from Jerry Ohlinger's Movie Memorabilia in Manhattan movie stills of military and war-themed films. I'd also like to thank those *many* historians whose voluminous books I have pored over. I've always been a student of military history (not Caesar or Alexander the Great; more recent centuries), and I bow low to those chroniclers of history who have busted their butts to give us these well-written tomes. Thanks to them, researching this book has not only been a great learning experience for a high school dropout like me, but an adventure I'll never forget. (See Bibliography of these authors in the back.)

Last but not least, I'd like to thank (I'd *better* thank) my wife of 24 years and counting, my beautiful Colleen. She has watched with me many a military or war-themed film, from the World War I films of the silent and early talkie period, through the service comedies of the 1930s, and into the World War II, postwar and Vietnam era flicks of recent decades—and even their coming attractions! These viewings also include many documentaries from the various history channels, particularly the American Heroes channel. Colleen and I have viewed countless documentaries (and a few poorly done reenactments with lookalike actors pretending to be Churchill, Roosevelt and Hitler) dealing with the Great War, Pearl Harbor, Midway, Iwo Jima, Vietnam and many other battlegrounds. I thank her for her patience and endurance (isn't that patience?) and especially for the love which she's given me for far longer than the last 24 years.

I hope this book both informs and entertains you.

TABLE OF CONTENTS

Acknowledgments vi

Introduction: Evasive Action 1

I—Forward March: 1917–1931   5
II—Covering Fire: 1932–1940   24
III—Collateral Damage: 1941–1945   44
IV—Section 8: 1946–1959   78
V—Lockdown: 1960–1970   123
VI—Ceasefire: A Quick Look
at the 1970s and Beyond   167

Chapter Notes 181
Bibliography 185
Index 187

INTRODUCTION
Evasive Action

"It's a lousy war, but it's the only one we've got!"
—Captain Flagg, *What Price Glory?*

For the decades that the U.S. military has been depicted on American screens, the portrayal of the Armed Forces has generally been positive, and with good reason. Men and women gave their lives fighting for this country, and they defeated foreign and domestic enemies who were a danger to this nation, or to democracy itself.

Yet what of the flip side of military professionalism: those who used their position as occupiers to further their own ends, or used deadly force upon a helpless populace? Further still, what does it say about a branch of the service that covers up a crime committed by armed service personnel? Or that excuses a military blunder that resulted in a tragic loss of life? Usually, with the discovery of a Tailhook scandal or My Lai Massacre, denial and cover-ups were the order of the day with the U.S. military—as it would be in *any* scandal-plagued institution. Every branch of the United States Armed Forces has its own public relations office, its mission being to present these branches in the most favorable light. These PR extensions of the military, operated by uniformed personnel, have had a permanent, and sometimes controversial, relationship with the movers and shakers of that bastion of heroic fantasies, Hollywood.

Usually, whenever Hollywood made war films or service-themed dramas or comedies, it was a given that they needed the cooperation of the Armed Forces. This was mandatory; war dramas and service comedies needed permission to shoot on battleships, Navy piers, Army installations, forts, Marine boot camps, Air Force hangars, airfields, tarmacs, submarine ports, barracks, firing ranges, and even mess halls. Hollywood cameras needed to show all that hardware and to show it in an authentic manner. In the early half of the 20th century, second units would shoot camp footage and sometimes rear-project it with actors in uniforms doing their dialogue in front of the screen. Actors playing sailors floating amidst the wreckage of a sinking battleship would have such obvious rear-projection screens behind them—sometimes with off-screen techies tossing buckets of water at them—with the result that the scene wouldn't be suspenseful, but laughable.

By the 1950s, this kind of B-movie budget-cutting was being abandoned in favor of the actual fulltime use of military locations. *The Caine Mutiny* may have started as a bestselling novel and a hit Broadway play (*The Caine Mutiny Court Martial*), but filmmakers Stanley Kramer and Edward Dmytryk wisely "opened it up" by getting Navy cooperation to film on battleships and naval ports, and to use uniformed personnel. Audiences never knew of the behind-the-scenes bureaucratic pissing matches between Columbia Pictures and the Navy. Nor would audiences know of the Army's stubbornness in allowing permission to use their property to film *From Here to Eternity*, though they were well aware of the controversial elements of James Jones' emphatically *anti*-military bestselling novel.

The stories behind these military films, the willingness of the armed services to conceal their own blunders and pressure Hollywood into presenting a benign version of the American military, is at the core of this book. You'll see how Hollywood fully cooperated in a whitewashed portrait of the United States Armed Forces. This will be coupled with the retelling of actual military missteps, many of which resulted in cover-ups, denials and outright censorship on the part of the government, as well as superior officers within the Armed Forces. Seeking the backing of the military, Hollywood went along with much of this censorship. The military-industrial complex, a phrase coined in the post–Vietnam era (but originated by, of all people, ex–Supreme Commander Dwight D. Eisenhower), had been around *long* before My Lai, Ribbon Creek, Monte Cassino or any of the other blunders, accidents and tragedies that marred the image of an infallible U.S. military.

This book will discuss the major wars of the 20th century, as well as the shaky peacetime years between them; from World War I, when the Armed Forces realized that they needed to enlist Hollywood in its efforts to project a positive image of the military during wartime and increase recruitment, to the immediate post–Vietnam War era, when the film industry openly attacked the military for atrocities committed during the conflict. I will go into studio production files and correspondence between representatives of the various branches of the military and Hollywood filmmakers, and between those filmmakers and the Production Code office; as well as excerpts from the works of military historians, biographers, authors of military-themed novels, and entertainment professionals on the periods being addressed. I also include excerpts from the reviews of contemporary critics.

During the period from the Great War up to the Korean War, armed service personnel were portrayed, more or less, as competent professionals, with special focus on American fighting men being lionized as heroes. This also meant that controversial issues concerning the military, like racism, anti–Semitism, sexism, homosexuality, physical and sexual abuse, oppression of locals in occupied countries, bureaucratic cover-ups, and military actions that resulted in unnecessary fatalities would be *verboten* on the American screen. However, with the breaking of Joseph Breen's Production Code Administration dictates in 1953 (as well as the end of the Korean War), more critical portrayals of the armed services could be produced.

In the aforementioned *From Here to Eternity* and *The Caine Mutiny*, there were depictions of brutality and incompetence, respectively, though much watered-down from their original source novels. Yet both branches of the Armed Forces allowed these mild critiques because, ultimately, both films indicted flawed officers, *not* the system. However, just a couple years after these two films, Robert Aldrich's *Attack!* showed the officer in charge as a coward, with an imminent military cover-up in the works, to conceal the officer's cowardice after he is killed. In *Crossfire*, it is revealed that there was anti–Semitism in the American military, but the film indicts a bigoted sergeant, not the system; 11 years later, in the post–PCA *The Young Lions*, the Jewish soldier played by Montgomery Clift faces bigotry from his fellow soldiers, though with the usual vindication that anti–Semitism is *not* tolerated by Army higher-ups. Similarly, in *Home of the Brave*, the racism felt by James Edwards' private is delivered by other soldiers in his platoon, not his superiors. Quite a change from *The Boys of Company C*, in which racism is systemic, with African-American soldiers purposely sent on dangerous tours of duty "in country." In the film version of *Reflections in a Golden Eye* and *The Sergeant*, filmmakers brought up the very controversial topic of homosexuality in the Army; however, both of these late 1960s films were set "safely" in the 1940s and '50s, respectively.

Even when the military tacitly gave its backing, there could still be hurdles. The silent World War I–era *The Unbeliever* (1918) had full Marine backing. Its plot dealt with the Marines fighting the Germans in occupied Belgium, despite the fact that in real life they were never deployed there. Though *What Price Glory?* was a groundbreaking Broadway play co-written by a World War I veteran, the USMC bitterly complained about the portrayal of the Corps as a bunch of foul-talking, womanizing sleazebags, a complaint that colored director Raoul Walsh's sanitized 1926 film version. Though *The Green Berets* (1968) would be pro–Army and pro-war, the Department of Defense, doubling as film critics, *still* found reasons to nitpick, though apparently not noticing that the sun was setting in the wrong horizon.

During the post–Korean War era, we started to see psychotic soldiers. In the 1958 film version of Norman Mailer's *The Naked and the Dead*, Aldo Ray (who would be seen frequently in uniform practically all through the 1950s and '60s) is a bigoted and homicidal sergeant. In *Seven Days in May* (1964), there is the danger of a military demagogue taking over the United States. Military blunders resulting in loss of life, the abuse and physical brutality of men under ambitious officers, bureaucratic cover-ups, power-hungry officers seeking promotion or national acclaim, all these controversial elements were glossed over or completely altered by military propagandists working hand in glove with Hollywood—at least until the 1960s and beyond. In this book, I'll point out the instances of censorship as compared with the actual history; as well as the behind-the-scenes political maneuvers and backroom deals that allowed a sometimes fallible military to be depicted in the most favorable light. In the following pages, the reader will see how the branches of the Armed Forces cast a long, and sometimes dark, shadow over a film industry that eagerly catered to its every whim.

In most of the productions calling for military cooperation, there *was* the very serious concern of accuracy from the point of view of the military. The people who populated the Armed Forces' public relations arms weren't sinister individuals; they were, like the military branches they represented, competent professionals. They had a job to do: present their officers and service personnel in the best light. They also desired accuracy, though it would be more technical and logistical rather than controversial. No one was going to be critical of the decisions of their superiors, or the actions of the men and women under them, no matter how wrong. Yet the truth, tenuous as it may be, was out there; and as time went on, even Hollywood couldn't ignore it. For incidents of rape committed by American soldiers in foreign lands, they would give us an *Apocalypse Now* (1979) and *Town Without Pity* (1961); for every blunder committed by a naval commander, there would be a *Caine Mutiny* (1954);

for every vainglorious superior officer, we would see a composite portrait in movies such as *Attack!* (1956), *They Came to Cordura* (1959) and *Seven Days in May*; for every wild, hellraising platoon sent overseas, we'd see a *What Price Glory?*, *Full Metal Jacket* (1987) or *Battle Cry* (1955); and for issues of prejudice, there would be *Crossfire* (1947), *Home of the Brave* (1949) and *The Young Lions* (1958).

Therefore, this book is *not* about the bulk of the U.S. Armed Forces, the men and women who do their jobs with skill and professionalism (and sometimes give their lives). Instead, it focuses on the neurotics in uniform, the military madmen, the incompetent generals, the captains who sail over their own towlines, the dysfunctional soldiers, the racists and anti–Semites who "fought for democracy," the Few and the Proud doing things they wouldn't be proud of, the accidents and the cover-ups; the blunders in battle and the efforts to sweep them under the rug. I will also discuss some cliché-ridden musicals, mysteries and comedies, all of which promoted a benign, yet pushy, military who *always* knew best.

I will also examine films that were unmistakably *pro*-military. Though many of them were unfailingly patriotic and uncritical of the military, some films concealed military mistakes, misconstrued orders, tragic incidents that could have been avoided, or battles that went wrong; with a nitpicking Department of Defense and the film offices of the various branches of the armed services frowning on certain projects that did not present a spotless depiction of America's fighting men.

It was obvious (and still is) that the U.S. Armed Forces have produced literally thousands of heroes who fought and died bravely. I would never write a book that slandered their memory. However, being a democracy, America highlights both its good and its bad; those who won the battles and those whose incompetence dragged out the battles and made it harder to win them.

Incompetency and blundering was the last thing you could say about the American military in early 1945. As Allied armies were heading non-stop for Berlin, as my mom and thousands of others were being rescued by the U.S. Army from the Mildorf concentration camp in occupied Romania, my dad was crowded with hundreds of other emaciated people in cattle cars headed deeper into Germany. Fortunately, their Final Journey was interrupted by the arrival of U.S. Army infantry units, with air support provided by fighter planes and bombers from the Army Air Corps. The Army pilots had been busy bombing the tracks ahead, forcing the train to a halt. My father saw SS troops fleeing the train and getting strafed by machine-gun fire from the fighter planes, as well as their getting riddled by Browning Automatic Rifle fire.

I can honestly say that without the United States military, I wouldn't be here.

Nor would thousands of other survivors who owe these soldiers their lives.

So as you read this book about those military incompetents who disgraced their uniforms by their abuse of power, also remember those American heroes who gave their lives as they saved so many.

To them, this book is dedicated.

Bob Herzberg
Brooklyn, New York

I

Forward March
1917–1931

> "Rascals, would you live forever?"
> —Frederick the Great, to hesitant soldiers
> before going into battle at Kolin

George Kleine was a Chicago film producer and distributor whose 18 film exchanges were spread all over the Midwest and South. On April 6, 1917, the day President Woodrow Wilson called for a declaration of war against Germany and her allies, Kleine sent a telegram to Congressman Fred Britton thanking him for his anti-war stand. While insisting that no one wants war, the producer also emphasized: "Never has Congress, an administration, or a press so misrepresented the popular will."[1]

But soon Kleine was singing a different tune. On September 25, 1918, he wrote a letter to George Creel, head of the Committee for Public Information, the main government agency dealing with censoring anti-war material in both films and print. A good 15 months after America joined the Allies, the previously anti-war producer wrote:

> I am prepared to deliver my 18 film exchanges to the United States for the distribution of its films.... If the interests of the government require it, I would accept no further films for distribution from private producers, and refrain from further production myself, for the period of the war.[2]

In September 1915, Kleine wrote to his bank, the Union Trust Company of Chicago, arguing against a massive loan they were going to make to help England and France. Three years later, the now-militant producer gave any of his employees who joined the military and were serving in France letters of introduction to a Paris bank that effectively authorized these employees to withdraw up to 250 francs. He generously bought thousands of dollars of Liberty bonds and encouraged his employees to do likewise. In fact, for the duration of the conflict, Kleine was best buds with the pro-war Wilson Administration; and he wrote to the brass-hats of the various branches of the Armed Forces, George Creel's CPI and even Secretary of War Newton Baker, offering to use his films and exchanges to strengthen the War Will the president was insisting upon.

In the spring of 1917, with America's declaration of war ringing in everyone's ears, Kleine's transformation from conscientious objector to war activist would soon take shape on celluloid. Released to Kleine's theaters on June 10, 1917, *The Star Spangled Banner* became one of the first American films to connect the United States Marine Corps with the film industry, and demonstrated how the two could benefit each other. According to the IMDb, this lost film was 30 minutes long, much of it filmed at the Navy Yard at Bremerton, Washington, by director Edward H. Griffith.

For the Marines, their survival as a separate branch was at stake. Bridling under the control of the Navy Department, sometimes overshadowed by the Army, and not receiving as big a budget from Congress as other branches of the service, the Marines needed help; or more to the point, *publicity*. Riding to their rescue was, of all people, the Edison Company.

Thomas Edison, known worldwide as an inventor, had his dark side. Displaying thuggish behavior *vis-à-vis* the young "upstart" movie moguls who intended to establish their own studios, Edison had a more personal ax to grind (he never forgot that his commercial rivals just happened to be Jewish). Harassed by goons hired by Edison to disrupt their films, Messrs. Laemmle, Goldwyn, DeMille *et al.* followed the lead of groundbreaking filmmaker Francis Boggs and fled to Southern California to set up operations. Filming mostly in the wilds of New Jersey, the Edison Company hoped to save money and increase its prestige as the possibility of a war with Germany loomed. For this purpose, Edison purchased a Mary Raymond Shipman Andrews short story whose plot dealt with the American widow of an Englishman. She marries a Marine colonel stationed in France as a military observer; when the officer is called back home to be stationed at Bremerton, they unfortunately bring along the widow's teenage son (former child star and future character actor Paul Kelly). Though the widow and her new husband thrive at Bremerton, their son proves to be a major headache to cadets and corpsmen. Raised in England, the boy has absorbed an all-too-English sense of entitlement and looks down at the Marines as if they were vermin. He makes no friends among the eager and patriotic boys of the Corps. You just *know* that some incident will make the obnoxious little slug change his tune. Then, before you can say *Semper fi*, the boy finds himself dangling from a cliff during maneuvers. Despite the fact that they hold him in contempt, the young corpsmen do what they're trained to do and rescue him. This act alone will make the boy come to respect Marine traditions and develop a love for the land of his mother and new father. He soon has an American flag on his mirror beside the Union Jack and the French flag, a not-so-subtle commentary on the new wartime alliance. For Kelly, his anti-military youth was an interesting early role for an actor who would thrive in Hollywood for the next half century (and go to prison for murder a dozen years after the release of *The Star Spangled Banner*), culminating in his portrayal of a tormented air base commander in the hit Broadway play *Command Decision*.

The short film impressed the USMC; and when Kleine offered a film clip of Captain Edward F. Fuller (who performed in *Star Spangled Banner* and was killed in France shortly after the film's release) to the young officer's parents, the Marines took note. Edison and Kleine had done right by them; and with America now shipping men and equipment to Europe *en masse*, the time was ripe for a *real* pro-war film, one that would put Marine involvement in the conflict front and center.

Based on the allegorical novelette *The Three Things* by (again) Mary Raymond Shipman Andrews, Edison's new film *The Unbeliever* (1918) continued Hollywood's newly born patriotic zeal. Serialized in the November and December 1915 issues of the *Ladies' Home Journal*, the novelette was so popular that it had gone through many printings during and after the war. Andrews was born in Mobile, Alabama, on April 2, 1860, a year *before* the start of the Civil War. Though growing up in a culture of

Southern racism and disenfranchisement, young Mary was also the daughter of a reverend; this enabled the burgeoning author (who had previously written a famous story of Lincoln's Gettysburg Address) to instill in her work some now cliché-ridden doses of self-righteous morality. In *The Three Things*, this child of the Confederacy focuses on the issue of equality though, typically, it was about a young man who's obsessed with social position, not skin color.

Now with a war on, the company moved Heaven and Earth to get Marine backing for the production, promising the leathernecks not only a morale-booster for the country, but a cinematic recruiting poster for the Corps. On-location filming was approved by Marine brass—not at the base at Bremerton, but the actual USMC barracks at Quantico, Virginia. Uniforms were provided, and actual Marines wore them. Very much in the clichéd spirit of *The Star Spangled Banner*, *The Unbeliever* depicts a prejudiced young man from the privileged classes learning that fighting for his country makes a great equalizer, and how wonderful the lesson is learned when you're a grunt in the United States Marines.

We meet the wealthy Landicutt family, especially Philip Landicutt (Raymond McKee); at first introduced in his golfing cap and sweater. The smiling young man is then seen standing proudly, rifle on shoulder, in a Marine uniform. At church, his folks bemoan the fact that Phil has "unbelief," a grammatical error which should mean the boy has "disbelief." In other words, Phil doesn't believe in God, and is a snob towards the working class. Still, watching a platoon of Marines go through their marches close to his favorite golf course, Phil is anxious to get "into the fight" with the evil Huns. In fact, his hatred of Germans is almost as fierce as his hatred of the working class. In the novel, the young man calls Germany "[a] nation of vulgarians glorified by brains—which can't save 'em!" He also calls them "a beastly swarm of day laborers."[3] He learns about equality the hard way when his ex-chauffeur, now a Marine, is killed in battle. Nevertheless, despite the wonderful teamwork and good feeling among the film's Marines (played by real-life Marines), neither the Corps nor the Edison Company bothered to mention that there were *never any Marines sent to Belgium*!

Like the previous collaboration between the Edison Company and the Marines, the feature-length *The Unbeliever* (1918) was a hit, with no small help from America's leathernecks, here doubling as Hollywood PR mavens. "Generally, the commanding officers are with us the whole way..." enthused director Alan Crosland in a November 10 letter to Edison company officer L.W. McChesney.[4] Though the weather at Quantico didn't always cooperate, and the soldiers' helmets and uniforms arrived late, Crosland completed shooting on November 23 and a final cut was finished in early December.

From the halls of Detroit's Majestic Theater to the shores of the Liberty Theater in Seattle, dozens of Marines made personal appearances at each and every showing of the film. With theaters across the country decorated with huge American flags and red-white-and-blue bunting, the Corps did all they could to promote the film. Patriotic songs were sung on stage, and there were audience sing-alongs (including, of course, Marine battle songs). Doubling as stage performers, Marines sang, blew bugles, marched in split-second precision on stage, gave speeches promoting the aims of the war and, with the cooperation of the management of every theater where *The Unbeliever* played, set up recruiting tables in the lobby.

Apparently, the Marine spirit was contagious and worked in unexpected ways: Star Raymond McKee soon joined the Corps. The actor's fate (he died in 1984 at the age of 91) was far better than that of his real-life Marine co-stars: They were sent to France soon after the film was completed, and many of them perished at Chateau Thierry and Belleau Wood—a fact Edison later exploited as publicity for the film. In fact, the company later added a "Roll of Honor" before the start of the film, an idea approved by Marine Colonel A.S. McLemore. In letter to producer George Kleine, McLemore wrote:

> Such a picture should bring home to the audiences of *The Unbeliever* more vividly than anything else, what these men have gone through, who a few months ago "played" the game of war before the movie camera.

Their sacrifice deserved a far better tribute than as a footnote in the ledgers of the Edison Company's balance sheets....[5]

In September 1924, thirteen months after Calvin Coolidge became President, the United States Army and Navy were thrown into a panic. A new play, *What Price Glory?* had debuted on Broadway that leveled withering criticism on the conduct of the Armed Forces and the men who controlled them during the recent world war.

Worse yet, it was a comedy.

> A play of war as it is, not as it has been presented theatrically for thousands of years.

This line from the program of the play, one of the most groundbreaking works on Broadway, certainly of the 1920s, written from the point of view of a conscientious objector and a wounded war veteran. Esteemed Broadway critic Heywood Broun proclaimed after its September 1924 debut, "This is certainly the best use the theater had yet made of the war, and it is entirely possible that it is the best American play about anything."[6]

How did this theatrical powerhouse come about?

After the end of the war, young writer Maxwell Anderson was fired from the *San Francisco Evening Bulletin* for maintaining that Germany would never be able to pay off its war debt. After also being fired by the *San Francisco Chronicle* and *The New Republic*, the anti-war writer fled to New York. While still working for the *New York World*, he wrote his first play, a 12-performance clinker called *White Desert*. However, all was not lost, for the play was lauded by the *World*'s chief drama critic, a 29-year-old veteran of the Great War named Laurence Stallings.

It is said that Stallings, as a young ad man, was so taken by his own ad copy promoting enlistment in the USMC that he did just that, joining the Marine Reserve unit in 1917. As a platoon commander for the 3rd Battalion, 5th Marines, he fought with honor at Chateau-Thirry. But it was at Belleau Wood that the young man's life was permanently changed. On June 25, 1918, Stallings charged a German machine gun nest and was hit in the leg. Severely wounded, Stallings begged Marine doctors not to amputate his leg (tragically, many military doctors of those days opted for this cruel "treatment" rather than a slow mending and what we now call physical therapy). After being sent home, Stallings spent two years recuperating at Brooklyn Hospital; unfortunately, after his release, a fall in the ice forced doctors to amputate the leg in 1922. Many years later, Stallings had his *other* leg amputated as well. His collaboration with Maxwell Anderson put the young writer's name on the map in a way that most of the nameless heroes of the Great War would never experience. However, Stallings *never* forgot them. He proved that with a play that skillfully merged the grim horrors of war with ribald and black humor that had never, up to that time, been done before. Used to this melding of tone in theater, film and TV today, one can only wonder what audiences of the day felt when faced with this innovative approach.

Debuting at Broadway's Plymouth Theater on September 3, 1924, less than six years after the 11th hour of the 11th day, *What Price Glory?* is the sometimes episodic and plotless wartime tale of a Marine platoon garrisoned at a French village. Commanded by Captain Flagg (combat veteran Louis Wolheim, who returned to the Great War in the 1930 film version of *All Quiet on the Western Front*), the platoon awaits the arrival of a new top sergeant named Quirt (William Boyd—then the star of DeMille silents, and the future Hopalong Cassidy). Flagg and Quirt detest each other, having been violent rivals for women around the globe, wherever the Corps was sent. However, though holding him in contempt, Flagg has need of a good top sergeant. The two drink, smoke and carouse throughout the play, though their Heaven, as well as their albatross, is Charmaine, barmaid daughter of Cognac Pete; she is gorgeous and neurotically promiscuous. Indeed, in this day of the #MeToo movement and the promotion of female empowerment, one will probably be appalled at this play and its subsequent film version. Charmaine is portrayed as a cheating slut, plain and simple. Not too bright, she goes for anything in pants as soon as the two chief rivals for her affections, Flagg and Quirt, so much as step out of the room. Equally appalling is our heroes' treatment of her. They think nothing of trading her back and forth as if she was some kind of trophy, in games of chance, or drinking bouts, or anything else.

Throughout the play, there are moments of tragedy, with dying Marines and bitter indictments of the war and the arrogant leaders, both military and political, who sent the men overseas. Flagg's constant humoring of his general's harebrained ideas barely hides his contempt for this strutting, insensitive ass:

> Damn headquarters! It's some more of that world-safe-for-democracy slush! Every time they come around here I've got to ask myself, is this an army or is it a stinking theological society for ethical culture and Bible-backing uplift! ... The side-whiskered butter eaters! I'd like to rub their noses in some of the latrines I've slept in, keeping up Army morale and losing men because some screaming fool back in the New Jersey sector thinks he's playing with paper dolls.

At another point, Flagg, who has the most bitter lines, declares, "I corrupt youth and lead little boys astray into the black shadows between the lines of hell, killing more men than any other company commander in the regiment and drawing all the dirty jobs in the world."

The play was also controversial for its liberal use of "Christ!" and "God damn!" unashamedly sprinkled throughout its three acts. Theater critic Burns Mantle wrote that *What Price Glory?* "cleared the stage forever of the type of war play that is no more than prettily heroic. It represents war, especially the great war of ten years back, as it is in truth and in fact...."[7]

However, a reaction of a different kind awaited the controversial play from a more pertinent source: the branches of the Armed Forces that the play was about.

Having received complaints about the play, Naval Intelligence officers (the Marines were under the aegis of the Navy Department), as well as Army Intelligence and two Department of Justice officials, attended a performance shortly after it opened. Unlike Burns Mantle or Heywood Broun, they were *not* full of praise. An inspector named Peterkin (it's unclear whether he was with the Army or the Navy) complained of the opening scenes when the Marines boasted of their female conquests and quoted one as making a sarcastic remark about Marine recruiting posters (instead of "Join the Marines and See the World," it should be "See the Girls!"). He described Flagg as "disgusting" and "uncouth." He complained that the men "convey to the audience the lack of discipline in the marine corps," with the "top sergeant (Quirt)" clearly stating that he does not take orders from the captain "and that he does what he damn well pleases." Besides the insulting comments about the Army, Peterkin also found the numerous scenes of drinking "very disgusting, insofar as they tell all about debauchery and seducing, the language of which is all obscene." Again, what Inspector Peterkin considered "obscene" were all the numerous damns, hells and mentions of Jesus. Peterkin hated the drinking contest between Flagg and Quirt so close to the battlefield, and the fact that they "gamble in front of the orderlies in possession of the girl...." Though Peterkin had a good point about this blatantly sexist scene, the officer continued to depict characters in the play as having "no system, no discipline, no morale in the U.S. Marine Corps or the U.S. Army." He was also displeased that "subordinates do not have respect for superior officers," and that the play depicted the two services as "drunkards most of the time [and] subject to debauchery and seducement."[8]

The officers went so far as to contact the Secretary of the Navy, and then, on September 24, almost three weeks after the play's opening, with New York's police commissioner to see if the play could be closed down. Back then, there *was* a law on the books that stated quite clearly that no play or film could "bring discredit or reproach upon the United States Army, Navy, or Marine Corps." However, the services, to their credit, backed off, claiming that they were "not interested in censoring of any play now or in the hereafter being produced in New York...."[9] What they *were* concerned with, fully realizing that the play's popularity practically ensured a sale to Hollywood, was cleaning up the film version, something that would have a potential worldwide audience that would dwarf the Broadway crowds. In fact, it's quite possible that the cleaning-up had already begun while the play was enjoying its first weeks of popularity. The New York City of crooked mayor James Walker, despite His Honor's personal corruption, was far more status quo than people might think, with both the city and the Manhattan D.A.'s office possibly "leaning on" the supposedly uncompromising playwrights to clean up the material before the play continued its run and before the property was published in book form (as most successful plays are). Certainly, the brass-hat pixies of both the War Department (the Army) and Navy Department put forth their own demands to cut out many expressions of what they would consider defeatist or bitter comments from the play's soldiers. There's a good possibility that Anderson and Stallings were forced to cut some of the play's over-the-top dialogue in order to save the production, both playwrights fully realizing that, backed by New York City's obscenity laws, the military could have closed the show.

After purchasing the play for his studio, Fox production chief Winfield Sheehan ordered director Raoul Walsh not to "pull any punches." According to Walsh many years later, he claimed that he told Sheehan he was going to shoot the film version, not as a "war play," but as an "anti-war film." He further maintained that war "is a bungled mess," and that "the ideas projected by the characters is that war is a farce."[10] He insisted repeatedly that this would be his approach.

WAR IS HELL ... KIND OF: Left to right: Dolores del Rio, Victor McLaglen and Edmund Lowe in the film version of the hit play *What Price Glory?* (1926). Director Raoul Walsh removed the play's more controversial elements.

However, this was emphatically *not* the way the film turned out. Though Victor McLaglen's Captain Flagg *does* lament "There's gotta be something rotten about a world that's got to be wet down every thirty years with the blood of boys like those," and other dialogue attacking the hell of war, totally gone were Anderson and Stallings' bitter comments indicting *this* particular war, as well as the political leaders and brass-hats who kept it going. Gone is the portrayal of a pompous general who thinks that hanging up placards around the countryside will make the enemy surrender. Throughout its two-hour running time, men do things like cry out "What price glory now?" and other laments, but these poor souls are clearly portrayed as hysterics who just can't "take it." Michael T. Isenberg, author of *War on Film*, writes that *What Price Glory?* "was never sure of itself, seeming to condemn war at one moment and worship it the next."[11] Walsh never once addressed the change from the play's bitterness in his *highly* inaccurate autobiography *Each Man in His Time*.

The film opens up the play as Marines go from one port to another around the globe. We are introduced to Flagg and Quirt's (Edmund Lowe) violent rivalry over women. In France, the film reaches the point where the play began, with the rivalry over Charmaine the love-em-and-leave-em bargirl. However *this* Charmaine was played by one of Hollywood's most beautiful women ever, the immortal Dolores del Rio. Here, through the unreality of the silent film, the Mexican star is cast as a French girl; and though Walsh's film version retains the ugly sexism of the play, it also radically changes Charmaine's character.

In the play, Charmaine was depicted as an unprincipled slut who went from one man to another. However, with the beautiful and talented del Rio playing her, Charmaine suddenly starts siding with the angels. Though the stage Charmaine says that she's "been keeping house for one regiment after another," she also uncharacteristically laments the men who "go into Hell to die—and they are not old enough to die." In the film version, when Flagg is forcing Quirt to marry her, the formerly cynical bargirl rebels, shouting that she knows her own heart and refuses to participate in the fake ceremony. In the play, there is a baby-faced young soldier who is known as a mama's boy and who, predictably, misses his mom and his hometown. He dies tragically in the play without a peep from Charmaine. In the film version, especially with Dolores playing the French gal, their relationship is the most powerful one in the whole film. More powerful than the fierce one between Flagg and Quirt, and far more loving, despite the fact that it's clearly platonic, than the relationships Charmaine has with Flagg *or* Quirt.

With Flagg and his men practically self-censoring themselves, and Charmaine relating to the doomed mama's boy as if he were her little brother, the film widened its appeal considerably and was a worldwide box office smash. Walsh handled the battle scenes expertly, with the helmsman claiming (without proof) that Fox destroyed the homes of several people in Southern California on the block where the battles were filmed. At least one scene during the bombardments had more echoes from the past than Walsh cared to admit. Walsh was mentored by D.W. Griffith, and he clearly steals a scene from the elder director's *Hearts of the World* (1918) in which soldiers are buried alive when a trench closes in on them. However, outside of this bit, the wounding of the mama's boy, and the pyrotechnics, it's the only time Walsh focuses on the battlefield. In fact, regarding its low budget (certainly not as great as those for films with numerous battle scenes such as 1925's *The Big Parade*), *What Price Glory?* barely leaves the confines of Cognac Pete's or the makeshift barracks where wounded men wander in to die and others passionately cry out, "What price glory?"

Not all is grim in *this* War to End All Wars. Walsh lightens the play with some glaring "comedy" moments. Walsh had McLaglen and Lowe actually curse at each other on-camera during their frequent verbal battles, infuriating lip-readers in the audience. Ted McNamara plays the Irish Marine (complete with exaggerated funny faces) and Sammy Cohen (in a dry run for his Jewish soldier in *The Fighting* 69th 14 years later) plays the Jewish Private Lipinsky (played on stage by future WB contract player George Tobias). Also in the play (but not in the film), delivering its opening lines as Corporal Kiper, is future star Brian Donlevy, a fighter pilot in the Great War. Unfortunately, whenever the Irish and Jewish soldiers are on screen, whoever laid down the post-talkie music soundtrack decided to do it according to stereotype. When the Irishman does his antics, the Irish revolutionary, song "The Orange and the Green" is played. Meanwhile, Sammy Cohen's bits of business are accompanied by a rendition of "Israel" (movingly popularized by Al Jolson in a far more serious vein in 1948).

The film practically made McLaglen's career, as he would play variations of the tough, combative soldier for the next 30 years, especially for John Ford. His performance points up the fact that the actor was never served so well in his talkie film period as he was in the silents. In the final drinking duel, it is Quirt who captures Charmaine's love. But just then, the company is called back to the line, and even though the sergeant is wounded in the leg and limping around, he follows Flagg and his platoon back into the war. Unlike the Charmaine of the play, the French girl's tearful cry implies that this time they will *not* come back. Of course, they did come back; if not the characters, then the actors playing them: They made a series of adventures starring Flagg and Quirt–like characters. Walsh and others directed them until audiences got tired of seeing the same film over and over.

Six years after the end of World War II, John Ford, always jealous that *he* was not offered a chance to direct the original, got his chance to remake *What Price Glory?* for 20th Century–Fox. Unfortunately, it starred the *very* over-aged James Cagney as Flagg and Dan Dailey as Quirt. Since the property could *only* be successful in the era it was first performed, as a bitter comment on the madness of the Great War performed only a few years after its conclusion, the 1952 film was a box-office bomb. Certainly, in the shadow of a more recent world war, with a victory that Americans could justifiably be proud of, the remake looked like a pathetic antique. The play itself would be condemned to the dustbin of theatrical history, its material so symbolic of a certain time and place that it is *never* revived.

While the assorted complaints, cover-ups and controversy was going on over a hit Broadway play about the wartime Marines and its film version, other, more tragic events were occurring. In the autumn of 1925, as *What Price Glory?* was still enjoying its healthy run and the film version had yet to see the light of day, the Corps' sister branch, the Navy, was going through its own turmoil. On the night of September 25, near Block Island (14 miles east of Montauk Point, Long Island, and 13 miles south of Rhode Island), one of two tragedies occurred that would shake the USN to its core. The USS-*51* submarine, or the *S-51*, was surfacing in Block Island Sound with its running lights on when it was approached by a merchant steamer, the *City of Rome*. To the captain and navigator of the *City of Rome*, all they saw was a single masthead light popping up out of the mists. However, the men of the *S-51* were able to make out far more details. They could clearly see the steamer's masthead light and its bright sidelights, *but* according to the rules of the road, or in this case the sea, the *S-51* remained on course, not giving way. They didn't understand that the *City of Rome still* couldn't make out what was in front of them until they got closer. Like a cranky motorist, the sub was fully expecting *the other guy* to give way. By the time the steamer finally made out the sub's bright red sidelights, it was too late. Though the *City of Rome* backed its engines, the steamer struck the *S-51* full force. Reversing engines and then attempting to steer away is no easy move for a large seagoing vessel. Imagine braking an 18-wheeler on an interstate highway—except that this was on water—and you get the idea. Only three of the 39 men aboard the *S-51* were able to abandon ship before the damaged sub sank to the bottom.

The courts found the *City of Rome* at fault for not reducing its speed, though it had certainly tried. However, the Circuit Court of Appeals found the *S-51* at fault for having improper lights. The USN responded that the *S-51* was a special kind of warship that didn't have to adhere to "the rules of the road," and that the service had no legal compunction to obey the marine laws followed by civilian shipping. The court, not to be outdone in a territorial pissing match by the USN brass-hats, replied that Navy submarines "should confine their operations to waters not being traversed by other ships." With the Navy's prestige on the line, already forgotten was the tragic loss of 36 young men who went to a watery grave.

This horrible calamity would pale in comparison to the next naval disaster to strike at the heart of the USN.

On December 17, 1927, the USS *S-4*, an eight-year-old Class S submarine, was submerged at Wood End, off the coast of Provincetown, Massachusetts, conducting routine tests in speed and maneuverability. Clearly marked white buoys bobbed on the surface. But this quite normal naval operation was about to meet another vessel which was on anything *but* normal operations. Heading southwest at 18 knots was a Coast Guard destroyer, the USCGC *Hiram Paulding* (*CG-17*). It was 1927 in Prohibition-era America, where Presidents Harding, Coolidge and Hoover maintained that the country would remain dry for the duration of their terms. Like many a Coast Guard vessel—and, for that matter, *Navy* vessel—the aim of the armed services, especially at sea, was to blockade all rum-running vessels and confiscate their cargo. In fact, the *Paulding* itself, which was fully armed, had been one of a half-dozen armed vessels loaned to the Coast Guard by the Navy for "finding and keeping under surveillance vessels suspected of importing liquor."[12] Since gangsters didn't exactly give up their illegal hooch willingly, in this case, the Coast Guard sent an armed destroyer to block shipments of booze from getting into Boston proper. Unfortunately, it wasn't Capone or the Purple Gang who were going to suffer for this day's work.

At 3:37 p.m., the *S-4* commenced to surface, causing the *Paulding*'s officer of the deck to shout, "Hard astern! Full right rudder!" The sub had been rising fast when it was spotted a mere 75 yards off the *Paulding*'s port bow. As in the case of the *S-51*, the warning was acted upon much too late. The *Paulding* rammed the *S-4* bow and went deep into it, punching two large holes into its hull in the process, one in the ballast tank and one in the pressure hull, striking it just forward of the four-inch gun on its starboard side. Blood-freezing water rushed through the sub's gaping holes; within minutes, she heeled to port and water rapidly filled its bow. At 3:50, the Boston Navy Yard commandant received this urgent message from Lieutenant Commander John S. Baylis of the *Paulding*: "Rammed and sank unknown submarine off Wood End, Provincetown."[13] Before the radio message left the *Paulding*, the ship's lifeboats had been lowered. Unfortunately, no member of the crew on the *S-4* was able to use them. Finding nothing before them but a small oil slick, the *Paulding*'s crew marked the spot with a buoy.

Meanwhile, 110 feet down on the bottom of the Atlantic, beleaguered crewmen in the *S-4*'s battery compartment tried to stuff clothing into the gaping two-foot gashes in the hull, to no avail. Thirty-four of the 40 men were in control room positions, the engine room and the motor room, while six others were trapped in the torpedo room. Then the rushing gallons of salt water mixed with battery acid and formed deadly chlorine gas; if water hadn't already filled any spaces left in the flooding submarine, the chlorine gas quickly filled the only breathable spaces left. The freezing water soon shorted the sub's switchboard, destroying all communication to the surface and cutting power as well, leaving the survivors in the dark as the *S-4* filled with freezing water and chlorine gas. At 8:00 the next morning, a rescue ship, the USS *Falcon*, arrived in Provincetown to pick up ten Navy divers. By the time they arrived at the spot of the sinking, the boats that carried the divers, as well as the one that was able to get a grappling hook onto the sunken sub, were buffeted about in freezing, rolling waters. At 1:45 p.m., veteran diver Thomas Eadie went below and spotted the sub in five minutes. The 34 men in the engine and motor rooms had not survived the night. Eadie banged on the hull near the torpedo room and carried on a "conversation" with the six survivors in code.

The messages were heartbreaking: "Is there any hope?" "There is hope," answered Eadie.[14] Later in the afternoon on the 18th, as a storm raged on the surface, an exhausted Eadie was able to save the life of diver Fred Michels, whose air hose was fouled; for saving Michels, Eadie received the Medal of Honor and the Navy Cross. (He later wrote an acclaimed book on his life's work, *I Like Diving*.) That night, as a storm made things tough for the crew and divers of the *Falcon*, another message was "sent" to Fitch through the *S-4* hull: "Lt. Fitch, your wife and mother constantly praying for you."[15]

When the weather finally improved two days later, a diver went down to tap a message on the *S-4* hull. This time there was no answer. Nor would there ever be. On December 23, six days after it was rammed, all hands were declared dead. While it was still submerged, the Navy was able to determine that the carbon dioxide level aboard the sub was at seven percent; no human being could have survived.

Many of the people who had helped with the salvage of the *S-51* two years before returned to raise the *S-4*, including future Naval author Commander Edward Ellsberg and then–Captain Ernest J. King, future admiral of the Pacific fleet and naval commander during World War II. It was King who reportedly drafted the reply to the trapped Lt. Fitch that there was still hope. The rescue effort itself was under the command of the chief of the Navy's Control Force (which encompassed Class-S submarines), Admiral Frank H. Brumby.

The Navy was now facing yet another Court of Inquiry. It seems that lookouts from the Coast Guard station at Wood End were able to see the *S-4* going through its test run—yet the Navy had not informed them of it. In fact, outside of the Wood End lookouts, neither the Navy, nor the Coast Guard, was aware that they each had a vessel in the vicinity, creating the chance of a collision. Though the *S-4* was careful to avoid all surface craft (as all Navy submarines usually do), in this case, several factors worked against them. One was the harsh weather, which would have caused much concern for larger subs and surface craft, with turbulent waters buffeting all ships in the area. By the time the *Falcon* and other ships arrived, storms were seriously impeding the rescue efforts of Navy divers and salvage teams. Another factor was that S-Class subs like the *S-4* were purposely designed and painted so that they could see, but not *be* seen.

The blame for the collision (but not the guilt) was ultimately fixed upon *S-4* Commander Roy K. Jones for his failure to take evasive action after becoming aware of the *Paulding*'s presence. Of course, Jones was dead, so assigning blame to him was easy. Next on the list to blame for the tragedy was Admiral Brumby: He had ordered air hoses down to the *S-4* to fill its ballast tanks so the trapped men could breathe, but both the chlorine gas and the rushing floodwaters had sucked out what air was left. Not only was Brumby blamed by the public and the newspapers for this failure, but they also criticized his decision to order the *Falcon* back into Provincetown Harbor to ride out the storm, which lasted for several days. It turned out that Brumby was *not* very knowledgeable about either the rescue operations he was supposedly in charge of, or the operations of the submarine service itself. "Ask the technical people," he said, under oath. "I am not familiar with the details of the construction of submarines, but those who were there thought the steps being taken were the proper ones...." Yet the result of Brumby's "proper steps" resulted in the deaths of 40 men. The court ruled that Brumby should be removed as head of the Control Force since he obviously had little knowledge of submarines, salvage operations or rescue efforts. Secretary of the Navy Curtis D. Wilbur couldn't fathom (pun intended) how the court could praise the rescue efforts, yet criticize its commander, and he struck down any talk of having Brumby removed from his post. It was also determined that Brumby's previously impeccable record of service (31-plus years) far outshone any "errors or oversights or failures" that could be inferred from his testimony.[16]

In other words, despite the fact that the head of the Court of Inquiry, Rear Admiral Richard H. Jackson, recommended Brumby's removal, the Navy ultimately protected its own.

In the Navy service film of the coming years, the 39 men of the *S-51* and the 40 men of the *S-4* hovered over the U.S. Navy and their dealings with Hollywood like a black cloud. Off screen, however, there was much to commend. Communication was improved between the USN and the Coast Guard concerning ship traffic, with much exchange of precious charts and schedules, as well as the Navy coming up with valuable inventions like the Mumford lung and the McCann diving bell (which aided in the rescue of sailors in the USS *Squalus* in 1939).

But despite these improvements which would ordinarily instill confidence in an agency, government or otherwise, the USN continued to frown on any effort by Hollywood to recreate the disasters of 1925 and 1927. Instead, when these tragedies *were* used as plot devices, it would be individual human error that would cause the disasters, *not* a lack of planning, command failures, poor communication between the services, or system-wide bureaucratic turf wars.

From then on, the Navy would be on the alert for any effort to depict these tragedies on screen just as much as they would now look out for submarines and cruisers approaching each other in the fog.

After the Navy suffered a black eye, the Marines stepped in, if only temporarily, to grab the spotlight. In December 1926, MGM, the same studio that made *The Big Parade*, released a film that was one of the first to depict a tough Marine sergeant turning young, fresh-faced recruits into fighting machines. What was unusual about this groundbreaking motion picture was that it starred a cinematic icon then known mainly as a horror star.

Lon Chaney was one of the greatest film actors ever. Known around the world as the Man of a Thousand Faces, he continually tormented himself as he used his own innovative makeup and costume expertise to transform himself into every sort of handicapped or physically challenged example of heartbreaking humanity an actor could play up to that time. To this very day, *no one* has approached Chaney's innate ability to play so many physically different human beings: He was in wheelchairs, he walked on stumps, he had no arms, he had a hump on his back, or his face was so hideous that he needed to hide it behind a mask. He also played other ethnicities and nationalities, but usually with great sympathy. He played gangsters and killers, stranglers and mad scientists, clowns and vengeance-crazed fiends. But Chaney the actor always let you see the reasons for his madness, the heartbreak behind even the most physically repulsive criminal, the set of twisted principles driving his deformed outlaws.

Another strong element in Chaney's films was his characters' persistent unrequited love for the gorgeous heroine. No matter whom he played, clown, killer, Paris phantom, hunchback or Russian peasant, Chaney's characters almost always gave their lives to save the heroine and make sure she could end up with the handsome hero, always eventually seeing himself, for one reason or another, as physically and morally inferior to the good-looking but unbearably vacuous leading man.

Under contract to MGM in the 1920s, Chaney was cast in a role that probably surprised his fans just a year after his performance in *The Phantom of the Opera*. Expecting another facially deformed fiend or wheelchair-bound criminal boss, his fans were shocked when the Man of a Thousand Faces was signed to play a member of the United States Marine Corps.

Tell It to the Marines told the story of a soft-living playboy who becomes a Marine recruit, and the veteran sergeant who toughens him up and makes him a man. Cast against type, Chaney excelled as the sergeant who, basically, looks like everyone else. Chaney was not only bereft of his usual face-altering makeup, he didn't put on *any* makeup for the camera. He felt that to do so would ruin the documentary-like feel of the film. With the exception of Chaney's tough non-com, the plot of *Tell It to the Marines* could have easily been taken out of any one of his "love triangle" films where he adores the heroine, but she really loves the good-looking lead—thus, *not* exactly a film with a documentary-like feel.

The plot is simple. Robert "Skeet" Burns (William Haines) joins the Marines merely to get a free train ride to San Diego (go figure). The happy-go-lucky young man is in the charge of veteran ballbuster Sgt. O'Hara (no first name, and played by Chaney). At the base, Skeet meets cute Navy nurse Norma Dale (Eleanor Boardman), but he is so full of himself that his overtures to her fail miserably. Also, to his horror, he finds that O'Hara loves the nurse as well. Throughout the film, Skeet must give up his own self-involvement and learn the Marine Way. Though Norma cold-shoulders him through most of the film, she, of course, really loves him. When the Marines are called to Tondo Island, a place that's "six miles this side of Hell," Skeet rejects a come-on by a native babe because he's still loyal to Norma. The Marines next arrive in China's Hangechow Province to save the city from both an epidemic and bandits (of course, Norma is there too), and Skeet rises to the occasion. Trapped on a bridge with

MAN OF A THOUSAND UNIFORMS: Marine recruit William Haines (left) gets a sour look from the great Lon Chaney in *Tell It to the Marines* (1926). Chaney considered his tough Marine, Sgt. O'Hara, his favorite role.

O'Hara and ordered to leave, the young man remains with his tormentor and the two leathernecks fight off the bandits until they're rescued by a platoon of Marines.

At the end of Skeet's four-year enlistment, he and Norma are going to be married and live on a ranch. Though Skeet invites O'Hara in as his partner, the sergeant refuses to be a fifth wheel, telling them that he's sticking with the Corps. After they depart, we see O'Hara about to drill his men—but with tears in his eyes.

Tell It to the Marines helped crystallize the now-clichéd plot of a cynical, flippant young recruit joining up and then having his branch of the armed services make him a man. Often, the sergeant-figure would be a towering, impressive and usually harsh veteran played by a charismatic actor (John Wayne in *Sands of Iwo Jima*, Jack Webb in *The D.I.*; to a lesser degree, Murray Hamilton in *The Girl He Left Behind*). Chaney more than fits the bill of charisma, as well as the threat of physical violence lurking underneath, to show the young upstart that the Corps knows best. However, Chaney the actor never lets you forget the heartbreak behind the gruff exterior, as when Norma cries on his shoulder about Skeet. She doesn't see his hand reaching out behind her back; he wants to embrace her in return, but he doesn't dare, now that he knows the score.

Shot on location at the Marine Corps Recruit Depot at San Diego, *Tell It to the Marines* had an actual Marine hero backing the production. Chaney befriended the base's commander, General Smedley D. Butler (later to be major general, then the USMC's highest rank), whom MGM had hired as technical advisor. Butler had been a major in charge of the 3rd Battalion, 1st Marines in Panama from 1909 to 1914, and that was only *one of* his many commands. He had done tours of duty in several wars, from the Philippines, Haiti and Cuba to revolutionary Mexico, and was also stationed in France during the Great War. Indeed, he *was* Sgt. O'Hara! He was also one of the few Marines to receive the Medal of Honor *twice*, and when he died in 1940, he was the most decorated Marine ever up to that time. In 1935, Butler authored a short and cynical anti-war book called *War Is a Racket* (which quickly disappeared by the time of Pearl Harbor). Originally an enforcer of American imperialist policy, Butler was well-aware of how corporate interests sometimes decided military policy, including war profiteering (think the jingoism of William Randolph Hearst and many others). Though he had morphed into an isolationist, Butler willingly testified before Congress in the 1930s, revealing a major fascist plot to kill President Roosevelt and overthrow the American government (with the group planning to make Butler their new leader). Though Butler was attacked by the same isolationists he had previously supported, Congressional investigators proved that his charges were true, and quickly took steps to arrest the plotters of the coup.

But that would be years later, long after the shooting of *Tell It to the Marines*. Besides the Recruit Depot at San Diego (the location of many future Marine films), the Corps also gave permission to film on the USS *California*, later to be heavily damaged by the Japanese at Pearl Harbor. The battleship was used for all the scenes on board ship as O'Hara, Skeet and the rest of the Marines are headed for other ports, as well as the final rescue scenes in China. The final shootout was filmed at Iverson's Ranch in Chatsworth, California.

Yet for Lon Chaney, playing a sergeant in the USMC was the role he was proudest. This pride was noticed by the writers of *Leatherneck*, the official magazine of the Corps:

> Few of us who observed Chaney's portrayal of his role were not carried away to the memory of some sergeant we had known whose behavior matched that of the actor in every minute detail.[17]

Because of his performance in this film, as well as his close friendship with Major General Butler, Chaney was chosen to be an honorary Marine. When the star died of lung cancer at age 47 on August 26, 1930, it was the United States Marine Corps who provided both a chaplain and an Honor Guard for his funeral.

In 1928, a year after the sinking of the *S-4*, a Hollywood studio finally endeavored to tackle the subject of a submarine disaster. This particular Navy film combined the all-important buddy movie and love triangle plots and a dramatic submarine rescue with a dark portrayal of an embittered diver who has to conquer his own feelings of hatred to display Navy courage and skill.

Columbia released the film as a part-talkie. Yet it was the Navy that would refuse to be silent....

In the summer of 1928, Columbia's Jack Cohn, brother of autocratic studio boss Harry, was able to convince his sibling to start moving away from the B movies they had been making and take a chance on producing an A. Harry was enough of a gambler to risk $150,000 on the new production (the TCM website says $250,000).[18] One innovative move, long before Warners put a lock on topical material on-screen: The new film would come straight from the headlines. In fact, Norman Springer's screen story was heavily "inspired" by the recent submarine disasters that collectively cost the lives of close to 80 men. Predictably, the new film was called *Submarine*. Not only would it be a rousing big-budget and suspenseful sea adventure, but Columbia execs had it in mind for this production to be the studio's first part-talkie. Since it was a seafaring adventure, Cohn went with a man who had *lots* of experience with sea adventures to helm the production, a well-established director named Irvin Willat. With a long career in silent film, he had directed works with such waterlogged titles as *Three Miles Out, Rugged Water, Fog Bound, On the High Seas* and *Below the Surface*. Willat's *Behind the Door* featured a dark portrayal of a Navy captain seeking revenge on the U-boat captain who ordered the rape and grisly murder of his young wife. The captain's subsequent torture of the captured German is controversial to this day, and showed an unusual portrayal of a American naval officer crossing over to the dark side that was rare for that post–World War I period. Now Willat was going to helm Columbia's most expensive project yet. It was a heavy gamble for the Cohns, especially for Harry, as he nervously watched the reaction of Columbia's New York stockholders.

To hedge its bets, the studio enlisted the aid of the Navy as a full partner in the production. Ultimately, the USN loaned cruisers and a submarine, supplied plenty of enlisted men as extras, and permitted location shooting at the waterfront near the San Pedro naval base and even allowed some shots of the aircraft carrier USS *Saratoga*. (These shots reappeared in other service-oriented films during the 1930s.) Already smarting over criticism of the recent submarine disasters, the USN hoped that the Columbia film would show its heroic efforts to rescue trapped men, and that said rescue operations would be *successful*! In this way, *Submarine* would be used as a vehicle to cover the Navy with glory and bask in a successful rescue effort that was denied the real-life men of the *S-51* and *S-4*.

The story is simple, though drowning in clichés. (*Sorry about that!*) The tobacco-chewing Jack Dorgan (Jack Holt, a talented action star who had a long career) is the Navy's top deep-sea diver. A kind of Thomas Eadie clone, he is the inseparable best-bud to sailor Bob Mason (Ralph Graves). They push each other around and fight over booze, women and whatever else is handy. Early in the film, Mason dives into the drink and saves Dorgan, who is tangled in an underwater line as a bomb ticks nearby. Instead of demonstrations of friendship, they end up shoving each other in the face and verbally insulting each other. For some odd reason, this was Hollywood's idea of camaraderie. In other words, these two armed services pixies are yet another incarnation of Flagg and Quirt.

Though they work together like a well-oiled machine, the Navy sends Dorgan to San Pedro and Mason on tours of the Pacific. Some time later, a lonely Dorgan wanders into a San Diego waterfront dive called the Palais and meets an exciting taxi dancer named Bessie but nicknamed Snuggles—we can guess why. A promiscuous woman who makes the stage version of Charmaine look like a nun, Bessie wants wine, men and song—and not necessarily in that order. She is played by Dorothy Revier, rumored to have been the model for the Statue of Liberty lady who graced the beginning of every Columbia film at the time.

The smitten Dorgan proposes marriage to the wayward tart and the two set up a *kinda* happy home not far away. Disgusted by the fact that Jack's Navy diving work keeps him away for weeks at a time, the bored floozy soon returns to the Palais ballroom looking for kicks. In record time, Bob Mason is on shore leave in San Diego and wanders into the Palais, *also* looking for kicks. The two young people dance and, before you know it, Mason is spending his leave with her, with Bessie rather carelessly neglecting to mention her marriage to Dorgan (she has removed her wedding ring). Remember, this is a pre–Code movie, before Will Hays and Joseph Breen moved in and took over. Before you know it, Jack returns to hearth and home and, inevitably, catches the two lovers in a passionate kiss, causing the diver to slug his pal, ending their long friendship.

Mason is assigned submarine duty and, again predictably, his sub collides with a destroyer, sending his vessel to the bottom. The crew is trapped on the ocean floor and oxygen is going fast. Only *one man* can save them! Though bitter, drunk, and self-pitying, Dorgan finally decides to answer the call to the colors (in this case, his superstition about dice-patterned garters—which Bessie happens to have). He rushes to the site of the collision and dives in. Merely by attaching an air hose to the hull, the submarine is raised, the men rescued. Never mentioned in the film is the fact that Navy divers *had* attempted to use an air hose to pump air into the ballasts of the S-4, but the effort failed. What the film *does* have is a tense scene of Dorgan communicating with the trapped men by tapping on the outer hull and hearing their weak responses.

At the end, with Bessie sitting at a Palais table with another poor sap, the two heroes reaffirm their friendship and go off together. And though this film might appear to be yet another sexist Hollywood screenplay slamming evil, two-timing women and promoting male bonding, remember that the screenplay (if not the story) was written by Dorothy Howell—a woman, by the way.

Despite the huge investment in the production, something was going wrong. Willat's cameraman, Joe Walker, attested to the fact that Harry Cohn was far more nervous and fidgety than usual when visiting the set, obviously preoccupied with the cost overruns. Having viewed the stiff, repressed performances of leads Hoyt and Graves in the rushes, the mogul asked Willat, "Can't you make them look tougher?"[19] After three weeks, the Cohn brothers finally realized that it wasn't the actors who were the problem, it was the *director*. And so, as hundreds of civilian and Navy extras waited on the San Pedro piers for the shoot to continue, and with a mere four hours' notice, Harry Cohn fired Willat in front of his cast and crew. After starting production in June, the helmsman was fired on July 7 and replaced by Columbia B director Frank Capra (billed on this film as Frank *R.* Capra). According to studio producer Sam Briskin, "It was like replacing Billy Wilder with a TV director."[20] Capra's films up to that time were mundane, with the possible exception of three of Harry Langdon's most successful features.

In his old age, Willat still grumbled about his firing. Referring to his replacement as a "little dago," the septuagenarian claimed that Harry Cohn wanted to build up Capra at the studio and *that* was the reason for his firing. He also claimed that most of the film was *his* footage and only the ending was shot by Capra, a claim disputed by cameraman Walker.

Holt and Graves resented Capra at first, especially his demand that they should wear no makeup and dirty up their immaculate uniforms. But the two actors apparently warmed to "Frank R.," appearing in other action movies for the director into the early talkies. One way or the other, it looked like "the Capra touch" worked. Calling Capra's direction "especially clever," Mordaunt Hall of the *New York Times* also confirmed that the director used the right tack with his actors when he took charge of the production: "[Capra] obtained from his players infinitely better characterization than one is apt to see on the screen, especially in a melodrama."[21] Hall also wrote that the audience at New York's Embassy Theater, where the film premiered on August 30, 1928, erupted in "hearty applause" when Holt sent an air line into the sunken sub.[22]

Still, Hall criticized Capra's use of sound effects, arguing that there were times when silence would have been best. *Variety* knew the film was "valuable propaganda" for the Navy, but erred when they referred to the "ill-fated *S-44*, rammed and sunk by a cruiser during battle maneuvers a few years ago in California waters."[23] Though called the *S-44* in the film, for some reason, the writer for *Variety* seemed to think that the sub in the movie had the same designation as the one that sank in real life. The *S-4* was rammed by a merchant steamer off the coast of Massachusetts, not California. As for the real *S-44*, it had yet to be sunk, and when it was, it happened on the night of October 7, 1943, off the Kuril Islands, courtesy of the Imperial Japanese Navy.

Further on in its review, *Variety* mentioned the sinking of a sub (they didn't say which one) on the Atlantic, "and between the east and west, the navy was on the receiving end of much criticism. The country's newspapers devoted considerable editorial energy to lambasting high naval officials." Also from the *Variety* review:

> Without entering the controversial aspects of the tragedies, *Submarine* presents to the public the navy's side. Use of the S-44 was not good judgment, either as story-telling or as propaganda. The S-44 did not end happily and heroically in real life, as in the film.[24]

Though rightly seeing the film as Navy-influenced propaganda to color the rescue efforts during the recent tragedies as heroic (they *were* heroic; they just weren't *successful*), *Variety* ended its rather confused and convoluted review by calling the new film "a box office clicker."[25]

Box office clicker it was. Still, despite the USN's loaning Columbia all those Navy personnel, amphibious planes, ships, etc., Cohn had demanded speed and budget-cutting to bring the film in on time, and it features the cheesy special effect of a toy sub and a doll in a diver's suit to simulate Jack Holt sending an air hose to the stricken sub. The film also shows that the sub had sunk a whopping 400 feet! Even the characters in the film acknowledged that no diver had ever gone that deep (the *S-51* sank 132 feet and the *S-4* 110 feet). But somehow Holt and his team have no such problem swimming in such depths, like being crushed by the pressure. Also, the Navy's efforts to free the *S-51* alone, with pauses to avoid bitter cold weather, took several exhausting days of rescue and salvage work, not the hop-skip-and-jump quickie effort enacted by Holt & Co. on screen.

Amazingly, the Navy had no major complaints about a Navy man conducting an affair with a married woman; perhaps this was because the cheater was an enlisted man, not an officer. Another controversy was the depiction of a Navy diver getting drunk and letting personal feelings affect how he does his job, even though lives are at stake. Though accepting these problems stoically, naval cooperation would change radically by the time Columbia attempted to remake *Submarine* a decade later.

Far from being "Capra-corn," *Submarine* opened the door to other cinematic depictions of naval rescue efforts. Though the characters involved in the movie rescues would be flawed human beings who could get drunk, petty or jealous, they would always come through in the end. Mason, hurt by his friend's anger, could still smile and attempt to cheer up his fellow crewmen as air slowly ebbs in the stricken submarine; the skipper could still be a brave man leading his crew despite the poor odds of survival; and even the enlisted men could still face death with dignity—as long as they're successfully rescued! It was for these reasons that the brass-hats finally approved *Submarine*, a blatant rewrite of two historical disasters that gave a black eye to the reputation of the Navy; that is, until it was rescued from the depths by the picture-makers of Hollywood.

Too bad the men of the *S-51* and the *S-4* did not live to see the film.

All through the 1920s and into the talkie era, it became acceptable for movies dealing with the armed services to show the Army, Navy and Marines freely being deployed in other lands wherever "trouble" occurs. From the days of the Spanish-American War and into the 1930s, peacetime American forces flew, sailed and marched into areas around the globe where regimes friendly to the U.S., or smaller nations within the northern hemisphere under American "protection," were being threatened by insurrections. Sometimes the rebels had valid reasons for their rebellions; sometimes they didn't. Nevertheless, it was obvious that much of this turmoil had to do with the influence of large corporate interests, sometimes American and sometimes European, who had a veritable stranglehold on these nations' economies. And oftentimes when trouble occurred in other lands, the U.S. Navy or Marines showed up. Major General Smedley Butler may have been a passionate isolationist, but the Marine hero was not talking out of his hat (or "cover") when he insisted that sometimes business interests had an awful lot to do with the deployment of American forces on foreign soil.

Hollywood filmmakers would freely give us stories where American soldiers, sailors and Marines would do battle against "bandits" and other such troublemakers. The audience wasn't supposed to question our suddenly sailing into China, or storming into Central America, the Caribbean and the Philippines; all we saw was the action and romance. On screen, our leading men were fighting for democracy as they romanced some comely nurse or native doll, as in *Tell It to the Marines* and *What Price Glory?*. The hero wasn't supposed to question why he was there or who was pulling the strings behind the scenes. Audiences of the day were not allowed to see the *whys* behind the deployments, just the shootouts, the romances and the military hardware, period.

As the movies went from silents to talkies, political and military chicanery remained behind closed doors. Instead, using Skeet in *Tell It to the Marines* as a yardstick, we would see sarcastic young wiseacres in crisp uniforms fighting to retain their independence in an American military demanding strict obedience.

In this particular cinematic battle of wills, guess who won…

II

COVERING FIRE
1932–1940

> If there is one basic element in our Constitution,
> it is civilian control of the military....
> —President Harry S. Truman

The World War Adjusted Compensation Act of 1924 was not the first benefit awarded to American veterans of the nation's wars, but thanks to the violence that occurred years after its enactment by Congress, it would be the most controversial. The law permitted Great War veterans to receive thousands of dollars in special certificates that were not to be redeemed until 1945. At the time, certainly no one in Congress or elsewhere could have predicted that 1945 would be the final year of yet another world war. This was 1924, the Roaring Twenties, when both violent gangsters and the nation's economy were on the rise and Americans relish their Years of Prosperity. In fact, the nation, victorious in war and thriving in peace, would presumably be solvent enough for the next 20-odd years to be able to compensate brave war veterans for their service. What could possibly go wrong?

Flash ahead to the summer of 1932, when just one in every four Americans had jobs, and the other three couldn't pay their rent, couldn't feed their families, and couldn't find work. This included the nation's veterans: the ex-warriors who had given themselves, and in some cases, their body parts, their sanity and probably their will to live, in places like Verdun, the Marne and Belleau Wood. Demanding that the bonus certificates be redeemed *immediately* rather than when they were middle-aged men in 1945, 43,000 marchers (17,000 Great War veterans plus their families) assembled on Washington, D.C.'s Anacostia Flats, a swampy area south of the 11th Street Bridge and within spitting distance of the Capitol's corridors of power. Thousands of these people lived there during the summer; a rude and painful reminder to President Herbert Hoover and those Congressmen who were well-fed and didn't have to worry about *their* jobs. The marchers, now referred to in the press as "the Bonus Army," referred to their tents, shacks and lean-tos as "Hoovervilles."

Calling themselves the "Bonus Expeditionary Force" or BEF (a black-humored parody of World War I's American Expeditionary Force), the marchers and their families harmed no one, committed no violent acts and, in fact, had gone into negotiations with the D.C. police and their superintendent Pelham D. Glassford (formerly a Great War general), to keep the protest peaceful. The police even helped the protesters maintain calm among the more hot-headed members of the group. Hardly mentioned in the press was the fact that the marchers laid out streets within their camps, maintained clean sanitation facilities, and held parades proclaiming their eternal love of country and pride in their service to the nation. Under their leader, former Army sergeant Walter W. Waters, the bonus marchers had to register to live in the camps, with ironclad proof that they were honorably discharged. D.C. police had no problems with the ex-veterans, a group that obviously knew how to obey orders. The only problem might have been when children on local class trips to see the Washington Monument and the Capitol Building would ask their teachers why these impoverished families, some with children their ages, were living in the open a stone's throw from where their leaders wrote our laws.

On June 15, 1932, as the Bonus Army was about to begin their first summer camped out on their makeshift Hoovervilles, the House of Representatives passed the Wright Patman Bonus Bill, an urgent piece of legislation designed to move up the date for the veterans to receive their bonuses. Unfortunately, the bill was defeated in a vote of 62–18. There are probably a variety of reasons why the bill was defeated in a year when money emphatically did *not* grow on trees, but chief among them was that the majority in control of government wasn't going to give the bill half a chance. Firmly believing that authorizing the payout would force them to raise taxes and thereby slow down the nation's economic recovery, President Hoover and Republican Congressmen vetoed the bill.

Disgusted by the Bonus Army, the president ordered Secretary of War Patrick J. Hurley (a veteran of the Army's 76th Field Artillery Regiment) to use any means necessary to remove the protesters from Anacostia Flats and the areas surrounding the 11th Street Bridges. That same day, July 28, Attorney General William D. Mitchell amended the decision with an order to remove the protesters from all government property. Now Superintendent Glassford and the D.C. police, ordered to act before Hurley's order to the Army was received, reluctantly moved on the protesters. In the next few days, despite the formerly good relations between the cops and the veterans, rioting ensued, with several policemen and marchers injured. But the Bonus Army did not disperse.

Having spoken one on one with protest leaders, Glassford had insisted to Mitchell and Hurley that allowing the marchers to voluntarily drift away would be the best approach. Army Intelligence quickly shot down that recommendation, maintaining that the Bonus Army intended to permanently occupy Capitol buildings and instigate street battles with armed forces that would be a signal for Communist uprisings in all major American cities. Indeed, in the early 1930s, the worst years of the Depression, from the Hoover administration to President Roosevelt's, there was always that very real fear that what happened in Russia, or even Germany, could very well happen in an economically disenfranchised United States, with the country put under the thumb of a totalitarian dictatorship that would promise to remove all poverty caused by the Depression. That the price for such a system of government would be Americans robbed of their freedom meant little to Fifth Columnists, isolationists, radicals and other anti-democratic organizations. Unfortunately, with very little evidence, the Hoover administration quickly assumed that the Bonus Army, despite their loudly proclaimed patriotism, was one of these groups.

With this nightmare scenario in mind, Hoover ordered Hurley to have General Douglas MacArthur, then Army Chief of Staff, to put down the protest. The "old soldier," himself a victorious commander in the Great War, gave orders to the 12th Infantry Regiment and the 3rd Cavalry Regiment, backed by six tanks, to rush the marchers, thereby giving a new meaning to the word "overkill." The six M1917 tanks were commanded by another veteran of the Great War and another officer (like MacArthur) who would find lasting fame in the next world war: a neurotic yet talented major general named George S. Patton. As the men and tanks formed on Pennsylvania Avenue, the Bonus Army, at first thinking the assembled troops were marching in their honor, cheered them. Their cheers turned to cries of horror when "Blood 'N Guts" ordered his tanks and his men to advance. In the wake of the cavalry charge, MacArthur had the infantry move forward with fixed bayonets amidst screaming mothers and crying infants. If that wasn't enough, the soldiers fired Adamsite, a potent arsenical tear gas that induced vomiting. After many of the marchers and their families fled across the 11th Street Bridge, a now-horrified President Hoover ordered MacArthur to halt the attack. But MacArthur, a man who believed in his own God-like instincts far more than the opinions of his civilian superiors, ignored his commander-in-chief and continued pursuing the marchers. Hundreds of protestors were injured, including family members of the veterans involved. Twelve-week-old Bernard Myers died of enteritis, but an investigation later revealed that liberal doses of the 12th Infantry's tear gas definitely accelerated the illness. A veteran's wife later miscarried. When some protesters tried to slip through MacArthur's net and get back to their camp, D.C. police drew their weapons and fatally shot two veterans who had served with distinction in France, William Huska and William Carlson.

Major Dwight D. Eisenhower, a smart and principled officer who happened to be MacArthur's junior aide, would always claim that he warned his superior *not* to appear at the battle scene and order his men to charge; Eisenhower felt that this was beneath the office of the Army's Chief of Staff. "I told that dumb son of a bitch not to go down there," maintained the future Supreme Commander of the Allied forces in the next world war.[1] Still, Ike's principles were on hiatus when the young major backed MacArthur's conduct during the operation.

The violent suppression and removal of the men and women of the Bonus Army did not adversely affect the careers of the operation's two most highly visible officers, MacArthur and Patton. However, it spelled finish to the presidency of Herbert Hoover, widely seen as the cold-blooded chief executive who not only sicced the Army on the starving families of war heroes, but seemed to do nothing to alleviate the nation's jobless situation and end the Depression.

To the end of his days, MacArthur believed, with his usual faith in his own judgment, that he had defeated a Communist plot and saved the nation. In the twilight of his life at age 84, the former general insisted that his suppression of the Bonus Army made him a "man to be destroyed, no matter how long the Communists ... had to wait, and no matter what means they would have to use. But it was 19 years before the bells of Moscow pealed out their glee at my eclipse."[2]

Despite MacArthur's flavorful imagery (were there ever any "bells of Moscow"?), or any evidence of alleged Communist "glee" at his downfall, the suppression of the Bonus Army had other, more immediate consequences. Besides tipping the scales against Hoover's presidency, it also killed off any attempt by Hollywood to make a film tribute to the U.S. Army. The late 1920s and well into the '30s would be the heyday of cinematic glory for its sister branch, the Navy. Having not participated in the suppression of jobless Americans and their families, the seagoing gobs and the USN's "silent service," the officers and crewmen of its submarine branch, saw a Golden Age of Navy films come out of Hollywood. This despite the recent spate of sea disasters which called into question the performance of both naval personnel *and* equipment. The Army would still appear in films, but the films would *not* be tributes so much as they were tales of Great War action and tragic romance. To film industry movers and shakers, with few exceptions, there would be no reason to ask the War Department for permission for massive use of Army facilities and personnel (as in the days of *The Big Parade*); nor would they need to submit scripts to them. To the War Department, most of these scripts would view the Army through the lens of the Great War, and not comment on the Army of that time; i.e., the early talkie era up to the immediate pre–World War II years.

With Army, Army Air Corps and Marine characters seemingly confined to fighting World War I on screen, it was left to the Navy to grab the imagination of young male viewers toying with the idea of joining an exciting branch of the service. The slaughterhouse of the Great War, sometimes depicted on screen in the films of the 1930s (though during the Code years, *never* with any actual realism), would rarely be the stuff that would attract Army and Marine recruitment, especially with the bloody deaths of likable characters and an almost neurotic need to show scenes of tragic self-sacrifice on the battlefield. Yet there was something about a band playing a lively rendition of "Anchors Aweigh" and movie audiences viewing all those majestic battleships, destroyers, sub-chasers, cruisers, aircraft carriers, PT boats and submarines that removed the bitter smell of cordite and the spilling of blood on the grounds of the nation's Capitol.

For better or worse, what happened to the Bonus Army, as far as the movies were concerned anyway, was the best thing to happen to the U.S. Navy.

> Sprawled on the bed in a room on the harbor side of the (Hotel) Espana, Thomas Knowlton, Lieutenant, U.S.N., stirred slightly as the windows rattled under the first blast, then relapsed into a stupor.[3]

So began the 1931 novel *Pigboats*, written by U.S. Navy Commander Edward Ellsberg. He was born in New Haven, Connecticut, in 1891, and grew up in Denver. One of the very few Jews accepted into the Annapolis Naval Academy, Ellsberg graduated with a Bachelor of Science degree in 1914. Twenty-three years old, the young officer was assigned as an assistant navigator on the USS *Texas*. As a torpedo officer, turret officer and defense officer, Ellsberg gained vast experience in structural engineering and naval architecture. With America's entry into the Great War, Ellsberg realized his true potential: Assigned to the Brooklyn Navy Yard in the spring of 1917, the young officer revealed a talent for turning old tubs and rust-buckets into usable vessels for the Atlantic fleet. At the Navy Yard, he refitted captured German passenger ships and turned them into troop transports for the U.S. military. After a spell refitting old minesweepers, his next assignment was in the building of the warship, the USS *Tennessee*. After the sinking of the *S-51* on the night of September 25, 1925, he was summoned to help with salvage operations. The following year, Lieutenant Commander Ellsberg was the chief salvage officer responsible for raising the sub (he shared this duty with future World War II Admiral Ernest J. King, then a captain). The now-wrecked sub was officially wiped off the Naval Vessel Register (or "struck from the list") on January 27, 1930, and sold for scrap six months later. As previously mentioned, Ellsberg distinguished himself during rescue and salvage operations after the *S-4* was struck by the *Paulding* on December 17, 1927.

A man who knew the inner workings of battle cruisers, submarines and all other combat-ready vessels, as well as knowing the Navy and its chain of command structure, Ellsberg had already published short stories and novels based on his service experiences. In 1931, one year after the *S-51* was sold for scrap, Ellsberg published a novel about a submarine having gone down with all hands, not because of a merchant steamer veering wildly off the coast of Rhode Island or Massachusetts, but due to the fault of an officer of the U.S. Navy.

Released on April 25, 1933, in New York City and opening wide on June 9, *Hell Below* was produced by mighty MGM, and starred leading man and future PT boat commander Robert Montgomery. It had romance, melodrama and wartime action to spare; what it didn't have was adherence to the original Ellsberg novel.

Published by Dodd, Mead & Company in 1931, the novel *Pigboats* begins in 1914, when the country was not yet at war with Germany. USN Lt. Thomas Knowlton has been put in charge of captured German seaman Hans Erhardt and is stuck with him in Manila. The novel begins in Knowlton's hotel room where he lies asleep after a drunken night sampling Manila's night life with his prisoner. When he wakes, the prisoner is gone, and so is Knowlton's uniform. Furthermore, while sleeping off his hangover, he missed being picked up by his submarine, which left without him. However, Knowlton's absence is covered by another officer, his friend and colleague, Baker. Due to Baker's inexperience, the sub meets disaster and sinks to the bottom, losing all hands. Now listed as having gone to Davy Jones' proverbial locker with the rest of his buddies, Knowlton realizes that he'll be arrested for desertion if caught.

Blaming the duplicitous Erhardt (who has boarded a Dutch liner to return to the "war to end all wars"), Knowlton vows revenge, changes his name, and travels the world as a hard-drinking and vengeance-crazed shipyard worker—though not necessarily in that order. After the U.S. enters the war, Knowlton joins up under an alias, takes command of a sub, and discovers that the scourge of Allied shipping in the war theater is a sub commanded by Guess Who. Will the obsessed American officer forget his personal quest for vengeance and do his job the Navy Way?

Written with special inside knowledge and a talent for blunt, to-the-point exposition and dialogue that not all military men-turned-authors have, *Pigboats is* a good, exciting read, even if the plot is a bit far-fetched. Instead of blaming himself for his lack of discipline while guarding a dangerous prisoner in wartime, as well as getting soused and treating one of the Kaiser's minions as a beloved drinking buddy, Knowlton blames his escaped prisoner for all his troubles. Still, Commander Ellsberg not only gives us an accurate look at the inner workings of a submarine and its crew in wartime, but tons (or shall I say tonnage) of valuable details about the building, refitting and salvaging of seagoing vessels.

Hell Below casts Robert Montgomery as Knowlton, Walter Huston as the martinet Lieutenant Commander T.J. Toler, and Robert Young as Knowlton's pal, Lt. Buck Walters. Remember, Ellsberg was a lieutenant commander in the 1920s. However, director Jack Conway and his screenwriters, including MGM's prolific John Lee Mahin, radically alter Ellsberg's story and change the focus of Knowlton's vengeance.

The movie is set in 1918 and the Great War is on. With their sub in Taranto, Italy, the crew, including the incredibly named Ptomaine (MGM comic Jimmy Durante) and Chief Torpedo Officer, Mac (Eugene Pallette), do what sailors always do on shore leave—run amok. The two fun-loving pixies delight in provoking the British shore patrol. In dialogue that would have been struck by the Breen Office had they been in charge of censorship before 1934 (and *was* deleted in a 1937 reissue of the film), Mac freely refers to our British allies as "Limeys," and the two salivate over the prospect of beating them up. One stereotypical Englishman even has horrible teeth.

At a party, Knowlton meets the comely Joan (Madge Evans), and soon learns that she is Commander Toler's daughter. When the town comes under bombardment, Knowlton takes the married woman to his home, where she has more to fear than German bombs.

Back out at sea, our heroes' sub destroys one German battleship and disables another, with Toler ordering some men, including Walters, topside in a dinghy to retrieve survivors. When enemy planes arrive, Toler orders the sub to dive. Walters and his men, out in the open, are strafed by German fighter planes.

Knowlton is ordered to just observe a couple German cruisers, but the vengeance-crazed officer orders the torpedo room to open fire on them. The Germans return fire and damage the ballast tanks that allow oxygen into the sub. Here, *Hell Below* lives up to its title with its grimmest scene; one that makes you really appreciate the screenplays of the pre–Code years, before Joseph Breen turned all American productions, including war films, into something wholesome enough for the whole family. As the air gets scarce, several crewmen suffocate to death, with one grabbing a gun and shooting himself so others will have more air. Another grim scene occurs when crewman Jenks (comic actor Sterling Holloway, the future voice of Winnie the Pooh), first seen as kind of a clown, is injured while stopping a loose torpedo from rolling around on the floor. As he lies on his cot in sickbay, the leak of deadly chlorine gas forces Toler and Knowlton to keep the door to sickbay closed. It's a heartbreaking scene, as we watch Jenks banging on the door and begging his buddies to open up as he suffocates, the men plainly seeing his agony through the door's glass pane. Soon the engines are running again and the sub surfaces for some much-needed fresh air.

After a Navy inquiry, Knowlton is kicked out of the service. He soon hears about Toler being assigned to blow up a German stronghold by sending an explosives-laden sub into the enemy's harbor (after crewman dive off it and get picked up by Navy boats). In record time, Knowlton sneaks aboard the sub, confesses his deception to Toler and, after the crew abandons ship, he tosses his former commander overboard. Sacrificing his life, Knowlton blows up the German harbor, and himself as well. His bloodstained Navy cap floats in the water as THE END comes up.

The New York Post proclaimed *Hell Below* a "spectacular submarine film ... crammed with thrills for landlubber eyes." Still, the landlubbers in Hollywood had quite a few problems getting the head gobs in the Navy Department to green-light the film.[4]

Boasting of its record of pro–Navy productions, MGM maintained its strict policy of depicting "by means of an entertaining story, the lives of the officers and men of the United States Navy in the submarine branch of the service during the war." They also were "showing the actions of the characters in a manner as true to life as practicable and has made a sincere and earnest attempt at presentation of the best traditions of the U.S. Military service."[5] Of course, going by this statement, we can then

SMOOTH SAILING: Robert Montgomery (left) as the Navy officer in love with the married Madge Evans in *Hell Below* (1933). The film was based on recent submarine disasters; the Navy was not happy about seeing them recreated on-screen.

assume that Navy officers and enlisted men have affairs with their married commanders' daughters, get into boxing matches with psychotic kangaroos, disobey orders during wartime, bring death onto their shipmates, and get into knockdown fights with other sailors belonging to a wartime ally.

In a September 24, 1931, letter to Secretary of the Navy Charles Adams, MGM exec William Orr officially asked for approval of the *Hell Boats* script, with the producer pointing out that, since *Pigboats* was written by an old Navy man (Ellsberg), the Commander of Naval Operations would have no problem with the production and also allow the studio to use Navy facilities and personnel. To his surprise, the Navy said *no*. CNO W.R. Sexton wrote Orr that the Navy "considers the picture entirely unfit for production." Orr had already ordered his writers to alter certain script elements which had been closer in line to Ellsberg's novel. For instance, the controversial plot point of the disgraced Knowlton being responsible for getting drunk and letting a dangerous enemy escape, his irresponsible act in allowing a novice officer to head their sub to disaster, and his obsession to rejoin the Navy so he can continue his vendetta against the man he allowed to escape. Apparently, according to Navy brass, *no one* was going to use the service as some kind of instrument of vengeance or anything else.

Responding to the rejection, Orr pointed out that when MGM purchased Ellsberg's novel, it was mainly because other studios (Orr doesn't mention which ones) had filmed stories so close to Ellsberg's book that the studio had to get far away from his original plot in order to look different: "I regret to say that in the attempt to construct a substitute story we made the mistake of submitting material which would not maintain our previous high record with the Department."[6]

This was a little face-saving statement for the bureaucrats with whom he was dealing; the Navy wasn't about to accept Ellsberg's plot without major changes. Conway, Mahin *et al.* worked on the script for the next nine months, addressing every concern and bowing to every USN demand. From August 11, 1931, onward, the CNO cited several instances of inappropriate actions by Navy characters that weren't considered representative of the service. With a red pen dripping with venom, the CNO insisted on the deletion of a scene showing a violation of safety rules that leads to the explosion of a gun turret. The CNO also slammed "the mutinous attitude of an officer on the bridge of a submarine, necessitating members of the crew taking forcible action."[7] This would entail the highly dramatic scene where Knowlton takes over the turret gun on the bridge to fire at attacking German planes. Knowlton's insistence at his continued firing at the planes even after Toler has ordered a submerge was now seen, not as insanely obsessive behavior, but as a dedicated officer getting the job done as he fights his nation's enemies. Knowlton is also trying to protect his friend and the other crewmen in the lifeboat. Now, the script's only "forcible action" to remove Knowlton from the bridge before the submerge is Chief McDonald knocking him out and carrying him down the hatch before the sub dives.

When the completed film was screened for the Navy Board in Washington, the brass-hats insisted upon several changes. They were minor, but it highlighted something else about the Navy at the time—or at least the image the brass-hats had of the USN in the days before the Breen Office took hold of the movies. In this case, Navy officials were clearly doubling as pre–Code censors. The Board insisted on cutting dialogue that stated quite plainly that the officers going ashore were doing so for "a definite immoral purpose."[8]

Also on the list was the scene where Knowlton and Joan are seeking shelter in his apartment. The two lovers are embracing, and then director Conway's camera goes to the usual burning candles—instead of the usual burning fireplace. After a slow fadeout, the next shot has the candles "considerably burned down," implying that something happened during that passage of time that was emphatically *not* a game of Dominoes. In fact, the Board deemed the lapse of time as "strongly insinuating coition," and they insisted on cutting the scene to the point of not having a reason to cut to the burning candles at all.[9]

The Navy Board also chafed at the death of Seaman Jenks, played by the likable Sterling Holloway. The scenes of the tragic sailor suffocating behind the hatchway door "are repeated so often as to be unduly oppressive."[10] Yet it is Jenks' death which is the most powerful scene in the film. Injured protecting his buddies, the brave sailor is rewarded for his heroism with a gruesome death by suffocation as the crewmen watch, helpless to save him—as if Jenks were sentenced to death in the gas chamber. Yet the scene had chilled Navy brass, hoping that Hollywood's new pro–Navy films would help with their efforts at recruitment. Scenes like Jenks' grisly death were *not* the kind to make young people run out and join the Navy. Again, the awful memories of the recent sea tragedies, both dealing with the collision and sinking of S-Class submarines and the subsequent drowning or suffocation of their crewmen, weighed heavily on Navy censors. To appease the brass-hats, director Jack Conway skillfully trims Jenks' death scene so that the Board would approve it, but not to the point where it lessens its power.

The Production Code Administration (PCA), and its usually draconian dictates, took effect in the film industry in July 1934. On principle, Will Hays, Joseph I. Breen and others in the Code office welcomed films that promoted America's armed services, striking an unwritten bargain with the nation's military branches to promote a far more positive image far beyond the sometimes controversial portrayals of the pre–Code years (at least in the early script drafts). Now backed by a strict censorship office that unofficially shut down any filmmaker's attempt at non-conformity to the status quo, the brass-hats need not ever worry about scenes such as Seaman Jenks' suffocation or the adulterous passions of a Lt. Knowlton or the randy libidos of rambunctious sailors on shore leave. Never mentioned in this caveat, but totally agreed upon, was the strict censoring of any and all screenplays which dealt, even by euphemism, with the recent sinkings of the *S-51* or *S-4*, or any other naval vessels. Or if said screenplay did depict submarines being sunk and their men in danger, then the denouements had to end happily, with all rescue attempts fully successful. Teamwork, as well as modern Navy inventions and skill, would save the day in a way they could never do for the men of the *S-51* and *S-4*. From now on, all systems were Go; and any deviation from the norm would be blamed less on the dictates and pressures of military life and more on an individual character's faults.

Hell Below was one of the last submarine films of the 1930s set during the Great War. But the Navy was not through yet with its cinematic efforts at recruitment. Soon, a new subgenre (pun intended) would arrive within the Hollywood armed services film; one that harked back to *Tell It to the Marines'* William Haines playing a wisecracking playboy who mocked the Corps. By the cynical Depression years, a veritable army of wisecracking young upstarts were expressing their hatred for whatever branch of the armed services he somehow ended up joining; for as these films progressed, he would eventually change from a cynical know-it-all to a fine, upstanding sailor, soldier, pilot or Marine.

And so, as these characters played by various leading men had to be convinced that they would be much better off being a member of the Armed Forces than, according to their officers in these films anyway, the dead-end, useless jobs these men had as civilians, new actors surfaced to play these parts to keep them fresh to the moviegoing public. Being confused about being an Army or Navy man was one thing, but what if a certain protagonist had a screen image as an angry, defiant rebel who had contempt for all authority figures, even the officers and enlisted men of the U.S. Navy?

Warners and the military bureaucracy (in this case, the USN) worked overtime during the Production Code years of the 1930s to raise the level of enlistment by showing us an on-screen transformation of the most rebellious street kid of them all into a model sailor.

There are those who have always believed that *G-Men* was the first Warner Brothers film in which James Cagney's screen character, basically that of a gangster, rebel, iconoclast and "professional againster," toed the line and gave his allegiance to authority figures. Yet this assumption totally ignores his service films in which the former New York street kid played shining examples of Armed Forces professionalism and skill. Cagney's screen character, even when not toting a gun or pushing a grapefruit into a woman's face, would always be a rebel, quick to use physical force to cut through bureaucratic BS, and a non-stop wiseass who punctured the pretentions of those in charge. Cagney didn't have to play a gangster to threaten the status quo, especially during the Depression years, but transferring his screen character to the Armed Forces was definitely a problem. In *Here Comes the* Navy, released a year before the FBI-themed *G-Men*, the solution was to start the film with Cagney as Cagney, *then* have him morph into a dedicated gob.

During a tour in a Navy yard, USN officer Biff Martin (Cagney pal and Warners star Pat O'Brien) gets into an argument with wiseguy iron worker Chesty O'Connor (Cagney). That night at the Ironworkers' Ball, Chesty and Biff fight and the brawl causes the ironworker to be fired from his job. Chesty decides to enlist in the Navy just to catch up with Biff and get even. Sure sounds like a good reason to join the Navy, right?

After training in San Diego, Chesty is coincidentally assigned to Biff's ship; in this case, the *Arizona*, which would be sunk during the Japanese attack on Pearl Harbor seven years later. Being a good Navy man who never ducks a fight, but obeys the rules, Biff tells Chesty that their fight will have to wait until they get ashore. While in port, Biff is visited by his sister Dorothy (Gloria Stuart, replacing Margaret Lindsay, who was recovering from an appendix operation). The rest of the film is standard boy-meets-girl, boy-loses-girl, boy-becomes-model-sailor stuff. Cagney is Cagney throughout, breaking rules and refusing to conform. When Biff denies him a pass to visit Dorothy, Chesty decides to quit the Navy once and for all, going AWOL. He puts on blackface and sneaks off the ship with a detail of African-American sailors. (It's nice to see Hollywood acknowledging black armed service personnel in the 1930s, but they appear just so Cagney can do this tasteless gag.) Dorothy rejects him because she can't stand a quitter, a reaction that many other leading ladies will have in other service-oriented films. Stung by her rejection, Chesty is even more hurt by his fellow sailors ostracizing him because of his anti–Navy attitude.

PUBLIC ENEMY GOES NAVY: James Cagney as the reluctant recruit who has to learn Navy discipline the hard way in *Here Comes the Navy* (1934). The Warners film also depicted an incident based on the USS *Akron* airship disaster.

However, there is a big heart in Chesty's chest, and in record, cliché-ridden time, the professional againster risks his life by putting out a fire in the ship's gun room. He is awarded a medal for bravery but, still a rebellious wiseacre, he refers to it as "a hunk of tin" and gives it away to his buddy Droopy (Frank McHugh). (Apparently, this cynicism concerning the awarding of medals was still a good dramatic device for military heroes a good 85 years later when one of the two young British soldiers of *1917* refers to the medal he gave away as "a piece of tin.") Witnessing Chesty's ingratitude, naval brasshats quickly transfer him to airship duty (the real-life USS *Macon*) at San Pedro. The following year, the *Macon* was actually downed in a storm, causing the USN to drop plans for the construction of more airships.

During a Navy Day celebration, Biff, on the ground, gets his feet tangled in the dirigible's ropes as it takes off and he ends up hovering over the Pacific. Denied permission to rescue him, Chesty disobeys orders and parachutes to safety with his tormentor. At the end, Chesty not only marries Dorothy, but he's promoted over Biff.

In an earlier scene in the USS *Macon*'s hangar, Chesty tells another crewman, "I want you to know, those boys on the *Arizona* are the best in the world," a line that must have pleased Navy brass viewing the film. Certainly, the USN didn't skimp on cooperation with Warners on the production. The film was not only shot on the USS *Arizona*, but the Naval base at San Pedro, the Naval Air Station at Moffet Field, California, the Navy Yard at Bremerton, Washington, the dirigible airfield at Sunnyvale, California, and the Naval Training Station at San Diego. Even the airship incident was based on reality. In 1932, two years before the film's release, two naval crewmen grabbed the ground ropes tied to the USS *Akron* as it lifted off the field and soon plunged to their deaths.

The film was released right at the dawn of the new Joseph Breen–enforced Production Code. Besides the blackface bit, Cagney and Frank McHugh throw in several "gay" jokes and general fooling-around that could have been ad-libbed. When Droopy blows a kiss to Chesty as he's leaving the ship, a CPO remarks, "What're you guys, a couple o' violets?" Somehow, Navy brass *didn't* demand the bit's removal; though not surprisingly, Breen *did*, at least in Kansas theaters. They also didn't like Chesty calling Dorothy a "twist" and Droopy blurting out, "It makes me feel like having a baby."[11]

The *New York Times* July 21 review picked up on Warners' attempt to use the Navy to clean up Cagney's image:

> A fast-moving comedy enriched by an authentic naval setting, this Warner production has the added advantage, in these parlous times, of being beyond censorial reproach. This last is even more remarkable since the chief player is none other than James Cagney, whose rough-and-tumble antics in several earlier pictures have been held up to scorn by those who would reform the screen. Mr. Cagney has not changed his style in this picture.... But the restraining hand of the producer, writer, director (or all three) never is relinquished.[12]

The American public certainly concurred with their approach. Budgeted at a negative cost of under $250,000, the film brought in over $800,000, more than twice what Cagney's recent films had reaped.[13] It also didn't hurt his image in the eyes of critics that "bad boy" Cagney could actually make it all the way through a Warners film without punching a woman once.

"Atten-*shun*!" cried the tagline. "Here comes the Warner Brothers military musical!"

Hollywood's usual m.o. has always been to make the same film again and again, and yet *again*, until the public gets sick of it, meaning that the last one loses money.

II. Covering Fire

Warner Brothers, in particular, never met a story idea they didn't beat to death. And so the follow-up to their successful armed services musical, *Flirtation Walk*, was already in the planning stages. Filmed during the summer of 1935, and released on October 12, *Shipmates Forever* took the leads from the previous film (Dick Powell, Ruby Keeler), the same actors who played his cadet buddies (Ross Alexander, John Arledge), the same director (Frank Borzage) and the same screenwriter (Delmer Daves), and transferred the setting from the Military Academy at West Point to the Naval Academy at Annapolis.

Even more boldly arrogant in its depiction of a wise and persuasive armed service branch that knows more about what an individual wants than he himself, *Shipmates Forever* takes its title far too seriously, depicting a Navy that never lets you go—even if you want to leave! Popular crooner Richard Melville III (popular WB crooner Powell) is the son of Admiral Melville (Lewis Stone, on loan from MGM). It is a tradition laid down, apparently in stone, that every son in the Melville family tree will be a Navy career man. When Melville and another officer heavily imply that Dick is too dumb to pass the courses at Annapolis, the crooner is shamed into proving them wrong. He not only passes the tests for midshipman, but decides to stay in the Navy despite his previously declared hatred for the service. (He eventually refers to the Academy as a "prison.") Adding to this conflicting character motivation is June Blackburn (Keeler), a tap-dancing teacher whose dances are inserted into the film rather clumsily. Her father and brother were killed while on duty with the USN and she absolutely refuses to marry a Navy man. Then, when Dick wants to leave the Navy, she refuses to see him again because she hates a quitter! It is pretty obvious that these two confused young people desperately need the admiral and the rest of the fleet to show them the way—meaning, "Go Navy and Nothing Else But!"

Just like in *Flirtation Walk*, the talented Ross Alexander provides the film's lighter moments, showing an enthusiasm in his comedy scenes that belied the turmoil in his own life. Pressured by Jack Warner *not* to go to Hollywood's gay hot spots, the depressed actor agreed to a bogus marriage to another tragic actor, Warner contract player Anne Nagel. Ultimately, he shot himself to death in 1938. In the film, it's not Alexander but Navy-loving cadet Johnny "Coxswain" Lawrence (John Arledge) who supplies the melodrama when he flunks his tests. Yet somehow, Lawrence is able to return for sea duty along with Melville and his pals. We see the admiral giving him the bad news, but somehow he's able to get an assignment on board—not only an assignment, but one in the boiler room! And as we all know, especially in service films featuring sacrificial lambs like Coxswain, working in a boiler room is an all-too-predictable death sentence. Predictably again, not only does the boiler blow up and Coxswain sacrifices his life, but it also proves that Melville is All Navy as he heroically attempts to rescue his fellow crewman.

Visited by his father in the hospital, Dick is bandaged from head to toe, except for his eyes. In no time at all, he is honored and promoted at Annapolis with absolutely no facial scars whatsoever. With no reason for her change of heart, June has decided she wants to marry Dick, whether he is Navy or not. In fact, for a woman who is supposedly embittered by the deaths of her dad and brother while on Navy duty, what in Sam Hill is she doing constantly hanging out at Annapolis? This is just one of the movie's many inconsistencies. At first, June's cousin, Ted (Robert Light), seems to be a grumpy, jealous rival to Dick, but he (Ted) warms to him in one brief scene, and then disappears from the film completely. Similarly, Gifford, Melville's superior officer and main tormentor (wonderfully played by singer-actor Dick Foran), also disappears at the midpoint after he is chastised for letting Dick sing and play the piano in a rec room (and steal the attention of the women away from their officer boyfriends). Both Powell and Foran reunited years later in yet another Navy setting, and in similar roles, in Abbott and Costello's *In the Navy*.

Perhaps the worst of all these dysfunctional characters is Admiral Melville, a man who apparently has little love for his own son, only showing him affection when he's carrying on the family tradition and joining the Navy. This is despite the fact that Dick was obviously far happier as a crooner. The snobbishness of the admiral and others in the USN towards Dick's chosen profession should have spoken volumes to the audience; being a crooner and making people happy with his songs, Dick is not considered adult and responsible by his officious father until he joins the Navy. One is almost sorry that a film with a plot like this wasn't made many decades later, when the son would have the gumption to tell his old man to get off his back; and while he was at it, not to judge him while Tailhook and other embarrassments to the Navy were still going on.

The message of *Here Comes the Navy*, *Shipmates Forever* and other 1930s service pictures was "You can't whip the Navy!" Seen as vehicles to promote recruitment by having a rebellious upstart learn Navy discipline the hard way—all amidst the background of a love triangle, of course—these films soon gave way to a newer, more urgent kind of pro-service film.

By the late 1930s, at the behest of the Roosevelt administration, Hollywood started to move away from melodramas like *Hell Below* and romantic triangles in uniform to a new subgenre called the War Preparedness Film. Of course, there were still romantic triangles (with Warner Brothers alone using the same plotlines over and over), but now the romances were buried under the Navy's attempts to perfect new inventions: planes, ships, subs, diving equipment, oxygen tanks, efforts to improve dive-bombing, underwater rescues, surgery and, of course, detecting enemy vessels.

By the mid–1930s, Frank Wead was one of Hollywood's busiest screenwriters. The former Navy pilot and commanding officer was flying high, well-paid and highly respected for his acumen, as well as his vast experience in the world of naval aviation. He had done the screen story for Frank Capra's post–*Submarine* hit *Dirigible* (again with Jack Holt); did the story for the Wallace Beery–Clark Gable opus *Hell Divers*, and penned *West Point of the Air*, *Midshipman Jack* and *Air Mail*, among several other Navy- and/or aviation-themed films. Pre-dating *Airport*, he even wrote a hit play about a commercial airline: *Ceiling Zero*. When made into a film, it featured the battling stars of *Here Comes the Navy* and other Warner pictures, James Cagney and Pat O'Brien.

In '35, again working for MGM, Wead did an original screenplay called *Murder in the Fleet*. Until World War II, it was probably the most violent film depicting the deaths of Navy personnel. Crashing their planes during a fog or some mechanical malfunction or suffocating to death on a damaged submarine was one thing. But in *Murder in the Fleet*, innocent sailors (never officers) are shot, stabbed, electrocuted and bludgeoned by a mystery killer who has come aboard a battle cruiser, along with other civilians. Though it would be an all-too-predictable conclusion that the killer was *not* a member of the Navy, the film is still a dark journey into Navy Hell.

"Join the thousand men on the warship who saw Duval die!" was the tagline for the film, which starred up-and-coming MGM leading man Robert Taylor (who obviously does *not* play Duval). The McGuffin is a new invention that will revolutionize naval warfare. Spies might want to steal it for a foreign power, or a corporate rival, or God knows who. Interest in the new gizmo results in a plethora of strangers, reporters, foreign officials, corporate heads, the hero's girlfriend—and a murderer—all boarding the ship with the invention. In real life, the USN would *not* reveal the existence of such a new weapon; and if they did, they sure as hell wouldn't invite so many people aboard the ship carrying it so they can commit murder and sabotage!

Taylor is Lt. Tom Randolph, in charge of safeguarding the device, and Jean Parker is Betty Lansing, his snotty, rich-bitch fiancée. Betty wants Tom to leave the Navy and work for her wealthy father. When the machine's engineer Al Duval (Raymond Hatton) gets shot dead during a naval gun salute, Captain Winslow (Arthur Byron) seals the ship, and nobody can return to shore. Future comic actor (still in his villain phase in the 1930s) Mischa Auer is a sinister dignitary from an Asian country called Kamchuka. Seeing as how disaster would strike the naval installations of Pearl Harbor six years later, it is tempting to think that Wead and his co-scenarists were ahead of their time and that Auer's ambassador is supposed to be from Japan. But this is doubtful (though Japanese belligerence in China and other locales must have been well-known to Wead and his collaborators).

Meanwhile, poor young sailors are shot, stabbed, clobbered and sizzled with hot wire for the cardinal sin of being in the murderer's way. After much *sturm* and *drang* between Tom and Betty and all concerned, the murderer is revealed to be Victor Hanson, the *real* inventor of the device, getting even with the company he believes stole it. Sober and thoughtful early in the film, Jean Hersholt's performance as Hanson gives way to laughing hysteria once he is unmasked. His attempt to drown Taylor in a flooded powder magazine is a camp highlight (Hanson had attempted to blow up the magazine, thereby blowing up the ship). Betty learns never to defy the will of the U.S. Navy and to accept her beau being a naval officer for the rest of his life—and like it! Shot in the spring of 1935, with the full cooperation of the San Pedro naval base, *Murder in the Fleet* made $216,000 for MGM. Wearing a Navy uniform early in his career certainly helped Taylor go on to bigger and better roles.

Released by Warners on January 22, 1938, *The Invisible Menace* was based on a short-lived Broadway play (17 performances after debuting on May 1, 1937) called *Without Warning* by little-known writer Ralph Spencer Zink. The plot is yet another potboiler of an insane murderer among the fighting men of the U.S. Armed Forces, in this case, the Army. Eddie Pratt (played by Eddie Craven, the *only* actor transferred from the Broadway play) smuggles his new bride Sally (played by the always lovable Marie Wilson) onto the Army base on Powder Island. Wilson again plays the role of a scatterbrain blonde perfectly. (Jane Wyman was originally set to play the part.) While Eddie is attempting to hide Sally in a rarely used armory, they see the body of the fort's ordnance expert pinned to the wall with a bayonet.

Boris Karloff's red hearing role had originally been played on Broadway by Philip Ober, later, the corrupt captain in *From Here to Eternity*. The horror film star had been under contract to Warners in the mid–1930s in decidedly *non*-horror roles. The play's title was changed to *The Invisible Menace* to take advantage of Karloff's casting. The murderer is revealed to be a member of the Armed Forces, and an officer to boot. *The Invisible Menace* also features Cy Kendall as a rather brutal Army investigator, freely beating up the handcuffed Karloff to make him confess. Unlike the post–Vietnam War era, when government conspiracies, sinister general staff officers and psychotic soldiers flooded the American screen, it was unusual in the '30s for an officer to be the murderer, and for the chief investigator "good guy" to be a sadist. One harks back to the psychotic submarine captain in the pre–Code *Devil and the Deep* (1932).

Karloff's Jevries saves the day, holding off the killer and getting wounded in the process. But before he's shot, Jevries says to his antagonist, "When the Army gets you, the first thing they'll do is tear off that uniform! You're not fit to wear it!" Here, even a convicted embezzler has respect for the Army, and it is certainly emphasized that the officer-killer is an aberration: a thief and a murderer, and emphatically *not* symbolic of This Man's Army.

Still, Joseph Breen and the Production Code Office had their complaints. Besides the "suggestiveness" in connection with Eddie and Sally wanting to be alone ("What about your duty to me?" the new bride whimpers at one point), one of the major problems was "[b]rutality in the portrayal of an Army officer using third degree methods." Indeed, Kendall's psycho Army investigator obviously disturbed Breen no end, as he stated in his July 29 letter to Jack Warner: "The business of Colonel Rogers beating up the witness seems decidedly offensive, especially in view of the fact that an Army officer is involved."[14] By August 3, Breen still complained about Colonel Rogers' beating up a handcuffed suspect, and "the scene showing Jevries pinned against the wall by a bayonet."[15] In fact, Jevries was played by a very much alive Karloff, not the dead ordnance officer who's really the victim. By January 1938, Breen also insisted on cutting Rogers' directive to officers (witnesses to his beating of Jevries) that they had *not* seen a thing![16]

Warner Brothers' *Submarine D-1* was released on November 27, 1937. Then, in an unusual move, the studio released a re-cut version of the film right after Christmas. Missing from the original cut were Broderick Crawford and a future American president named Ronald Reagan. Directed by WB helmsman Lloyd Bacon, who fought for the Navy during the Great War, the film tells the story of yet another conceited lout who has to get his ears boxed by the Navy. In a role that might have been slated for James Cagney had he not briefly abandoned Warners for Grand National in a salary dispute, future hero bomber pilot Wayne Morris is "Socks" McGillis, said conceited lout. He vies for the affections of Ann (Doris Weston) with "Butch" Rogers (Pat O'Brien again, hence the Cagney connection). Also along for the ride is Lt. Commander Matthews (George Brent). Ann's fiancé Tom Callan (Regis Toomey, the murderer of *The Invisible Menace*) is killed when his sub sinks during a drill near the Navy's actual base in New London, Connecticut (it sinks and doesn't come up, that is). Rogers works to improve Navy rescue operations while at the same time trying to keep showboat Socks in place.

The USN respected Bacon, an old Navy man, and genuinely liked helping to Warners, who, like MGM, made pro–Navy films. But with *Submarine D-1*, the Navy was able to show audiences its enormous progress in perfecting rescue chambers (as Rogers promotes in the film), amazing inventions like the Momson Lung and new rescue diving bells, thus making the tragic entrapment and deaths of crewmen in stricken subs a thing of the past.

While Warners was promoting (with the USN's help) the Navy's new rescue operations, Harry Cohn's Columbia seemed stuck in the past. In the spring of 1936, Cohn gave the go-ahead to remake Frank Capra's creaky early talkie *Submarine*.

However, unlike their cooperation with the original version, the United States Navy insisted on deep-sixing it.

The property scripted by Dorothy Howell, eventually making it to the screen in 1928 as *Submarine*, had a long, sometimes tortuous route to its eventual remake.

Submarine had been a hit for Columbia, so Cohn ordered the production of another version of the property, including putting the same screenwriter, Dorothy Howell, on assignment to come up with a variation that included a love triangle and dangerous occupations for the male protagonists. *Fifty Fathoms Deep* starred Jack Holt and future director Richard Cromwell as salvage divers; not exactly Navy, but dangerous nevertheless. Not only did Howell participate in the project, but Capra's *Submarine* cameraman Joe Walker was the cinematographer of the new version.

Flash ahead to 1936 when Cohn ordered the production of yet another version of the same tale. Originally called *The Depths Below*, the completed screenplay had no less than *five* screenwriters, three of whom were Communists (one of them being Dalton Trumbo). This time, with perhaps a subversive anti–American slant in mind, the screenwriters put the Navy back into the property. Whether the presence of Party members Trumbo and Edward and Joseph Chodorov made the Navy nervous is not known. What is known is that *this* version, produced during the Production Code years, was not going to get a pass the way *Submarine* did. Not only were the *S-4* and *S-51* disasters a decade or so in the past, but the Navy had not had a sea disaster, certainly not on the level of its previous catastrophes, since 1927. Rescue operations and inter-service communications had improved considerably, resulting in much safer voyages for the brave men of the submarine service. In 1928, when Columbia and the USN collaborated on depicting a submarine disaster, the Navy needed Hollywood to rescue its damaged reputation in much the same way the endangered crewmen needed air from the surface. Now, in the mid–1930s, with Hollywood already making pro–Navy films that helped with recruitment, and with the Breen Office heeding to the Navy's dictate to avoid depicting naval disasters, the USN became uncomfortable with Cohn's remake of an incident that they preferred to forget.

However, before they could complain, Joseph Breen entered the fray. Sensitive to brass-hat concerns, he wrote Harry Cohn a February 15, 1936, letter, pointing out a problem with Scene 112:

> [T]he battle between the marine and the sailors. It was just such a scene which got the entire industry into trouble with the Government at Washington and brought about the setting up of certain regulations by the Navy Department which makes it most difficult for any company to secure naval cooperation in the production of pictures. The objection is in picturizing enlisted men as brutish louts who engage themselves in barroom brawls.[17]

This was only the beginning of the complaints. Breen also didn't like the rough demeanor of the Navy characters, especially when dancing with Myrtle, the slutty female protagonist. He didn't like her sexy dances, nor the randy behavior of sailors on shore leave. One even tells Myrtle that he is looking for a "playmate."[18]

In a July 21, 1936, letter to Cohn, Breen applauded the changes in a revised script, yet the stuffy censor still complained about allegedly sleazy scenes in Charley Wong's place. He huffed about the goings-on in Scene 45, particularly shots "showing the 'girls' in the streets, the 'women,' etc., will have to be carefully handled so that the girls should not be suggestive of prostitutes."[19] Supporting the industry's chief censor, the Navy also put in their two cents.

Three weeks later, Captain H.A. Badt, a senior officer with the USN's Motion Picture Board, replied to Columbia's July 28 request for assistance. In an August 12 letter to Cohn, , the officer wrote that the project would give "the public false ideas of Navy married life and of the enlisted men of the Navy."[20] However, it was revealed in the same letter that their *big* complaint had little to do with the married life of a Navy diver.

According to Badt, "the scene in the stricken submarine is sure to cause unnecessary worry to the families of enlisted men in submarine service. Also, the parents of young boys who desire to enlist in the Navy, will, in a great many cases, be unwilling to consent in the enlistment of their sons."[21]

Going full steam ahead, Badt condemned the script's

> horrors of doomed and dying Navy personnel, the remarks and craven actions of men who are apparently doomed to a slow and agonizing death; the hysterical scenes of the families of the trapped men; the master diver, who tries to forget his unfortunate marriage in drink, and practically refuses to return to duty and go to the assistance of his doomed shipmates—are not favorable publicity for the Navy or its personnel.[22]

One wonders how much of this derogatory portrayal of panicky American sailors and their equally panicky families were the work of Trumbo & Co. (Within four years, Trumbo would write the brutally anti-military *Johnny Got His Gun*.) Certainly, the Communist screenwriters had no interest in furthering Navy recruitment; and depicting panicky sailors in airless submarines and reminding audiences of the dangers young Navy recruits would face certainly helped along this pessimistic agenda. (Breen had also suggested cutting scenes of a rescue diver with "blood streaming down from nose, etc."[23]) Topping this off was the scenarists' portrayal of Navy men going into sleazy dives and lusting after sleazy women, one of Breen's major complaints. These takes on the Navy would *not* prompt audience members to whistle "Anchors Aweigh"!

An officer on the USN's Motion Picture Board noticed something frighteningly familiar about the script for *The Depths Below*—soon to be retitled *Devil's Playground*: It was a sound remake of *Submarine*, a little detail Cohn didn't bother to mention to them. However, the screenplay's numerous "horrors" did the trick: Badt recommended that the CNO withhold naval assistance.

The USN also complained that Cohn was going to use shots of naval vessels and facilities that the Navy had lent Columbia back in '28 for *Submarine*. In an October 20 letter from MPPDA honcho Anthony Muto to Columbia's Washington rep, Fred W. Beetson, Breen's hatchet man wrote, "Captain Jacobs, Commander Rienecke and [Lt. A.J.] Bolton have made it clear to me that if Columbia proceeds to make the picture and uses stock shots made with naval cooperation, the Navy will 'take steps.'"[24]

Even CNO (and FDR advisor) Admiral William D. Leahy got into the act, citing Columbia for violating the Navy Department's policy concerning cooperation with the film industry: "The [Navy] Motion Picture Board has under advisement recommending action which will bar Columbia Pictures Corporation from any future naval cooperation that may be requested."[25] In a February 24, 1937, letter from Fred

II. Covering Fire

Beetson, Muto warned that "Captain Badt (senior member), Commander Reinecke and Lt. Bolton (members) [of the board] will recommend for cooperation from Columbia be turned down."[26]

Still, negotiations continued. Holding firm against the Navy's insistence on making their personnel look better in the film, Cohn continued to order Trumbo and the Chodorovs to change things *just* enough to get their approval. However, while the USN was hunkering down, costs were rising on the project. In September, the Motion Picture Board's Lt. Young received a call from an arrogant Jerome Chodorov, the playwright brother of associate producer–screenwriter Edward Chodorov. The scenarist announced that he and his collaborators were refusing to make the changes the Navy wanted, i.e., *not* having the Navy diver drunk and bitter and having the trapped crew showing far more panic than USN censors would like. While they were at it, Chodorov proclaimed, the studio was also refusing the offer of a technical advisor. For Cohn, however, it was less a matter of showing the Navy in a bad light as much as lowering an already rising budget; and it was obvious that he figured to save money by merely utilizing stock footage clips from the original part-talkie and dubbing in voices and sound when necessary. From the USN, however, there was angry talk of their Motion Picture Board blacklisting all cooperation with Columbia on

A SENORITA IN EVERY PORT: Beautiful Dolores del Rio as the cheating Navy wife, leading officer Chester Morris astray in *Devil's Playground* (1937), Columbia's remake of its part-talkie *Submarine* (1928).

future Navy-themed projects—a frightening prospect for the studio with war on the horizon. By the New Year, however, things had calmed down considerably, with both Cohn and the USN eventually coming to an understanding.

The controversial *Devil's Playground* was shot quickly and released in early 1937. Richard Dix plays crack Navy diver Jack Dorgan (the same name as Jack Holt's *Submarine* character) and Chester Morris co-stars as his buddy Robert Mason (again, the same name as in the original). Mason is assigned to a sub while Dorgan is sent to San Diego. In this remake, Dolores del Rio plays the slutty nightclub dancer. The Mexican icon had gone from major studio films to Bs but, still beautiful and talented, she made a tremendous comeback in 1943 by rejecting Hollywood's racism and ageism and returning to Mexico to, as she said, "become an actress again." However, in 1937, it seems she was back to playing the kind of exotic vamps she had perfected in her silent films. When told of del Rio's casting, the Communist screenwriters decided to Latinize the formerly Anglo slut (Myrtle in earlier drafts) and renamed her "Carmen."

Dorgan and Mason fight over the conniving Latina; Mason's sub sinks; Dorgan gets drunk and refuses to help. Then, out of the blue, and unlike the first two versions of the story, Carmen verbally condemns Dorgan for not doing his duty and rescuing his buddy and the others. In her career, Dolores had rarely played a villainess; perhaps her possessive, wealthy aristocrat in *La Dona Perfecta,* shot in Mexico City in 1946, came closest to her playing an evil woman. In fact, her sudden conversion to righteousness in *Devil's Playground* almost reminds one of Fox's whitewash of her Charmaine character in the film *What Price Glory?*.

In another subplot, before Dorgan meets the enticing Carmen, he has pretentions of being a member of the staid middle-class. He purchases a house; however, typically in a screenplay by Communist writers, his neighbor is snotty (apparently his only neighbor is one middle-aged woman), and every effort to forget his working-class roots ends in failure. His attempt at middle-class domesticity with the two-timing Carmen is a pathetic joke; a justifiable punishment for Dorgan's thinking he's "better than others," according to Trumbo and his pals anyway.

In the meantime, as the end of the 1930s approached, Warners filmed *Wings of the Navy*, another war preparedness film, this one starring George Brent, John Payne, and Olivia de Havilland as the usual love triangle. The story dealt with the problems Navy pilots face with losing consciousness during dive-bombing runs. At one point, Brent delivers an excellent monologue to younger brother Payne about the horrible physical reactions a Navy pilot feels when his plane goes into a dive during the test flight. Michael Fessier's original screenplay almost sounds like it could have been written by Frank Wead.

One critique of the film came from an unusual source. In a confidential memo from Joseph Breen to Warners dated November 21, four days after *Wings of the Navy* was released in Japan, the censor wrote, "Japanese authorities objected to a sequence showing target practice. They claimed that the targets, consisting of a white background with a round spot in the middle, resembled the Japanese flag and therefore wanted to eliminate the entire sequence."[27]

How different things would look in exactly two years and 16 days after Breen apprised the studio of Japanese complaints; and how by that time it would be the Japanese military who would be honing their skills on *American* targets.

Still, the message in *Wings of the Navy*'s tagline was blunt, and perfectly meshed with the pro-war footing of the Roosevelt administration: "FOR ALL THE WORLD TO WITNESS THAT AMERICA WILL NOT BE UNPREPARED!"

Wings of the Navy was released in the U.S. on February 11, 1939. Within seven months, Europe would explode into another world war. In less than three years, America itself would be attacked by those same sensitive souls who complained that we were targeting their flag.

Yet despite all the war preparedness films put out by Warners and MGM, and despite the optimistically flag-waving tagline of *Wings of the Navy*, America was *not* prepared...

III

Collateral Damage
1941–1945

> I fear that all we have done is awaken a sleeping giant
> and filled him with a terrible resolve....
> —Admiral Isoroku Yamamoto, *Tora! Tora! Tora!*

The Roosevelt administration did *not* want a war with Japan. The objective was to find an excuse to tackle Nazi Germany, save England, and liberate the rest of Europe. However, Messrs. Hirohito, Yamamoto, and Tojo had other ideas.

Taking a cue from FDR's Washington, Hollywood had emphasized war preparedness, and by the turning point year of 1941, even its comedies reflected this choice. The up-and-coming Bob Hope made *Caught in the Draft* at Paramount and the declining Laurel and Hardy filmed the unfunny *Great Guns* for Fox. However, while the world was at war and America was still at peace, two comics from New Jersey made the nation laugh all through the war years and beyond. In 1941, Bud Abbott and Lou Costello's first three released films were military comedies, with Bud and Lou causing mayhem in three different branches of the Armed Forces. (Actually *Keep 'Em Flying* dealt with the Army Air Corps, since there wasn't an Air Force yet.) *Buck Privates* even started with documentary footage showing the signing of the peacetime draft.

Released on May 30, *In the Navy* (originally titled *They're in the Navy*) has Bud and Lou as sailors—despite the fact that both men were too old to serve—doing their routines on a naval cruiser in peacetime. However, towards the end, Bud and Lou accidentally give their captain a doped drink. Then, trying to impress the Andrews Sisters, Costello dresses up in the captain's uniform (though with an ancient Horatio Hornblower outfit) and broadcasts orders to the crew that sends the ship into all sorts of crazy and suicidal maneuvers, one of which almost has it collide with a destroyer.

The USN, which had cooperated with the production, was *not* happy about the bizarre sight of Costello commanding a battleship and the sailors under him blindly following his wacky orders like robots. (In the original synopsis, Navy bigwigs compliment the now-revived captain on his maneuvers![1]) In fact, at a time when Herman Wouk, future author of *The Caine Mutiny*, was still submitting scripts for radio programs, Universal was filming a scene depicting an incompetent man at the helm of an American warship.

As the film's producer, Alex Gottlieb, explained, "We sent a rough cut of the

III. Collateral Damage 45

ABBOTT & COSTELLO VS. THE NAVY!: CPO Dick Foran (left) harasses sailor Lou Costello in *In the Navy* (1941). Under pressure from Navy brass, Universal was forced to alter the film's comic climax.

picture to Washington after it was all done. And the Navy wouldn't allow it to be released…. Universal was stuck, no second Abbott and Costello picture."[2]

Apparently, the Navy Department brass-hats had originally approved the sequence in the script, but were horrified at actually seeing it performed on screen. Gottlieb's brainstorm: The sequence was all a dream (Costello had accidentally doped himself with the captain's drink). According to Gottlieb, this solution was enthusiastically accepted by the admirals.[3]

Released on May 27, 1941, *In the Navy* ended up delighting audiences around the country who never knew about the controversy over the climax.

"I feel that any move west [to Pearl Harbor] means hostilities," Admiral James O. Richardson, commander of the Pacific Fleet, wrote to CNO Harold Stark on May 13, 1940.[4]

Richardson was pure Navy, a crack officer who rose through the ranks (he had attended Naval War College in Rhode Island) to become the top Commander of Naval Operations in the western U.S. The Pacific fleet had always been based in San Diego and Long Beach when Richardson took command in January 1940. Known as serious and dedicated to his job, Richardson also impressed some as opinionated and a know-it-all. Still, he was aware of the hostile intentions of the Japanese in the Pacific. He also didn't think much of FDR or his being a so-called expert in naval operations. Despite having been the Navy's assistant secretary during World War I (and ruthlessly angling for Navy Secretary Josephus Daniel's job), the president fancied himself an expert on the Navy despite the fact that his expertise never really went beyond amassing a huge collection of model ships in his second-floor study in the White House. "Stamp collecting and playing with the Navy," is how Richardson disdainfully described his superior's interest in naval affairs.[5] After the move to the shallower waters at Pearl, Richardson kept bombarding Secretary of the Navy Frank Knox with memos warning him that the fleet at Oahu would not be, as Roosevelt claimed, a "restraining influence" against Japanese attack, but a provocation.

After many more months of this back and forth, matters came to a head during a contentious White House meeting with the president on October 8, 1940. Roosevelt, a vain man who already prided himself on being a naval expert (as well as most other things he knew nothing about) did not like Richardson's brutally honest remarks about the Navy not having "trust and confidence in the civilian leadership in this country that is essential for the successful prosecution of a war in the Pacific."[6] To FDR, the CNO's statements sounded defeatist, though he would never admit to anyone else that they also must have hurt. The result of the meeting came on January 5 of the following year (and two months after Roosevelt's second reelection) when an aide gave Richardson a message informing him of his dismissal as Commander of the Pacific Fleet while he was on a golf course in Oahu. Richardson had been publicly fired by a vindictive commander-in-chief, but he also had the satisfaction of *not* being the man in charge in Hawaii on December 7.

That thankless position was taken by Admiral Husband E. Kimmel, another outstanding naval commander. Kimmel, as well as the Army's Lieutenant General Walter C. Short, were the commanders responsible for the defense of Pearl Harbor. They were also the ones the Roosevelt administration, as well as fellow Democrats, would blame for what happened in subsequent Congressional hearings on the Japanese attack that lasted well after the president's death in April 1945.

However, thanks to the Magic intercepts, the Roosevelt administration was aware of Japanese duplicity. The Japanese expressed only friendship and peaceful intentions to the Americans, but the decoded messages seen by the president, the secretaries of War, State and the Navy, and other top officials revealed dissembling and stalling tactics while the Japanese made even *more* plans for conquest in the Pacific.

Armed with the Magic intercepts, looking for an "excuse" to get into the war, did Roosevelt and his aides know that the Japanese were going to attack Pearl Harbor? The answer to that is *extremely* doubtful, to say the least. One would have to believe that everyone within military and civilian intelligence circles who would have been privy to such vital information, literally hundreds of people, would have had to remain silent while knowing that several thousand Americans in uniform were going to be killed and that all the battleships of the Pacific fleet destroyed. Ultimately, Roosevelt and his aides suspected there would soon be a Japanese attack at the Philippines, Wake Island, Guam or the Dutch West Indies. As it turned out, they were right; however, these attacks came about almost immediately *after* they attacked Pearl Harbor.

And whether American stenographers were slow in transcribing Japan's message about breaking off negotiations in their talks with the U.S., or whether adequate personnel were available in Oahu on a Sunday morning to alert everyone to an impending attack, or that a totally unaware General George C. Marshall was out horseback-riding as Hawaii burned, ultimately didn't matter. At no point in any message the Japanese had sent to the Americans did they ever issue a Declaration of War. They had just said that they were breaking off "negotiations" (the Roosevelt administration promised renewed supplies of oil if they would leave China and abandon their goals of conquest). In fact, under radio silence, the strike force code-named *Kido Butai* had set sail from Hitokappu Bay in the Kuril Islands on November 26, and their plans had been made, with enthusiastic approval by Emperor Hirohito himself, many months before. (Cadets at Tokyo's naval war college had actually promoted an attack on the U.S. as far back as the 1930s.) For them, there was no turning back. Defying the American boycott, Hirohito and his militarists sought to conquer the Dutch West Indies for its supply of oil and tin; but first, the goal was to knock out the U.S. Navy who had hegemony over the area. The attack would take place on a quiet Sunday morning: a day of rest when the supposedly hedonistic Americans were sleeping off a Saturday night out at the canteens. Japanese scientists and engineers had purposely fitted their Navy's air torpedoes with special fins so that they could skim *above* the shallow waters at Pearl and not be caught in the mud beneath the surface; this development took place many years *before* Japan opened up so-called "peace negotiations" with the U.S. The goal was to hit the battleships and destroyers while they were still docked, just as they would hit American planes on the tarmac at Clark Field when they bombed the Philippines later that day. The attack on Pearl was brilliantly planned and executed, but it was also dirty and underhanded and, yes, a brutal act of aggression against another nation that had never suspected anything was amiss. In fact, the Japanese had essentially pulled the same move on the Russian Imperial Fleet at Port Arthur which handed them an easy victory during the Russo-Japanese War of 1904–1905.

We *were* caught napping. However, despite the apologies and revisionism of some so-called historians, the inescapable fact was that the Japanese government, the same leaders who ordered their military to brutalize and murder so many innocents across Asia, had been talking peace to us while they were really making war.

Years later, on March 2, 1944, at the Academy Awards ceremony at Grauman's Chinese Theater, at a time when it looked like the war in Europe and the Pacific was finally turning towards an Allied victory, the Oscar was given out for Best Documentary/Short Subject of 1944. In a choice that hardly seemed a surprise considering all the time and effort involved in the production—as well as the involvement of the country's most powerful men—the Best Documentary turned out to be a 34-minute film called *December 7*th. How this wartime production was conceived, shot and then butchered to the point that it suddenly became Oscar-worthy, was a long and, to some, painful journey. It once again laid bare America's military bureaucracy and its almost neurotic need to control all Hollywood product that attempted to depict them, even in a positive light, and twist a filmmaker's original intentions into adhering to its own idea of a flawless image. It is a tale of bureaucratic interference, wartime propaganda and finally, the stigma of racism and xenophobia which sometimes surfaced during those tumultuous years.

On the morning of Sunday, December 7, John Ford, his wife Mary and their daughter Barbara were in the dining room of the home of an Admiral Pickens in Alexandria, Virginia. The commander was called to the phone; when he returned to his guests, he announced the Japanese attack on Pearl Harbor, a tragedy that shocked everyone at the table—everyone, that is, except John Ford.

Since the beginning of the war back in 1939, naval reserve man Ford had run a government-backed field photographic unit that put naval preparedness operations on film. The Eleventh Naval District Motion Picture and Still Photographic Group consisted of over 200 men, most of them from the Hollywood studios, who were trained and equipped by the Navy in reconnaissance and field photography, including possible battlefield conditions. Merian C. Cooper, a Great War pilot and a future partner with Ford in Argosy Pictures, was part of the unit. In January 1941, the two men exchanged correspondence discussing budget outlays for a proposed Field Photographic Unit, or Field Photo. Also gladly joining the unit were talented cinematographer Gregg Toland and a future writer-director named Robert Parrish. All through 1940 and into '41, the future Hollywood combat photographers were trained at either Fox or some other studio, all under the auspices of the Navy. Sometimes they would take their "classes" at the Naval Reserve Armory in downtown Los Angeles. No one suspected that they would have to use their training in actual battlefield conditions. After all, the country was still at peace.

Then on September 9, the head of the Office of Strategic Services, "Wild Bill" Donovan, wrote a letter to Secretary of the Navy Frank Knox requesting that Ford immediately be put on active status. Ford and his people had actually been to Pearl Harbor months before the attack, but the director and his crew had also been to San Diego, Pensacola, Florida and Panama; some members of Field Photo had even been to London to witness British responses to Nazi aerial bombardments.

Ford did not have a crystal ball; he was not, by any stretch of the imagination, a far-seeking visionary on the subject of a future attack by Japan. A talented filmmaker, certainly one of our greatest ever, Ford was also a drunk, a dictator, a sadistic bully, a bigot (in a letter to General Albert Wedemeyer in October 1944, he referred to Hollywood as "mockie-land"[7]) and a generally obnoxious human being, even where his friends were concerned. Yet given the opportunity to be far away from Hollywood (as well as his wife and family), Ford seized the opportunity to "serve" in the USN. Yet despite his obvious wanderlust, the director did rise to the occasion when his country needed him and he proved himself, beyond all doubt, to be a brave man.

In the days following the sneak attack, Frank Knox authorized the first of several investigations into just *why* the Japanese Naval and Air Commands were able to successfully bomb Pearl Harbor and supposedly get away scot-free, a move that did *not* please the Democrats. Also, around this time, Wild Bill Donovan proposed to Knox the making of a film that would clarify the American, particularly the Navy, response to the attack. Knox wholeheartedly approved the idea of

> a complete motion picture presentation of the attack on Pearl Harbor on 7 December 1941. As you well know, the president has stressed the highly historic importance of this date, and I believe that this should be handled by the best talent available.[8]

In 1942, the best talent available was the man who had already won three Academy Awards for Best Director (with number four coming up in 1953). Elevated to the rank of lieutenant commander in the USN, Ford was the undisputed head of Field Photo. Though officially a member of the Navy, in reality, his *only* superior was the head of the OSS, William Donovan—and Wild Bill answered to *no one* but President Franklin D. Roosevelt. Despite the fact that Knox was an old friend and longtime colleague in the military-industrial complex of the day (both men were Republicans in an administration packed with Democrats), Wild Bill was not a well-liked man, despite his personal charm and charisma. The OSS was a major rival to intelligence agencies like the FBI (J. Edgar Hoover reportedly detested him), as well as Army G-2 and Naval Intelligence. The other brass-hats, and Hoover especially, were jealous of Donavan's relationship to the president, and made their feelings plain by purposely *not* sharing vital intelligence with him—and sometimes, not sharing any intel with each other—even in wartime!

Today, some might justifiably see *December 7*th as Donovan's revenge against the military establishment who had kept him out of the loop of Washington power politics and highly classified intelligence briefings. Ford detested Navy brass-hats; always pro–military preparedness, he had only contempt for those self-satisfied men who sat behind desks and regaled in their position as powerful bureaucrats. Beholden only to Donovan, Ford used his unit as he pleased; and though sometimes palling around with Navy brass, he had no interest in their opinions on how to make a film promoting them. His feelings about them, as well as his deep respect for Wild Bill, colored the point of view of this new government-sanctioned project.

Gregg Toland co-directed and handled the cinematography, and Jack Mackenzie was the camera operator (he also collaborated with Ford on *The Battle of Midway*). Fox screenwriter Lt. Samuel Engel was Ford's writer and co-producer. It was planned as a quick newsreel-like operation, but somehow it became a full-length dramatization, using already shot footage of the attack. The story, dealing with America's lack of preparedness, featured Hollywood actors in certain roles.

A tall, bearded character named Uncle Sam (get it?), played by Walter Huston, relaxes in the then-peaceful paradise of pre-war Hawaii. His reverie is rudely interrupted by the appearance of a certain "Mr. C" (for Conscience; and played by Harry Davenport). Uncle Sam is unusually complacent, and he resents Mr. C's taking him to task for his lack of military preparedness. Despite the fact that both Huston and Davenport are talented, seasoned performers, they cannot keep viewers from coming to the conclusion that the whole premise is absolutely ridiculous. Yet the film *really* takes a dive when Mr. C decides to be an expert on the Japanese citizens of Hawaii. Heralding their culture, religion and loyalty one moment, Mr. C then comes down on those same loyal citizens by heavily implying that they're also traitors. "When Tokyo speaks, they all listen!" remarks Mr. C in Davenport's usual folksy manner. Showing Japanese citizens of Hawaii in their temples and with their families (including their cute children), we also see Japanese hairdressers, taxi dancers, gardeners and cab drivers closely listening in to the conversations of American service personnel, especially when they just happen to be discussing the islands' defenses—which, we all know, servicemen are *always* talking about. Indeed, according to Mr. C, there are no secrets in Hawaii where the Japanese are concerned. In fact, as soon as Mr. C's conversation turns from Japanese loyalty to their alleged penchant for treason, horror music plays on the soundtrack. We even see scenes in Hawaii's Japanese embassy, which is soon visited by a Sieg-Heil–ing Nazi agent (the talented Lionel Royce, former star of the Yiddish theater in Berlin). After the attack, Japanese-owned businesses are closed. These expository scenes have the obvious approval of the filmmakers, including, apparently, John Ford.

The film also boasts the participation of other Fox contract actors, with Ralph Byrd (the screen's best Dick Tracy) as a reporter persistently quizzing the Japanese ambassador about the smoke coming out of his chimney (we assume the burning of incriminating documents, which was actually based on fact); Irving Pichel, who narrated Ford's *How Green Was My Valley* (1941), does the narration here; Ford veteran George O'Brien (*The Iron Horse, Fort Apache*) as the voice of a dead sailor; Philip Ahn as a Shinto priest of notoriously dual loyalties; Robert Lowery as a radio operator who indirectly brings about the tragedy: and a young Karl Swenson and Charles Tannen as Navy gunners. Though Ford would attempt to wash his hands of this version of the film, he *was* the producer; and though many of these actors were under contract to Fox, many of them had *also* worked for Ford.

Perhaps the strangest scenes in this highly biased film were the ones near the end with Fox contract star Dana Andrews as the ghost of an American sailor (or the symbol of *all* U.S. Armed Forces personnel who died in the war), as well as Paul Hurst as the ghost of a World War I soldier. At the time, both Andrews and Hurst had appeared, as lynching victim and lyncher, respectively, in William Wellman's *The Ox-Bow Incident* at Fox. There's a strangely haunting and sentimental scene that *could* have been directed by Ford, but also could have been helmed by Toland. (Ford was notorious for static camera setups; Toland, as a cinematographer, would have kept the camera moving.) In the scene, Andrews and Hurst, their faces unseen, walk down a path in a cemetery of dead war veterans (shot at the National Cemetery in Westwood, California). Andrews sees World War II as a conflict which will end all wars, while the cynical Great War soldier Hurst argues that the Second World War will be no different than the first. Though restraining themselves from openly criticizing President Woodrow Wilson, when Andrews reminds him that World War II will "make the world safe for democracy," the scornful Hurst replies, "Where have I heard that before?" Then the dialogue descends into baseball jargon, with terms like "striking out" and "home runs." Still, it *is* a fascinating scene, imaginatively performed by two fine actors, and shot in an innovative way, especially as they talk about the pros and cons of our involvement in the war. Yet it's already 1943 at the time of the film's release, and one wonders why we still need convincing in order to fight the war when we were already well into it to the tune of thousands of American lives already lost in battle—as if the filmmakers *still* had to sway the minds of longtime isolationists.

The film's point of view *vis-à-vis* the military's lack of preparedness became a touchy subject to the brass-hats in Washington, and particularly those in charge in Hawaii on that fateful day in December. The official government report produced by the highly biased Roberts Commission investigating the lack of intelligence dealing with the Pearl Harbor attack, led to the forced retirement of Admiral Kimmel, commander of the Pacific Fleet, and Lieutenant General Short, Army commander of the Hawaiian Department. In time, more heads rolled, though not enough, according to some. Wild Bill Donovan biographer Anthony Cave Brown wrote that the "root cause of the intelligence failure" at Pearl Harbor was the result of military gridlock and bureaucratic jealousy. To Brown, "the Army and the Navy had ignored the presidential order that Donovan was to see all intelligence having a bearing on national security." The U.S. had broken Japanese foreign office code traffic with their MAGIC intercepts, yet both military branches of the service refused to trust civilian Intel man Donovan *or* his agency. And so, "vital intelligence was withheld ... before, during, and after the attack," wrote the author.[9]

Army G-2 and Navy Intelligence were already fighting vicious turf wars with the head of that other civilian intelligence agency, J. Edgar Hoover, and his extraordinarily pushy FBI. Vindictive to a fault, they insisted that Donovan be barred from green-lighting any clandestine operations on U.S. soil. To the military-industrial complex, the OSS people were a bunch of uncontrollable wild boys who blew up German power stations in occupied countries, slipped poison into the drinks of fascist collaborators, and bedded the girlfriends of Nazi officers to get the skinny on secret plans and military moves. They didn't have the skill or the discipline to fight a war out in the open like traditional warriors, nor make the supreme sacrifice that thousands of soldiers, sailors and Marines were making for their country. Rather predictably, thanks to the brass-hats of Washington exerting pressure on Hollywood, there would be no film tributes to the OSS until 1945 and '46 (*Cloak and Dagger* and *O.S.S.*, respectively), at the end of the war, long after their usefulness was over.

With this thinking in mind, it would not be a surprise to learn that the brass-hats of the USN fairly detested John Ford, Donovan's close friend and filmmaking Golden Boy (or, rather, Golden Old Man). Needless to say, Ford, a man with a vicious temper (*especially* when sober), returned the contempt. Yet the veteran filmmaker had more immediate problems.

When Toland and Engel neglected to ship any footage of their work back to Fox after six weeks on location in Hawaii, the helmsman flew out to Pearl on January 24, 1942, to see what was going on. Envisioning a quickie, newsreel-like semi-documentary, the director was shocked to see that the two men were filming a feature-length docu-drama, decades before that term came into being. Robert Parrish, then a cameraman with Field Photo, backed up Ford, claiming that the director had no idea what his two assistants were planning. Yet the "Fordian" elements were obviously there, especially when showing scenes of American families on the homefront, as well as the previously mentioned use of Ford actors. Still, it's pretty obvious that Toland, the master cinematographer, directed the excellent scenes of the Pearl Harbor attack, shots so realistic that other filmmakers, especially Frank Capra (in his highly propagandistic *Why We Fight* series), used these clips and pretended that they were actual footage from the day of the attack.

After Ford berated an admiral who had the temerity to suggest how to set up a shot, Navy brass almost gleefully banished the filmmaker from returning to the Pearl Harbor location. Indeed, it would not have come as a surprise that Gregg Toland also inspired the Navy's wrath; in fact, according to Parrish, many of the brass-hats "were anxious to scuttle the Toland operation."[10]

Things finally came to a head when naval brass finally saw the film, a joint effort between Ford (despite Parrish's persistent arguments that the director had little to do with the long version), Toland and Engel. Rather predictably, the Navy was *not* pleased. Already angry over Ford's high-handed treatment of them, they turned thumbs-down on the production. Admiral Harold R. Stark, commander of American naval operations in Europe, had been the CNO at the time of Pearl Harbor. Instead of demoting him, after Hitler's declaration of war against the U.S., the USN quietly transferred him to Europe, a theater of war where the Navy was emphatically playing second-fiddle to Army operations against the land-based *Wehrmacht*. To put it mildly, Stark's fury knew no end:

> This picture leaves the distinct impression that the Navy was not on the job, and this is not true.... I am not concerned with minor inaccuracies, but great harm will be done and sleeping dogs awakened if the picture is released as it now stands, leaving the impression that the Navy was asleep.[11]

Though the Navy was reportedly concerned about the film's allegedly detrimental effect on national morale, it was pretty obvious that they were actually concerned about its image, with the former CNO doubly concerned about reopening an embarrassing can of worms *vis-à-vis* his own lack of preparedness in the weeks leading up to the attack.

Lowell Mellett was the head of the Office of War Information, which was a liaison between Washington and the studios. Having perused the script, Mellett had a very good idea that *December 7*th was *not* going to be released in its present form, and in late 1942, he expressed his concern to the undersecretary of the Navy, James Forrestal. Insisting that the project should be stopped,

> not merely because it seems certain to be a very, very bad picture per se, but because the whole approach is, in my opinion, unwise from the government's standpoint. It is a fictional treatment of a very real fact, the tragic disaster at Pearl Harbor, and I do not believe the government should engage in fiction.[12]

Meanwhile, the Roosevelt Administration, which had been engaging in fiction all through the war, had their own take on Ford and Toland's Pearl Harbor reenactment. In fact, the Navy had little, if any, concern about scenes shot by Ford and Toland that clearly stated that the Japanese citizens of Hawaii were spies and traitors. FDR had signed into law the roundup of all Japanese-Americans on the West Coast and herded them into internment camps. Therefore, out-and-out racism didn't shake up the brass-hats as much as latent accusations that naval commanders were "asleep" before an enemy attack. Secretary of War Henry Stimson agreed, as did the president, with FDR issuing a spring 1943 order stipulating that all Field Photo works would be severely censored before release, whether they played before the public or military personnel. The Navy got their revenge on the ornery Ford by confiscating a print of the film and ordering him to lock up the negative. Working fast, Ford ordered Parrish to recut the film; ultimately, *December 7*th went from 83 minutes to 34. Budd Schulberg and MGM scenarist-producer James Kevin McGuinness rewrote the screenplay, effectively removing the racist Mr. C and the incredibly lazy Uncle Sam character. Ford's new emasculated version of *December 7*th won the Oscar for Best Short Subject for 1944 (his wonderful *The Battle of Midway* won the year before). Rather vindictively, despite his obvious bravery in risking his life and limb while shooting a Japanese aerial attack from the powerhouse of the Naval Air Station at Midway, Ford stole entire ideas from Toland and Engel's original version of *December 7*th and put them into his *Battle of Midway*, an act of blatant plagiarism that infuriated the two men. Thanks to Ford and the brass-hats, the talented Toland, crushed by the duplicity of the former and the bureaucratic overkill of the latter, never directed another film. Bitterly, he requested (and got) a Field Photo assignment to South America.

Ford was the most Oscar-winning director ever; however, his boastful claim that he had won *six* Oscars, rather than four for his feature films, was but another lie in a long history of easily proven fibs. As one of his biographers, Joseph McBride, noted, "Ford was "ignoring the fact that the Oscars for *The Battle of Midway* and *December 7*th were not awarded to him personally. The Oscar for *The Battle of Midway* was awarded to the navy and 20th Century–Fox, and the navy and Field Photo won the Oscar for *December 7th*."[13]

Ford returned to the topic of the Navy's lack of preparedness in the far less controversial *They Were Expendable*, with a release date in the far less controversial last year of the war, 1945. Between *December 7th* and the war's end, Ford traveled thousands of miles shooting films for the Navy and, on far too many occasions, getting horribly drunk, all on the government's dime. The war would change him; and though it would never temper his bullying ways, his films became darker and more pessimistic; at the same time, his slapstick fight scenes would become sillier. *The Searchers*, *The Horse Soldiers*, *Fort Apache*, *The Man Who Shot Liberty Valence* and especially the Navy-themed *They Were Expendable* all pointed to a director who didn't see armed conflict as a soldier's call to glory, but an end to everything he had known before.

On June 3, 1943, MGM released a film that told the real-life story of the U.S. Army and Marines' heroic defense of an American outpost against ruthless Japanese invaders. What MGM and military censors papered over was the still-controversial theory that their heroic sacrifice was the result of the military's desire to save the face of a famous Army commander.

In many ways, *Bataan* was symbolic of so many World War II propaganda films. Made at a point in the war when the tide was beginning to turn against the Axis, the film purportedly told the story of the American and Filipino defenders of the Bataan peninsula.

The War Department had drafted a plan for the defense of the Philippines. Called WPO-3 (War Plan Number 3), it called for the Philippine garrison to bar the entrance of Manila Bay to Imperial Japanese forces. Recalled to active duty in July 1941, the islands' military governor, General Douglas MacArthur, was to mobilize the Philippine army, though in a defensive posture, to protect the coastline. If the Filipinos failed, then American troops were to fight the Japanese while also retreating to the Bataan peninsula, with the aim of preventing Japanese naval vessels from crossing into Manila Bay. MacArthur turned thumbs down on the plan because it was too "defeatist." He wanted a combined frontal assault against the invaders, should they arrive. There was also squawking among military brass that the plan made no preparations in case other Axis powers joined Japan in attacking Manila Bay. As it turned out, the Japanese needed no outside help in their goals to conquer the Philippines.

MacArthur had ruled the Philippines for years, doggedly trying to create an army from the ground up, with a target date for full readiness by 1946. The Japanese rampage throughout China, and later throughout the Pacific, lent urgency to this goal. But by the time of Pearl Harbor, the Philippines had *still* not come near being the crack army that could defend themselves against a military the size and ruthlessness of the Japanese Imperial forces. Perhaps MacArthur knew it as well. For after the shock of Pearl Harbor, the man who had called WPO-3 plans "defeatist" and ordered his army to charge unarmed families on the grounds of the Capital some nine years before, was strangely lethargic.

As the commander-in-chief of the Philippines, the autocratic (some say, downright dictatorial) MacArthur believed that he had to inspire awe and unbending respect for his command with people of the Far East, to whom he obviously felt superior. Believing that they respected pomp and much swaggering in public, he dressed in loud, attention-getting white uniforms (reportedly made of sharkskin) and his gold-braided Army cap. Carrying his riding prop and wearing his signature dark sunglasses, he was supremely aloof, never allowing himself to get close to his "subjects," or the other way around. The Philippines already had a president, Manuel L. Quezon, but as far as MacArthur, the Filipino people and the U.S. government were concerned, the *real* ruler of the Philippines had four stars on his shoulders and smoked a corncob pipe. Predictably, Quezon appointed MacArthur chief of the Philippines armed forces and a field marshal to boot—as if he had a choice.

Though a commander with a history of winning during the Great War, MacArthur had trouble adjusting to the complications of the new world war. A heroic commanding officer against the Imperial German Army in France, MacArthur most definitely dropped the ball trying to figure out the Japanese; yet the general didn't think there *was* a problem. Fancying himself an expert on Asian peoples, he pooh-poohed the idea of Japanese aggression in the Philippines: "[It] would cost the enemy ... at least a half million of men as casualties and upward of five billion of dollars in money."[14] Still in World War I mode, he thought that the British Navy's failure (then under Lord of the Admiralty, Sir Winston Churchill) to strike Turkish positions on the beaches of Gallipoli would be repeated if the Japanese invaded the Philippines. Again, thinking of himself as one of the few white men to understand "Orientals," he felt that those who feared an invasion were alarmists who "fail fully to credit the Japanese mind."[15] He also believed that the Philippine islands would have no economic or military value to Imperial Japan. With this mindset, he failed to realize that, though the Commonwealth had no oil or rubber deposits which Japan would covet, the enemy might *still* have a problem with American hegemony over the region that would interfere with her plans for conquest in the Pacific.

Army Chief of Staff George C. Marshall was an organizational genius and former officer and senior planner in the Great War. Though he would drop the ball in shoring up defenses for Pearl Harbor, he knew that a Japanese amphibious attack on the Philippines was very possible. So did the Joint Chiefs of Staff, the War Department, Navy brass and the president. But, arrogant as usual and cut off from up-to-date military thought and tactics by his own self-isolation, MacArthur had no contingency plan in the event of a Japanese invasion since, to him, the "Japanese mind" would never conceive of their forces ever going near the Philippines.

On December 7, as Pearl Harbor was still smoldering, the War Department sent an urgent radio message to MacArthur informing him of the sneak attack and that America was now in a state of war. When his pilot, Lewis Brereton, volunteered to attack Japanese positions in Formosa, MacArthur refused his request. Four hours after MacArthur received the War Department message about Pearl Harbor, the Japanese bombed Clark Field, effectively destroying dozens of American B-17s while they were still on the ground, lined up wingtip to wingtip as if they were pins in a bowling alley. MacArthur later lied that Brereton made no request to attack Formosa, which he couldn't have led anyway since he had no fighter planes. Of course, this made sense since the Japanese had already destroyed his planes while they were still on the tarmac. Continuing the lies, MacArthur also claimed that the War Department never once informed him about Pearl Harbor, though government archives proved this to be false.

He had stockpiled few rations for his men, forcing them to go on half-rations; he was slow to order the pullback to the peninsula that he had originally detested; and he refused to believe the intelligence he received of Japanese victories as they got nearer and nearer to Bataan. Directing anti-aircraft fire on Corregidor, MacArthur frantically requested naval support. However, Marshall and the Washington brass-hats had other ideas, the most important being their direct order for MacArthur to leave the Philippines, and leave quickly! He was to take his wife and son on a PT boat and sail for Mindanao, transfer to an Army B-17 and fly to a newly built airbase in Australia to continue the fight. Marshall and the War Department refused to risk the few naval vessels they had to break an already tightening Japanese blockade. There are still unverified stories that MacArthur wanted to go inland so that he could direct a guerrilla campaign against the occupying Japanese. Though there might have been some doubt about this, one thing was certain: The decision was made in the highest corridors of power in Washington to "neutralize" the Philippines. With the Japanese Third Fleet already in Philippine harbors and Lieutenant General Masaharu Homma's 14th Army storming Manila, the endgame was never in any doubt.

No one ever questioned Douglas MacArthur's bravery, including exposing himself to enemy fire and bombardment during the Great War, on Corregidor and other battlefields; he truly *wanted* to stay behind. But to FDR, Marshall, Secretary of War Henry Stimson and the Joint Chiefs, there would be no argument. Not without reason, all of these men probably had nightmarish visions of a captured and tortured MacArthur, blindfolded and led around for Japanese news media (this happened to American hostages in Iran in a much later era). For the Japanese fascists, this would have been an enormous propaganda triumph. A terrified Roosevelt couldn't possibly allow such a thing to occur.

The Americans on Bataan angrily called themselves the "battling bastards of Bataan, with no mother, no father, and no Uncle Sam." MacArthur and other senior officials were on their way to Australia, while the American and Filipino garrisons on Bataan were left to the tender mercies of General Homma and his men.

Safely settled in at the American base in Australia, MacArthur famously vowed, "I shall return!" However, typical of MacArthur, even this sentiment didn't escape controversy. He had defied Roosevelt's order that his vow to the American people should actually be "*We* shall return!" and insisted on using *I* instead.

As usual with Douglas MacArthur, it was all about him.

> Through the Bloody Haze of Bataan's last Reverberating Shot, I shall always seem to see the vision of those grim, gaunt, ghostly men still unafraid.

So proclaimed General MacArthur in the movie crawl for the coming attractions for MGM's new entry into wartime propaganda.

By November 1942, Tay Garnett had commenced filming *Bataan*, the film version of one of America's worst defeats, with superstar Robert Taylor, character man Lloyd Nolan and an MGM stock company cast as a diverse group of American soldiers blowing up bridges to prevent the Japanese from moving inland.

Playwright Robert Hardy Andrews (author of the insightful play *Thunder Rock*) told MGM producer Dore Schary that he had an idea for a film depicting the Army's brave stand against Japanese invaders of the Philippines. Andrews wanted to essentially do a remake of RKO's 1934 desert adventure *The Lost Patrol* which had been directed by John Ford. In that film, Victor McLaglen played the head of a besieged British platoon gradually picked off by Arab snipers. After all the British troops are killed off, McLaglen gets revenge by killing every one of the Arabs as they come out into the open. Schary loved the idea so much that he authorized the studio to purchase the rights to *The Lost Patrol* for $6500.[16]

The movie opens with Japanese Zeros bombing and strafing Red Cross hospitals and encampments in the Philippines, murdering hundreds of soldiers, nurses and children. Though the film itself was morale-raising propaganda, there was no doubt that the Japanese *were* indeed this brutal. Sgt. Bill Dane (Taylor) runs his small squad after Lt. Steve Bentley (George Murphy) is killed. "Assisting" Dane is Corporal Barney Todd (Nolan), a cynical cuss and suspected murderer, who knows in his gut that there is no rescue coming for the "Battling Bastards of Bataan." (The B word is, of course, never used.) The cast also features Robert Walker, Desi Arnaz (as a Cuban-American soldier), Barry Newman, Lee Bowman, Philip Terry and a-far-too-old-for-the-battlefield Thomas Mitchell; the Irish actor is unbelievably cast as Corporal *Jake Feingold*.

Far more interesting is African-American actor Kenneth Spencer as machine-gunner Wesley Epps. Dore Schary wanted a black actor as Epps, and knew that, had he told Robert Hardy Andrews of his plan, the screenwriter would have given him a speech emphasizing his race. The casting choice won praise from the NAACP, but was not realistic since the U.S. Armed Forces at the time was segregated. There were no black soldiers on Bataan.

The propaganda is strong; the various American characters discuss their hopes and dreams, where they're from, as we know full well that these lovable soldiers will be picked off by a merciless enemy—making us hate the Japanese even more. Sgt. Dane and the others have no problem referring to their Japanese enemies as "monkeys." Furthering this racist propaganda, the Japanese soldiers are depicted as half-pint trolls whose faces you barely see; making guttural noises, the Japanese attackers usually appear to be hunched over on all fours as they attempt to overrun the Americans. In fact, Japanese troops wouldn't have had full frontal assaults on their enemies until much later in the war, when all was lost for them. According to the film, these sons of the Rising Sun routinely stick their valuable Samurai swords into fallen Americans and leave them there, the filmmakers neglecting to consider that a Samurai sword handed down from his ancestors was not something a Japanese soldier would abandon in such a cavalier fashion. Besides the inaccuracies about segregation in the Army, the racist portrayals, and the what-the-hell use of Samurai swords, Garnett and Andrews have our heroes use their grenades—an anti-personnel weapon—to blow up bridges. Grenades would hardly damage a bridge.

The *real* rewriting of history was MacArthur's perceived "abandonment" of the men of the Philippines. In *Bataan*, we are told that MacArthur "needs time to reorganize." Reorganize *what*? His men needed outside help, not reorganization. Other World War II films of the times also repeated this lie. "He's needed more [in Australia] than he is here [the Philippines]" is a bit of dialogue from 1943's *So Proudly We Hail!* It's hard to believe that a base in far-off Australia that wasn't under attack was going to need help more than the Philippines. Throughout the war years, and even afterward, Hollywood continued to make excuses for the general. MacArthur "never made a date he didn't keep," says a not-too-bright character in *Manila Calling* (1942). At no time is it ever mentioned that MacArthur had ignored the Japanese rampage over the South Pacific or neglected to beef up his forces in the Philippines. Nor was it

III. Collateral Damage

THE "BATTLIN' BASTARDS OF BATAAN" BATTLIN' EACH OTHER: Left to right: Kenneth Spencer, Phillip Terry, Robert Taylor, Lloyd Nolan and Alex Havier in *Bataan* (1943). The film glossed over the government's—and especially General Douglas MacArthur's—abandonment of its forces in the Philippines.

ever mentioned that MacArthur always claimed that he was never told by the Army that Pearl Harbor had been attacked—an easily proven lie. The systematic destruction of all his planes while still on the ground was emphatically *not* something any character in a studio-bound World War II B film would want to remind a wartime audience.

Ultimately, after all the Americans are picked off by Japanese marauders, only Sgt. Dane (not coincidentally, the star of the film) is left alive for the final assault. The ending will be far different from that of *The Lost Patrol*. Having dug his own grave, Dane fires a machine gun at the enemy and takes several of the sons of the Rising Sun with him before they overwhelm him, with director Garnett focusing on the hot machine gun barrel as a final shot instead of showing the death of a star of Taylor's, pardon the pun, caliber. In another ahead-of-its-time move, Taylor actually mouths "Come and get it, you sons of bitches!" with the noise of the machine gun obscuring the then-forbidden curse word.

Released on June 3, 1943, at a point in the war when Imperial Japanese forces were on the retreat, *Bataan* did well at the box office and was praised by the critics. Their quibbles were reserved for the obviously phony indoor set, with the words "studio-bound" being the biggest complaint about the film. Of course, Garnett praised Cedric Gibbon's work on MGM Sound Stage 16, where the film was shot, claiming that all it needed for total realism were 16-foot snakes. Not concerning itself over the wildlife on Bataan, *Time* magazine thought the film was "constantly loud and over-emphatic," adding: "[T]here are a few stretches where the military situation calls for silence...." *The New York Times* said that *Bataan* "gives a shocking conception of the defense of that bloody point of land. And it doesn't insult the honor of dead soldiers, which is something to say for a Hollywood film these days."[17]

Since the film was entirely shot on MGM stages, the Department of Defense gave no assistance to *Bataan* outside of an offer to lend the production a technical advisor. Looking at the results of his work on the film, he *wasn't* very accurate.

On April 9, 1942, Japanese troops captured Bataan three months and two days after the battle for the peninsula started. Any of the American or Filipino prisoners caught with Japanese money or possessions on them were quickly taken out of sight and shot dead, because the Japanese assumed that the articles came off the dead bodies of their soldiers. Beatings and attacks with rifle butts were common, with many Japanese soldiers punching out the teeth of their captives for the gold fillings. Sitting or standing in the sweltering sun without any head cover, thirsty men who begged for water were routinely shot or bayoneted; trucks drove over those prisoners who passed out and fell in the road. In a chilling parallel to starving, emaciated Jews being squeezed into cattle cars and headed for concentration camps like Auschwitz, American and Filipino P.O.W.s were squeezed into airless cattle cars, and then forced to walk the final nine miles to the recently captured Camp O'Donnell. Ultimately, the march from Mariveles to San Fernando, and from Capas to Camp O'Donnell, was roughly between 60 and 69 miles; add to this that the men were beaten and starving and it was obvious that the Japanese were guilty of Holocaust-like war crimes. (General Homma and other officers were sentenced to death for crimes against humanity after the war.) Between 500 and 650 Americans died on the Bataan Death March, as did between 5000 and 18,000 Filipinos.

Shockingly, America at large had no idea that atrocities were being committed by Japanese troops in the Philippines. They had known about the capture and occupation of the Philippines, but not the horrors of the march. This was a form of wartime censorship refined to a sinister art by the Roosevelt administration, with the aim of releasing information only at opportune moments for purposes of angering the public and boosting morale. On January 28, 1944, the government finally revealed the full details of the Bataan Death March, with a *Life* magazine cover story appearing a short time later. Imperial Japan was on the run, but more than ready for a fight to the death. The story's release was done with the full connivance of the War Department to get the American people ready for a final onslaught of Japanese forces.

Military censorship of wartime atrocities, a commander being ordered to abandon his post and leave his men to the enemy, and a Washington-Hollywood alliance to rewrite the blunder as a World War II version of Custer's Last Stand; all these and even more chicanery would occur as the second "War to End All Wars" continued.

The sneak attack on Pearl Harbor galvanized the formerly Depression-ridden nation into a sudden wave of patriotism. The millions of young American men rushing to join the varied branches of the Armed Forces were angered by the duplicity of the Japanese government and its military. Just as innocent about the ways of war as their predecessors in the previous global conflict, these young men were certainly sincere in their desire to serve their country. This included a group of five young Irish-American brothers from the Midwest cornbelt.

III. Collateral Damage

The Sullivan brothers, George Thomas, Francis Henry (or "Frank"), Joseph Eugene ("Joe" or "Gene"), Madison Abel (or "Matt") and Albert Leo (or "Al") were all born during or immediately after the years of World War I, an ironic counterpoint to their future immortality. On December 26, with the USN already sending its ships out to the South Pacific to face the Imperial Japanese Fleet head-on, the five young men from Waterloo, Iowa, traveled en masse to their local post office, which was doubling as a naval recruiting station, and enlisted in the Navy. Oldest brother George had already written to the USN practically demanding that they all serve together on the same ship, along with two other childhood friends from Waterloo. Lieutenant Commander Truman Jones, a reserve officer whose status was reactivated during the conflict, watched them enlist at the post office.

Jones would also deliver the news of their deaths to their parents in early January 1943.

The Navy acceded to the wishes of five young men whose father was a conductor for the Illinois Central, allowing them to serve on the same ship. The decision fuels controversy to this day. Yet when the brothers Sullivan "jerned up," the USN's public relations office considered it a recruitment gold mine. The War needed men, no matter who they were, and as long as they were sincere—and it was always a good idea if they joined up willingly and didn't *have* to be drafted. It must have surprised the brothers when they were called upon to participate in photo ops, such as when they removed their shirts and stood in line to get their physicals, something they had already done. Navy PR (and Army and USMC) had already focused their publicity efforts on patriotic brothers enlisting all at once in the wake of Pearl Harbor. But here were *five*—count 'em, five—brothers all wanting to serve on the same ship! The boys' image as innocent but patriotic young men dedicated to each other enough to risk dying together, had a far more complicated family dynamic than either the Navy PR office or the Hollywood movers and shakers cared to address.

Their father Thomas was born in 1883 to Irish immigrants. He worked for years at various jobs with the Illinois Central, and befriended a supervisor named George Abel, who had a teenage daughter named Alleta. Leaving school early and devoid of many social graces, Alleta was a simple soul (some might say not very bright); and, seeing very few prospects for his by-now not-so-little girl, George encouraged her wedding to Tom. She was 19, he was 30, which meant that his mother-in-law May was scarcely older than the groom. After George's untimely death, May moved in with her daughter and her husband. In time, there would be far more residents in the Sullivans' rapidly expanding household—five boys, as well as a girl named Genevieve, or "Gen." (In 1931, another child, a daughter, died shortly after birth.)

Though Gen stayed out of trouble, one could not say the same for the five boys. One student at their public school claimed that if you got into a fight with one Sullivan boy, then you had to fight *all* the Sullivan boys, with the unhealthy implication that all the brothers ganged up on lone antagonists. Rowdy and undisciplined, the boys were known to actually travel a few blocks south into the area's black neighborhoods and provoke racial fights with young residents. They also rarely took jobs. None of them had an education beyond the first two years of high school (kind of like their parents). Since their father was still making a respectable salary with the Illinois Central, the boys saw no need to contribute to their town or society at large by consistently being part of its workforce. Though eventually they would attain sporadic work at Rath's meat-packing plant or a pal's garage (where several of the boys developed an interest in motorcycle racing and joining a club afterwards), the brothers Sullivan were never cursed with the ailment their old man possessed. Quiet and reserved, Tom had been an alcoholic for decades. Traveling all over the state in his runs for the railroad, he drank incessantly at many company-owned roadhouses and taverns. Whether he was drinking due to his marriage to the eccentric and sometimes hypochondriac Alleta was never verified. There certainly were frequent fights between the two, with her rage at his drinking a major reason for the clashes. Still, with rare exceptions, Tom almost never drank on the job, and, in fact, performed it competently in the many years he was worked for the Illinois Central. However, sometimes Alleta had to make excuses for Tom when the railroad called to see if he could make an emergency run. The poor woman claimed he was "sick," when he was actually dead-drunk or sleeping off a hangover.

Then, in May 1937, in a rare act of direction in their up-to-then aimless young lives, the two older boys, George and Frank, went down to the naval recruiting station in Cedar Falls and joined the Navy. They soon began their training in Des Moines. It would be the first and *only* time the five Sullivan boys were split up.

They learned skills, attained some discipline in their lives, and even grew up to the point where they absorbed the need for patriotism and moral responsibility. But they were still Sullivans. This meant that, besides benefiting from the peacetime Navy's promise to see the world (with both boys stationed on a light cruiser, the USS *Hovey*), they were still cited for "minor" infractions, like sneaking liquor aboard ship. However, despite the rewarding personal experience of military service and all they had learned, the two boys never went beyond their four-year hitch and left the Navy in mid–1941. Coincidentally, others in the family changed as well. Alleta became a charter member for the Waterloo chapter of the Navy Mothers of America. Genevieve started having a romantic relationship with a young Navy enlisted man, Bill Ball. Very soon, he and his brother Masten, also in the Navy, were transferred to the USS *Arizona*, stationed in Pearl Harbor. The youngest, Al, would ultimately meet a nice young woman named Katherine—called Kena by all who knew her—and he became the father to a baby boy named Jimmy within months of their marriage. In his biography of the Sullivans, Bruce Kuklick writes that the wedding might have been, in reality, a shotgun marriage, with Kena already impregnated. Meanwhile, Tom's employment with the railroad, as well as his drinking, continued.

Then the Japanese bombed Pearl Harbor. Masten Ball survived the attack, but his brother Bill, Gen's boyfriend, perished when the *Arizona* went down while it was still moored in the harbor. Outraged in a way they probably had never been before, all five boys decided to join the Navy. The five brothers joined up together and wanted to serve on the same ship together—despite the fact that they could all go down together. This made national news.

The brothers were assigned to the light cruiser, the USS *Juneau*. They went around the world on this ship, doing mostly convoy duty for British warships, and never got into any kind of serious engagement with the enemy. But the brothers sometimes got into their usual mishaps, like sneaking booze aboard ship and the occasional discipline problem. Still, oldest boy George was responsible enough to man the ship's depth charges; Frank was elevated to coxswain, a job which included relaying orders from the bridge to the gunners on-deck and the torpedo room; Red, Matt and

III. Collateral Damage

Al loaded shells into the *Juneau*'s gun turrets for firing at enemy ships and subs. The Navy was a team, and the Sullivan brothers, whatever their past foibles, became fully committed members of that team.

On November 8, 1942, the *Juneau* set sail from Noumea, New Caledonia, as a major part of Task Force 67 to escort a convoy of naval and Marine reinforcements to Guadalcanal. The Marines had captured a Japanese airfield on the island and renamed it Henderson Field. For several brutal weeks, Marine battalions and Army units fought off attempts by Japanese forces to recapture the field and use it to land their own troops on the island, all while Navy guns took turns along with the Japanese Navy in shelling each others' troops. The American defenders referred to the nightly unloading of enemy troops and supplies as "the Japanese Express." The *Juneau* was part of the protective screen around the various American troop transports and supply ships. Unloading personnel and supplies went on without incident until 2:05 p.m., when a wave of 30 Japanese planes attacked in force. Anti-aircraft fire, much of it from the *Juneau*, shot down six of them, including deadly torpedo bombers (the ships at Pearl Harbor were destroyed by mostly torpedo bombers). American fighter planes destroyed the balance of the Japanese formation except one.

However, at 0148 (1:48 a.m.) on the morning of Friday, November 13, under the command of the incompetent Rear Admiral Daniel J. Callaghan, naval forces, including the *Juneau*, faced off against two Japanese battleships, one light cruiser and nine destroyers. Callaghan's communications were faulty, his radar useless with American ships close by, and the need *not* to turn on searchlights (which would attract enemy fire) resulted in one of the most chaotic sea battles of the war. American ships were so close that they were firing on each other; so were the Japanese. Many were killed by friendly fire on both sides. In the middle of the melee, the Japanese destroyer *Amatsukaze* fired a torpedo at the *Juneau*. Hit on the port side, the *Juneau* started to list. Hours after sunrise, long after the Japanese had retreated, the *Juneau* joined the other two cruisers in the battle, the *Helena* and the *San Francisco*, in heading for the base at Espiritu Santo for repairs. The Sullivans and their shipmates now attained the full level of battle-hardened veterans.

Tragically, their luck was about to run out. Just a few minutes after 11 a.m., a Japanese submarine, the *I-26*, fired two torpedoes at the already damaged and listing *San Francisco*. However, officers and crewmen had spotted the sub and orders were given to stop all engines. The *San Francisco*, against all odds, was indeed able to stop. Unfortunately, even as one of the torpedoes shot harmlessly by the battle group, thanks to the *San Francisco* stopping where it had, the second torpedo sailed past where the ship would have been and struck the vessel behind it, the *Juneau*.

Captain Lyman K. Swenson quickly ordered the ship to turn hard right rudder, but the already damaged *Juneau*'s engines could not muster enough power to complete the turn and the torpedo struck the ship's powder magazine. At that point, the *Juneau* literally disintegrated. According to Lieutenant Commander Bruce McCandless of the nearby *San Francisco*, "The *Juneau* didn't sink. She blew up with all the fury of an erupting volcano. There was a terrific thunderclap and a plume of white water that was blotted out by a huge brown hemisphere a thousand yards across."[18]

George, who was at his post on-deck, was blown into the air along with many others. Most of his brothers were below-decks, where they died immediately with hundreds of other men as the ship blew apart. The 140 or so survivors ended up in the oil-topped sea, bloody and mutilated, some with limbs torn off and massive head wounds. With three of his brothers blown to bits and young Al reportedly drowning some time later, George pathetically continued to call out to them as he crowded into a raft with others.

Tragically, these men, victimized by the Japanese, were now about to be victimized by their own Navy. Captain Gilbert C. Hoover, the *Helena*'s commanding officer, was now the senior officer present afloat. With little evidence, he totally dismissed the possibility that there were any *Juneau* survivors and, not wanting to expose his already damaged ships to further enemy torpedoes, ordered his task force to continue heading to the base at Espiritu Santo. Blood-soaked and hanging onto whatever floating wreckage they could find, the men were horrified to see their fellow crewmen sailing away as if nothing had happened.

A B-17 bombing crew spotted them shortly afterwards but, under orders to maintain radio silence, did not relay the sighting to headquarters. After they returned to base, their report was stupidly filed with dozens of other routine reports. When Admiral William "Bull" Halsey heard that Hoover had cavalierly left the survivors of the *Juneau* floating in the sea, he flew into a rage and ordered the captain's dismissal. Hoover's blunder had left the men of the *Juneau*, starving, wounded, delirious and plagued by sharks, floating in the ocean for the next week and a half. Only ten of the 140 men who went into the water alive survived. Still looking for his brothers, George Sullivan reportedly lost what little sanity he had, stripped off his bloody clothes and dived into the water; at least one of the survivors reported his being devoured by a shark. It was said that he was still searching for his brothers.

Alleta Sullivan heard nothing from her sons for close to two months. Wartime security required that the Navy not reveal the loss of the *Juneau* or other sunken ships so as not to provide information to the enemy; a strict policy to be sure, but cruel to the loved ones of slain heroes. By the time Commander Jones arrived at the Sullivan home at 98 Adams Street, the rumors that the Sullivans were "missing in action" were all over town. Jones' visit and President Roosevelt reply letter to Alleta's query about the boys confirmed the inevitable. Instead of comforting the grieving women under his roof (his wife, her mother, his newly widowed daughter-in-law), Tom fled and went on a bender, not returning home until the following day.

The USN enlisted Tom and Alleta to tour war plants, christen ships and give speeches to thousands of Americans on radio, in newsreels, and at live events to promote war production. Perhaps the USN was exploiting them for the benefit of their recruitment rolls, or perhaps they were doing what was necessary during wartime to guarantee that the nation's war will was kept at a high level. For four months, from February to May 1943, Admiral Clark Howell Woodward, head of the USN's Industrial Incentive Division, looked after their affairs while on tour.

Alleta, the sometimes flighty former high school dropout, became the spokesman for those mothers across the country who had lost their sons in battle. Navy PR experts and the press repeatedly coached her through her many fumbles, which were edited out of newsreel footage and radio broadcasts, and also basically provided the copy she was to read that supposedly came spontaneously from her lips. Not that she didn't have these sentiments promoting a final victory over America's enemies, particularly the Japanese who had killed her sons, but the Navy, prompted by the Roosevelt administration, also larded her pep talk with slogans like "Keep your chins up!"

These exhortations included praise for allies Russia and England, two nations it was obvious she never gave a hoot about. Still, during her appearances before newsreel cameras and radio hookups, Alleta sometimes had to do take after take because she'd cry while thinking about her lost boys. Meanwhile, Navy PR flacks and local newsmen would insist she do the take again, and *this* time, try to restrain her tears.

During the tours, the Navy covered all costs for train transportation, hotels and meals. Tom also agreed to the tours because the Illinois Central promised it would still pay him his regular salary while he was away. Then in May 1943, after dozens of appearances, the Navy suddenly cancelled the tours. Just before the USN cancellation, the Sullivans had suddenly left Hollywood and returned to Waterloo when they heard a family member was sick; though as it turned out, the illness was not serious. Whether the Navy was insulted by the Sullivans rushing home to attend to a family member's illness in the middle of the PR tour is not known. However, the sudden cancellation of the tour raised suspicions. Generally, brass-hats do *not* like anyone cancelling tours they paid for—especially if they felt the cancellation, no matter how legitimate the reason, would jeopardize their recruitment drive. The trips and speeches around the country had given the wounded parents a chance to delay their grief. Now, with Gen joining the WAVES, and without the tours that kept them busy, the aging couple would have no children to deal with, except grandson Jimmy. It wasn't enough; the pain was too great. Tom's alcohol consumption increased.

After leaving the survivors of the *Juneau* floating in the sea for 11 days, it seems the USN decided to cast adrift two more victims of the war.

Though Tom and Alleta continued to be invited to make speeches, christen ships and even receive awards and gifts commemorating their sons' sacrifice far into the postwar years, the two parents were forced to face much of their grief alone. Their own town didn't help, with many residents openly jealous of the attention Tom and Alleta were getting, while the world ignored the sacrifices of their own offspring killed during the war.

In late 1943, while the war was still going on and the Sullivans were still very much in the news, former Warner Brothers helmsman and World War I Navy veteran, Lloyd Bacon, and agent-producer Sam Jaffe proposed to make a film version of the Sullivan brothers' life story. Warners would miss out on producing the film (with a childishly vindictive Jack Warner spreading rumors that the Sullivans were really Jewish!); it was produced by Darryl F. Zanuck's 20th Century–Fox. Released on February 3, 1944, after a title change from *The Sullivans* to *The Fighting Sullivans*, the film was a hugely sentimental drama about a Middle-American wartime family and its doomed sons.

Yet the finished film was not exactly what you'd call accurate.

While the dead officers and crewmen of the *Juneau* were barely in their watery graves, Hollywood had sent feelers to the Sullivans on a film version of their sons' life story. There was talk of an independent production to be released through United Artists; Jack Warner and David O. Selznick also expressed interest.

In 1942, young producer Jules Schermer's one credit was a Republic B movie, *True to the Army*, a comedy starring their number one comedienne Judy Canova. (Schermer would produce more films into the postwar era, and produce the TV Westerns *Lawman, Cheyenne* and the groundbreaking *The Dakotas*.) Schermer had been developing the outline for a story of the Sullivans along with Edward Doherty, a reporter for the *Chicago Sun*; much of his material was based on human interest pieces on the Sullivans by *Chicago Herald-American* reporter Basil Talbot. Admiral Woodward and the Navy brass-hats loved the idea of a film about the Sullivan brothers, and made efforts to introduce the elder Sullivans to the "right people." Thrust into a show business world they had no knowledge of or previous connection to, the two grieving parents were advised by Navy PR people that a film about their boys would help the war effort. Though the Sullivans were undoubtedly patriotic and sincere about helping their country, it probably never occurred to them that some people, like, for instance, their neighbors in their hometown and elsewhere, just might see this new film project as "cashing in" on their boys' deaths. In their conversations with the Sullivans, it was doubtful that their Navy "handlers" ever brought up the subject.

Schermer and Doherty took their Sullivan story to powerful Hollywood agent Sam Jaffe. Known around Hollywood as a "bundler," that is, an agent who could put together casts, scripts, directors and other creative personnel for film projects, Jaffe liked their idea for a film about the Sullivans. However, this being Hollywood, the agent decided to continue with the project on his own, and though Schermer and Doherty were still officially with the project, their participation in it would diminish considerably when a new player entered the picture. For instance, Jaffe had an advantage over the two neophyte writers besides his position with the industry: his friendship with former WB director Lloyd Bacon. A dependable helmsman at Warners, Bacon had directed dozens of their films, including their service films, dramas dealing with the Navy. Of course, this was easy; Bacon was in the Navy during the Great War, doing battleship duty in the Atlantic. Predictably, the helmsman would have no problem using his old Navy connections to help green-light the Warner naval films *Here Comes the Navy*, *Devil Dogs of the Air* and *Wings of the Navy*. In early 1943, Bacon was working on another Navy film for Warners, *Action in the North Atlantic*, this time dealing with the Merchant Marines fighting Nazi U-boats starring Humphrey Bogart. However, Bacon's contract ran out in the middle of filming. Jack Warner told him to keep filming and *then* they'd talk about a new contract. Bacon's reply: no contract, no film. Jack Warner, being Jack Warner, vindictively fired Bacon, who, in mid–1943, was now *very* open to Sam Jaffe's overtures about a partnership to produce and direct a film about the Sullivans. Rather predictably, the USN wholeheartedly approved Bacon's participation in the project. Indeed, using his Navy contacts, Bacon ensured that the Sullivans would sign with him and Jaffe—and *not* Jack Warner—a development Bacon surely enjoyed.

Jaffe hooked up with the Sullivans in March during their swing through the Midwest, eventually arranging a meeting between them and Bacon in Minneapolis. Besides even this overkill, the naval officers traveling with the Sullivans *also* sang Bacon's praises. He was a Navy man, they said; and he'd instill compassion, sympathy and good ol' Midwest family values into the film, reminding the two parents that only *they* can produce the perfect film tribute to their dead sons. They even mentioned Bacon's direction of *Knute Rockne, All American* (1940) to show the parents that only Bacon could provide the necessary sentiment.

At first, realizing that Alleta was going to christen the USS *The Sullivans* around that time, Jaffe and Bacon thought they could use the event as the title for their film, an idea deep-sixed by the Navy. However, it was perfectly okay to use the ceremony at the beginning of the new film, with actors playing the Sullivan parents and Navy brass and cutting in the actual launching of the ship.

Jaffe and Bacon did get the Sullivan boys' parents to give them the rights to film their sons' story. As it turned out, the filmmakers would contribute to Jimmy's education, give a sizable amount to Navy charities (which the Navy loved), etc. Jaffe also signed the parents and their daughter, Gen, as technical advisors. Still, despite this big Hollywood deal, some things remained disturbingly the same. As Jaffe recalled years later, Tom drank a lot at the end of each day. In a letter to Waterloo neighbor Nell Turner, Alleta lamented that she'll have to "hogtie" her husband to keep him from the film community's free-flowing booze culture.[19]

Around this time, Tom and Alleta visited Allen Heyn, one of the *Juneau* survivors who had seen George being devoured by a shark. "They didn't take it well, of course," Heyn said later.[20]

Jaffe and Bacon paid author and scenarist Mary McCall Jr. $25,000 to write the screenplay. Then, not unexpectedly, Jaffe spent another $25,000 to buy Schermer and Doherty out of their participation in the project—more of the spoils for himself and Bacon that way (and the 25G also blocked any attempt by the young writers to file a lawsuit).[21] Schermer and Doherty still get credit for the original story. Then, in July, it was arranged for the movie to be released by Darryl F. Zanuck's 20th Century–Fox. By September, McCall had finished her script. Under Zanuck's guidance, the screenplay was to be an American version of the Welsh family of director John Ford's *How Green Was My Valley* (1941), a Best Picture Oscar winner. The new project would be an all-too-blatant film about a lovable Midwest family who end up sacrificing their sons to the war. It was also to have a 97 percent focus on the Sullivan family and three percent on the war.

Called *The Sullivans*, the film was quickly withdrawn from theaters and then re-released as *The Fighting Sullivans*. However, as one can tell from viewing the finished film, the only ones the Sullivans seem to be fighting in the first hour and 45 minutes are *each other*!

Alleta had wanted James Cagney cast as her eldest George; a laughable suggestion considering the actor was then 44 years old. (It also showed how naïve the Sullivan parents were about the movies.[22]) Oscar-winning character actor Thomas Mitchell plays Tom, who works for the Illinois Central; tall and regal Selena Royle plays the short and dumpy Alleta; top-billed in the film, Fox contract starlet Anne Baxter plays Kena; B starlet Trudy Marshal is Gen; Ward Bond is the Navy officer who inducts the Sullivan boys; Roy Roberts is Father Francis, who baptizes each of the boys at the beginning of the film. Everyone else in the film, that is, the young actors who played the Sullivan boys, were unknown. Unfortunately, like their onscreen roles as doomed young men, three of the actors portraying the boys died young. James Cardwell (who played George) shot himself in the head in 1954, despondent over his failed career; George Offerman, Jr., (who played Joe) died at 45 in 1963; and Bobby Driscoll (who played Al as a child) died of a drug overdose in 1968; his body was found in an abandoned building on New York's Lower East Side. Of the men playing the brothers, John Alvin (who played Matt) had the most successful career, first, as a contract player for Warner Brothers, then as a frequently hired performer in films and TV. He died in Los Angeles at the ripe old age of 94.

McCall and company took many of the real-life dramas and mishaps of the brood and put them into the film. There is the time the four boys abandoned a leaky boat in the middle of the river and left their crying little brother Al to drown. In fact, it was *Gen* who alerted adults by the river to save Al—the film ignores the fact that the other four brothers didn't attempt a rescue. We see the brothers fighting against other boys, not the black youths they attempted to start racial fights with, or the single boys all five would tackle at once. Yet the most melodramatic real event put into the film is when the boys cut out a section of the house's outer wall in order to make an opening to the outside to easily gain access to piled-up firewood. Eldest George refuses to be involved in the scheme, yet Tom thinks George was responsible and beats him. It's a painful scene, with Tom brutally smacking the boy around. Even with Breen Office restraints on brutality, this obvious child abuse is still upsetting to see.

When the brothers find Al's love letters to Kena, they rudely embarrass him at the dinner table while Kena is present. After Kena flees in tears, it seems that only Alleta cares, demanding that Tom (who apparently thought this embarrassment was funny) and the other boys go to the young woman's house and apologize. Soon, Kena and Al are married and Jimmy is born. There's no talk of shotgun marriages; in fact, we don't even see Kena's parents.

When Pearl Harbor is bombed, the boys are outraged. Gen's boyfriend Bill Bascom (*not* Bill Ball) is killed in the attack. After bringing up the idea of joining either the Army or the Marines, the boys finally march to the local naval recruiting station and practically bully their way into signing up as a unit—an attitude that would have gotten them kicked out of there in real life. Reluctantly, Lt. Commander Robinson (Ward Bond) signs them up to all serve on one ship, a controversy that would *not* be repeated, certainly not often, after the boys were killed in action. In reality, there was no such thing as a "Sullivan Law." However, there would be a Sole Survivor Policy; *this* time it would be strictly enforced.

Another glaring inaccuracy in this film is the fact that McCall neglects to mention that George and Frank had already served four years in the Navy in the late '30s. In fact, it was at their behest—having experience as sailors years before Pearl Harbor—that the other three brothers join the Navy. There was *never* any debate about joining the Army or Marines.

Finally, for just five minutes towards the end of the film, we see the boys serving on the *Juneau* during a night attack—not the daytime when the already damaged ship was torpedoed. The four brothers visit George in sick bay, though he was in reality on deck during the attack and his brothers were mostly below-decks. The lights suddenly go out and there is an explosion, a Breen Office soft-pedaling of the real-life horror of a ship being torpedoed. And, needless to say, we *won't* see a Navy captain order his task force to abandon 140 wounded men bobbing in a shark-infested sea.

Robinson (alone; not with another officer) informs the boys' family that they are "missing in action." In the film, May Bell, Alleta's mom, is nowhere to be seen. Tom stridently announces that he has to go to work, and leaves; we do not see him go on a drunken binge. Later, when he rides his railroad car past the water tower the boys played on as kids, he quickly turns away from us as he's about to shed tears. In the film, Alleta seems to take the boys' deaths very well, actually making some coffee for Robinson without shedding a tear.

In a moving scene, which *could* be seen as corny today, the boys all wave goodbye to us from Heaven (though I'll honestly admit, show me a film that ends with the ghosts of war heroes and I'll blubber like a baby).

In his February 10, 1944, *New York Times* review, Bosley Crowther praised the film, calling it "a deeply touching story, because of the personal sacrifice it represents." Later in the review, he concluded, "We might add that the tragic battle action is but a brief descriptive sequence in the film and that the tearful aspects are handled tactfully. This is the story of why the Sullivans fought, not how."[23]

Originally, there were to be war scenes filmed on-location at the San Diego Naval Base, and other scenes of the boys in uniform, but they were scrapped by Zanuck, who wanted to focus on the boys at home in Waterloo. The film was a sleeper hit; encouraging Zanuck to make a film about another notable figure from small-town America who became nationally known in a time of war, Woodrow Wilson. Unfortunately for Zanuck and Fox, *Wilson* (1944) bombed.

Tom Sullivan died on March 2, 1966, Alleta on April 22, 1972, and Gen, after inheriting Tom's problems with alcohol abuse, died less than three years after her mom, on February 11, 1975. May Abel, Alleta's mother, outlasted them all, dying at 102 in 1980.

President Ronald Reagan, who had played "The Gipper" in Lloyd Bacon's *Knute Rockne, All American*, eulogized Tom and Alleta's sacrifice in 1987:

WE BAND OF BROTHERS: The five Sullivan brothers—left to right: Joe, Frank, Al, Matt and George—in a Navy publicity photo in February 1942, months before their tragic fate aboard the USS *Juneau*.

[N]one of us who were alive then can forget the special burden of grief borne by Mr. and Mrs. Thomas Sullivan of Waterloo, Iowa. They would remember forever the afternoon they learned that their sons, the Five Sullivans as we knew them then, would not be coming home.[24]

The Fighting Sullivans was not only made as a tribute to a group of brothers who died for their country, but to infuriate Americans even more against our Japanese enemies. In early 1944, as *The Fighting Sullivans* was being released, the Imperial Japanese military was only *beginning* to exact a deadly toll on young Americans. For the next year and a half, the Army, Navy and Marines conquered island after island as they got closer to the Japanese mainland, losing thousands of brave men to a fanatical enemy.

In the war's last year, a director who was already a combat veteran made one of Hollywood's finest films about the war. Shot with realism in mind rather than cinematic heroism or phony flag-waving, this production's maverick director held his own prejudices against one of the branches of the Armed Forces and even lied in his cinematic depiction of a controversial bombing.

Independent producer Lester Cowan had been trying to bring to the screen a tribute to the Army fighting in the European theater since September 1943. Though his ideas for the story were vague at first, Cowan contacted the Department of Defense and told them of his plan. As usual with War Department brass-hats, they expressed great interest, but they were wary of wholeheartedly endorsing a project they were sure they would find fault with—especially as the services were fully experienced with Hollywood's tendency to fabricate the narrative, as well as their failure to adhere to the military's strict ideas of its own self-image. Nevertheless, by October, Cowan conceived the idea to make a film version of the book by groundbreaking war correspondent Ernie Pyle, with much of this work consisting of the reporter's "Here Is Your War" columns. The proposed project would show the Infantry during training and their war experiences as they slog through the Italian campaign. On November 27, the Army approved Cowan's brief outline; however, typically, they also pointed out, "It must be realized that many modifications will occur before this picture is completed."[25]

In other words, "This pipe dream of yours better be good, pal."

Unfortunately, Cowan had trouble coming up with a good script, and another year passed. Much of the problem was due to Cowan's exacting standards. He envisioned a tribute to the infantry but he did *not* want it to be the usual propaganda pap, filled with scenes of battle where heroism was glorified and the enemy was stereotyped to the point of absurdity. He wanted to focus on the *real* foot soldier, not Hollywood's typical portrayal of the American fighting man as a Superman who always wins as movie stars fight their way through either sound stages dressed up with tree and shrubbery props or parks in Southern California masquerading as battle zones.

In a letter to the Army's Bureau of Public Relations, the producer wrote just why it was taking so long to get the project off the ground:

In our script, we are undertaking something quite without precedent. It is a challenge to undertake the writing of a dramatic story about the war and the soldier during the war. As you know, in the past the best war stories evolved during the 10-year period following the war, when issues and events had become resolved and could be viewed with some perspective.[26]

Sticking with his idea of paying tribute to Ernie Pyle as well as the infantry, Cowan wanted the film to be "a love story, figuratively speaking, between Pyle and the soldier."²⁷ When Cowan wrote this letter to the Army on June 28, the successful invasion of Normandy three weeks before had given the producer the catalyst he was looking for. U.S forces had gone forward on the field of battle in spectacular fashion. Having freed France, they were now fighting vicious uphill battles as they advanced towards Rome. Mussolini and his fascists had been deposed, but the *Wehrmacht* had moved back into the Italian mainland and Sicily to fill the void left by the defeated *fasciste*. The U.S. Infantry would be the main fighting force against them. The Yanks were coming, and the film would now not only be seen as a victory for the American foot soldier advancing on the ground, but its constant chronicler, Pyle, a civilian who shared the same crappy food, the same discomforts, the same dirty conditions, and the same frustrating roadblocks that they had suffered on their way to Victory.

What Cowan needed was a director who would fight tooth and nail against any and all clichés of the war film, not an easy task under any circumstances in 1940s Hollywood.

Impressed by the wartime footage (if not the blatant military-approved propaganda) of the so-called documentary shorts in the *Why We Fight?* series, Cowan asked one of its main directors, John Huston, to make a film out of Pyle's book. Liking Huston's short *Report from the Aleutians*, and well aware that the helmsman had completed *The Battle of San Pietro*, set in wartime Italy, Cowan thought these projects gave Huston "irreplaceable experience of living with soldiers under frontline conditions, so that he knows and feels the difference between the real thing and the Hollywood version."²⁸ As he progressed in his goal of depicting the real-life sufferings of the infantry during wartime, it was obvious that Cowan was now holding Hollywood's fantasy version of the American soldier in contempt.

After perusing the latest draft of the script, Huston gave the producer some "very constructive and helpful criticisms."²⁹ Unfortunately, the director of *The Maltese Falcon*, still making films for the Pictorial Branch of the War Department, had to turn him down. Coupled with this rejection was the fact that the Army wouldn't let Huston go anyway. Like John Ford, who was also filming the war as it was actually happening, Huston reveled in his battlefield assignment, getting more out of his combat photography mission than he would have back in safe and pampered Hollywood. Especially impressive to the military was Huston's seamless melding of documentary footage and brass-hat propaganda; bombs and bullets and flag-waving, except that the sets were real.

What Cowan desperately needed was someone who was still on Hollywood's radar, someone who was experienced with war, someone who was *not* attached to the *Why We Fight* unit, and therefore be under Department of Defense jurisdiction. Where would he find such an independently minded crack helmsman and war veteran, one who could respect the infantry and bring forth a brutally realistic portrait of the foot soldier in battle, as well as a tribute to their own personal Boswell, Ernie Pyle?

When Cowan showed up uninvited on William Wellman's doorstep one day in 1944 with his offer to direct his film, he was *not* exactly welcomed with open arms. After telling Wellman that both he and Pyle wanted him to direct, Wellman turned him down. Cowan persisted, wanting to know exactly *why* the director who helmed the first Best Picture Oscar winner, *Wings* (1927), and whose best work had dealt with men in battle, felt like turning thumbs-down on his film. Getting mad (which, to "Wild Bill" Wellman, was relatively easy), the director blurted out that he was not interested in "working my ass off" for the Infantry.[30] Cowan was showed the door.

A combat pilot with the French Foreign Legion during the Great War, Wellman never articulated just *why* he detested fighting men who had to slog through the mud while he fought his wars gliding through the air above them. Indeed, considering that the U.S. Infantry would suffer thousands of casualties from the Civil War onward while still doing its job, one wonders why Wellman had had this kind of inter-service snobbery. And though he knew Pyle by reputation, Wellman steadfastly refused to read the correspondent's usually complimentary columns to the Infantry because, according to the director, "it would be like waving a red flag in front of a bull...." When Cowan returned with a letter from Pyle, Wellman "slammed the door in his face."[31] Cowan risked bodily harm by returning, again uninvited, a few days later with Christmas presents for Wellman's kids. This time the director threatened to put Cowan in the hospital.

From his home in Albuquerque, New Mexico, Pyle called Wellman. Pyle had been "in the line" along with the men he wrote about; even an obnoxious SOB like Wellman had to hold his tongue for five minutes as the war correspondent explained what he wanted of him *vis-à-vis* the new film. Before you knew it, according to Wellman, Pyle had him "close to tears," and he surprisingly agreed to visit the correspondent at his home two days later.

The visit was *not* what the director expected. According to Lee Server, author of the definitive biography of Robert Mitchum, *Baby, I Don't Care*:

> The writer who had been traipsing around the European war fronts turned out to be a frail, gray-haired, middle-aged man. Pyle's home life was modest and lonesome. His wife stayed in her room and drank. Ernie slept in the garage. Wellman slept in the guest room, uncertain what he was doing there. He had yet to read a word of Pyle's writings, and with nothing to do that night but listen to the clink of Mrs. Pyle's ice cubes, he cracked open Ernie's latest, called *Brave Men*.[32]

Though one can hardly say that Pyle had been "traipsing around the European war fronts," nevertheless, Wellman was up most of the night reading his book. It affected the helmsman, a veteran of another world war, in a way he didn't expect, even if the main subject of the tome was the hated Infantry.[33] By the following morning, the red flag in front of the bull had completely faded. Lester Cowan finally got his director.

The producer, who had also showed up in New Mexico for the meeting with Pyle, flew back to Hollywood with the director to work on the script. By late 1944, it was starting to take shape, but Cowan still brought in three scenarists who were credited with the completed screenplay. Ironically, they were all Communist Party members: Guy Endore, author of the anti-religious horror novel *Werewolf of Paris* ("*not* a Pulitzer Prize winner," wrote Lee Server[34]); Leopold Atlas, who later broke with the Party and testified before HUAC; and Philip Stevenson, who co-wrote the pro–Soviet *Counter-Attack* (and later died in the Soviet Union). If there was any left-wing propaganda in the film attacking America's Armed Forces, it was quickly scrapped by Wellman and Pyle's very real desire to portray the American fighting man in a sympathetic but realistic way. There would be no psychotic officers like Sgt. Croft (from *The Naked and the Dead*); nor would there be any Supermen soldiers of the kind that was featured in practically *any* American war film up to that time.

III. Collateral Damage

The project was now called *The Story of G.I. Joe* (Wellman heavily implied that *he* had come up with the title). To the director, the film would be "cruel, factual, unaffected, genuine, with a heart as big as Ernie's."[35]

For the role of Pyle, who was 44 at the time, Cowan considered several middle-aged character actors, including Oscar winners Walter Brennan and Barry Fitzgerald. He even considered Fred Astaire. Instead, Cowan followed Pyle's advice and chose Burgess Meredith, who was seven years younger than the correspondent. At the time, the actor actually *was* in the Army as a captain (some sources say a lieutenant). Typically, Army bureaucrats gave Cowan a choice: If they gave him Meredith, the producer would have to turn over all of his profits to the Army Emergency Relief Fund, or the actor would have to resign his commission. Instead, Cowan was able to arrange to have Meredith put on inactive duty. As expected, the Army did *not* collapse due to the absence of the future portrayer of the Penguin.

Robert Mitchum was a different matter. Though already in the Army, the actor had seen no action and, a wild and undisciplined man offscreen, had not obtained Meredith's rank of captain or anything even close to it. He was also a contract player for RKO; he was no star yet. Passing the audition, Mitchum was cast as the mythical Captain Bill Walker, supposedly a conglomeration of brave but weary battlefield officers whom Pyle himself had known. Cowan arranged the loan-out from RKO for Mitchum's services for a total of six weeks at a salary of $800 a week. However, the actor was only to get his standard $350 a week. RKO pocketed the rest.[36]

For further realism, Wellman got from the War Department 150 hardened combat veterans from the North Africa and Italian campaigns. The soldiers were given six weeks of active duty, or a "working leave," to shoot Wellman's film at Iverson's Ranch in Chatsworth and sound stage shooting at Selznick Studios. This was but a brief respite for these infantrymen. After filming, they were to face the fanatics of the Japanese Imperial Army in the South Pacific. In a speech to the men before filming started, Wellman announced that he was just "a broken-down old flyer" who still hated the Infantry; however, he also promised he wouldn't "double-cross them."[37]

Meredith, Mitchum, Wally Cassell (cast as the wiseguy Private Dondaro) and other actors were to sleep with the soldiers in battlefield conditions, eat K-rations along with them, and carry 80-pound backpacks during scenes of marching. These actors were to be fully integrated into the film's depiction of C Company (or Charlie Company) of the 18th Infantry Regiment, 1st Infantry Division. And despite all this "realism" from Wellman, there was still the uncomfortable fact that the 18th Infantry never fought in the Italian campaign. In fact, after serving in Sicily, the 18th (which Pyle traveled with) was sent to England to prepare for the Normandy invasion; and the 1st Division would be one of the first to hit Omaha Beach, not the Italian mainland.

The film is basically plotless; with various soldiers' deaths and Pyle receiving a letter midway through the film informing him that he won the Pulitzer Prize any indication of a passage of time. Throughout, however, Wellman's realism is plain for us to see. The men seem to slog through mud, torrential downpours and enemy fire with a grim sense of duty. From Meredith and Mitchum on down, the men have beards, and no one appears before us without at least a pound of grime and a cup of sweat on his face. Topping this off, the actors' constant diet of K-rations added to the picture of soldiers deprived of the comforts of home, and surviving on guts alone.

Having visited the set and witnessed Wellman's version of Basic Training for his cast of actors and Infantrymen, Hedda Hopper wrote in her column:

> Actors in *G.I. Joe* were pleading to be shipped to a real combat zone before Wellman finished with them. His set was filled with four feet of ice-cold mud and every night he had the special effects department soup it up.
>
> When the actors showed up at 8 a.m. and donned their full packs...they were ordered to fall in, in the mud. "That's how the soldiers live," howled Wellman, "so get in there." As a result, the actors looked like combat soldiers on the screen. They knew what slogging through mud meant.[38]

The plot, if one can call it that, has the 18th slogging their way through war-torn Italy. But before they slog, they will ride. The movie starts with the men getting into trucks as Lt. Bill Walker (Mitchum) watches over them. He and the men grudgingly accept Scripps correspondent Pyle (Meredith). Another passenger is a puppy who is beloved by the dogfaces. A lovable pooch, with a tendency to whimper piteously, the poor thing will instill terror in audience members who happen to be dog lovers (like me!); and as we watch the film, we're in dread that the adorable pup will be horribly killed. In fact, all through the film, not one grunt will think of doing the puppy a good turn and leaving him with some loving family (with children) in some newly liberated Italian village. This goes to prove that, during a war, lovable puppies and kittens should *not* be in the line! The dog does not die, but no thanks to the men of Charlie Company, who insist on taking him practically everywhere they go.

During the men's drive in the Italian desert, Wellman's partiality to the flyboys first makes itself felt, as a truck's gunner warns the men, "Just *one plane* and you're all dead ducks!" Sure enough, Charlie Company is attacked by the *Luftwaffe*. After they fly away, the men come out from their hiding places and one of them chortles, "Hey, what did I tell you about the Air Corps?" and another soldier calls the attackers "Yellow bellies!" Then the soldiers suddenly see horror in front of them. Wellman doesn't show it and the music on the soundtrack turns grim, so we can assume one of the trucks was strafed, with dead bodies everywhere. Despite the Breen Office, Wellman could have at least given us a quick shot of what the men were staring at.

Still, the scene shows where Wellman's real admiration lies: Trumping the boastful American soldiers who had contempt for the Air Corps, the director still puts combat pilots above his hated Infantry even when the flyers are Nazis.

When one private tries to convince an Infantry-hating private named Murphy (or "Murph"), that "the Infantry ain't so worse," Murph's response could have come directly from Wellman: "Look, this is a modern war, ain't it? And I'm a modern guy. The modern age is up in the air. That's where I belong, not down here."

As the men march through burning sun and torrential downpours, they ridiculously call the 44-year-old correspondent "Pop." Though it is plain for all to see that Pyle is not used to the hardships of war, the ink-slinger stubbornly keeps up with the men; leaving behind his duffle bag to cross a river alongside them, getting soaked in the rain, and having mud on his face just like the men he's writing about. Resting alongside a road as the troops march by, Pyle listens to the dogfaces as they shout out their names so that he'll write about them. Realizing that he's no better than they are, he doggedly gets up and marches along with them, knowing full well that these men can't sit at the side of the road and rest whenever they please.

Storming into a Nazi-held town, Private Dondaro (Wally Cassell), the smart-mouthed Italian-American soldier ("Tonight I dream in Technicolor!"), breaks into a bar and finds a cute young Italian lady named Amelia (Yolanda Lacca). She's the first woman he's seen in God knows how long, and despite their obvious *sympatico*, he's got to get back into the war. It's a sweet, semi-comic scene. Another standout scene is the big shootout amidst the ruins of a bombed-out church, with Walker and Sgt. Warnicki (played by boxer Freddie Steele) having a firefight with German snipers, eventually gunning down all of them. "This is a funny place to be killing men in, isn't it?" says Warnicki before he kneels in front of an altar. When a sniper hanging from a bell rope shoots Warnicki's helmet off, Warnicki and Walker riddle him with bullets. The ringing bell becomes a death knell for all the German snipers.

Indeed, all through the film, the church is uncomfortably juxtaposed with the brutal realities of the war. Besides the gun battle and grenade explosions within the ruins of a church, there are *Wehrmacht* snipers hiding behind church bells. When Warnicki saves Captain Walker's life by machine-gunning a sniper, the dead Nazi knocks down the damaged statue of a saint. Later, when Murph is married to an American nurse in another ruined church, the priest says the words "No man shall tear asunder," than blurts out, "Hit the dirt!" During the war itself, Hollywood war films would still have religious characters expressing their faith (of course, as long as they were *Christian*), but now these scenes of piety are merged with the violence of war. In Andre de Toth's *None Shall Escape* (1944), a young *Wehrmacht* officer, disgusted with Nazism, rips off his Swastika armband and kneels before the Host in a church, only to be gunned down by his fanatical superior. In Lewis Milestone's *Edge of Darkness* (1943), as Norwegian guerrillas rebel against their Nazi conquerors, the village priest grabs a Thompson and riddles the Germans from his perch in the bell-tower. In real life, Nazis would use church property as a killing field in the controversial Battle of Monte Cassino.

Or *would* they? And here too, Wellman and his leftist screenwriters use the juxtaposing of religious institutions with the violence of war; however, Monte Cassino was no fabrication of a screenwriter's imagination. A massive abbey set high in the hills overlooking the village of Cassino, it was founded by Benedict of Nursia in 529 A.D. In January 1944, months before *The Story of G.I. Joe* started production, the abbey was at the center of what became known as the Gustav Line, with the *Wehrmacht* effectively dominating the hilltop peaks overlooking Cassino, as well as the entrances to the Liri, Garigliano and the Rapido-Gari Valleys. In the film, as Charlie Company gets within sight of Monte Cassino, the lieutenant remarks how quiet it is and the men think the Germans have pulled all the way back to Rome. Of course, their optimism is destroyed by a devastating artillery barrage. In his communications to headquarters, Walker remarks, "Well, you can call it [a monastery] if you want to, but in *military* terms, I call it an observation post!" When the artillery commander calls it a religious shrine and an explosion comes too close to the Company, Walker shouts into his walkie-talkie, "Does that sound like religion to you?!" It should be pointed out that at no time do the characters refer to the place as Monte Cassino, though Pyle remarks that it's been around over a thousand years; it's just called "the monastery." (Incidentally, we are never shown the abbey.)

Whether it was the work of the film's Communist screenwriters (who wouldn't have been enthusiastic about ancient religious institutions), or uncredited screenwriters who later punched up the script (including Western author Alan LeMay), or for that matter Wellman himself, the film's point of view clearly backed the Army's decision to bomb the monastery into oblivion. In the film, the men below the monastery are targeted by both snipers and artillery fire for what seem like days, not the actual months that the Germans held sway. Still, the verdict is already predetermined by the dialogue of the men who are being fired upon:

> I'm a Catholic, and I say bomb it!
> Think I want to die for a piece of stone?

Perhaps to the film's Communist screenwriters, it was a "piece of stone," but to the world's Christians it was far more than that. Nevertheless, the film backed the military's decision. Therefore, when American bombers finally fly overhead and reduce the monastery to rubble, the troops cheer their arrival. Yet again, in a film saluting the Infantry, Wellman has his characters cheer the Air Corps. (At another point, Pyle comments that Infantrymen die in dirt and mud while flyers look immaculate before being shot down.) Yet Wellman totally ignored the fact that the destruction of Monte Cassino was a collaboration between the Air Corps and ground troops. And it was carried out despite serious miscommunications—mostly by the Air Corps. Ultimately, there were no less than four major assaults against the monastery, not just the quickie air bombardment the filmmakers showed. To Wellman and his screenwriters, one simple bombing raid and all was well with the world. The reality was far more complicated.

Commander-in-Chief of the Mediterranean Allied Air Forces, Lieutenant General Ira C. Eaker, accompanied by other top brass from the Mediterranean theater, had flown over the monastery and Eaker reported "a radio mast.... German uniforms hanging on a clothesline in the abbey courtyard [and] machine gun emplacements 50 yards from the abbey's walls."[39] Major General Geoffrey Keyes of the U.S. II Corps *also* flew over the monastery, and apparently a lot more times than Eaker & Co. (One wonders why the Germans didn't shoot these reconnaissance planes down.) Keyes promptly reported to the Fifth Army G-2 (Army intelligence division) that he had seen no *Wehrmacht* troops anywhere in the abbey, nor any hard evidence that they had ever been there. Commenting on the "findings" of Eaker and his group, the major general remarked, "They've been looking so long, they're seeing things."[40]

Unfortunately, others in more influential positions than Keyes were also seeing things, and they were hundreds of miles away from the battle zone. The British press, as well as C.L. Sulzberger of the *New York Times* (who had their own journalistic lapses in not reporting the discovery of Hitler's concentration camps), without any proof, freely backed Eaker's assertions that Monte Cassino was saturated with Nazis.

In assaults from the left by X Corps on January 17, and then from the center by II Corps three days later, the Army made *not one dent* in German defenses. The French tried, then the British. Then British Major General Francis Tuker, who headed the 4th Indian Division, suggested massive aerial bombing with blockbuster bombs, since 1,000-lb. bombs would be useless, he claimed. Apparently, he had made a study of the monastery from an 1879 book he had picked up at a Naples bookshop. Armed with this information, Tuker pointed out to Army brass that the walls of the abbey were 150 feet high and consisted of masonry that was ten feet thick.[41] Perhaps they were, but the general's findings were emphatically *not* backed by Army G-2, who relied on far more substantial intelligence than half-price books from wartime Naples' version of Barnes & Noble.

Tuker's "findings" were backed by Lieutenant General Ira Eaker and Lieutenant General Jacob Devers, both of whom wanted to impress the enemy (and apparently, their allies as well) with American air power, something William Wellman would have definitely approved. However, their plans made absolutely no impression on Lieutenant General Mark Clark, commander of the Fifth Army, and his Chief of Staff, Major General Alfred Gruenther: They saw no military necessity in the bombing. Still, Clark told the British Commander-in-Chief, Allied Armies in Italy, General Sir Harold Alexander, "You give me a direct order and we'll do it."[42]

On the morning of February 15, 142 Boeing Flying Fortresses (B-17 heavy bombers), accompanied by 47 B-25 and 40 B-26 medium bombers, dropped over 1,150 tons of explosives and incendiary bombs on the centuries-old monastery and reduced it to smoldering rubble. Not stopping there, the Air Corps also dropped their payloads on the surrounding hillside. And, as in Wellman's film, both ground forces and correspondents cheered the destruction. Wisely, General Clark made sure that he and his chief of staff were nowhere near the scene; he was at Fifth Army headquarters at Prevenzano, 17 miles away. They knew it was a fiasco, yet Clark followed orders. The following day, 59 more bombers dropped another payload on the destroyed structure and its surroundings. Unfortunately, the Air Corps never once coordinated their

BOSWELL, MEET JOHNSON: The wiseguy sergeant (Wally Cassell) lights correspondent Ernie Pyle's (Burgess Meredith) cigar in director William A. Wellman's *The Story of G.I. Joe* (1945).

operations with the Infantry so they could initiate "mopping up" operations on the ground. This was, after all, a time for the flyboys to strut their stuff, not Wellman's hated foot soldiers. Typically, Army red tape delayed the arrival of much-needed food and supplies for the Infantry, with priorities given to the Air Corps. Also, with bad weather predicted, and the Infantry always bogged down in mud due to flooding in the valley, it was felt by the generals that the foot soldiers were no longer needed. All those bombs should have done the trick by now…right?

Then, to the horror of military brass, something went wrong.

German troops seemed to come out of the woodwork, or more likely, the broken remnants of stone walls that used to be ten feet thick. According to historian Andrew Roberts in his *Masters and Commanders: How Four Titans Won the War in the West, 1941–1945*:

> Cassino's sixth-century Benedictine abbey—once it was severely damaged by Allied aerial bombardment on 15 February 1944—provided in its rubble a highly effective strongpoint to hold up the Allied advance. The battle of Monte Cassino was one of the most hard-fought engagements of the Second World War, and after the flooding of the Rapido [Valley] meant that tanks and motorized equipment could not be employed.[43]

On March 27, Churchill complained bitterly to his War Cabinet that the RAF was "not able to knock out Monte Cassino!"[44] Furious at the lack of results in dislodging the Germans, the prime minister told the commander of British forces, Field Marshal Sir Alan Brooke, that he had written privately to General Alexander a week before and wondered why there were "no attacks on the flanks." Continuing his tirade, Churchill wrote, "Why was Cassino the only point of attack? Please explain why no flank movements can be made. We've broken the teeth of six divisions."[45] Alexander answered that Monte Cassino "blocked and dominated" the main valley leading to Rome.[46]

Yet now there *wasn't* any more Monte Cassino blocking anything, so why were the Allies still stalled? Didn't they get rid of the Germans?

In fact, despite the insistence of several Allied officers to the contrary, there was never *any* verifiable proof that the Nazis had hunkered down amidst the walls of Monte Cassino; they had avoided it before, seeing no military objective in being pinned down within four walls of an ancient edifice, something they knew could be a prime target for Allied bombing despite the complaints of the world's Catholics. Also, it was later revealed that the Germans had made a deal with the Benedictine abbot *not* to occupy the monastery. It would probably be one of the few times that the Nazis kept their word. Instead, the *Wehrmacht* had skillfully used the surrounding hills and draws to mount successful mortar and artillery assaults within sight of the ancient structure, *not* within it. But now, with Monte Cassino in ruins, the Germans cunningly used the monastery's rubble as observation posts, breastworks and machine gun nests. It would take two more major assaults and many more smaller ones, before Allied armies were able to send the Germans packing on May 18, 123 days after the Allies attempted to get the Germans out of Monte Cassino. All in all, Allied troops suffered over 55,000 casualties, while the Germans received less than half that number wounded and killed.

Unlike the unanimous opinions of the soldiers in *The Story of G.I. Joe*, the Vatican was not pleased. Pope Pius XII said nothing publicly, but his Secretary of State,

Cardinal Luigi Maglione, called it "a colossal blunder ... a piece of gross stupidity."[47] In his memoir, General Mark Clark called the bombing "a military and propaganda mistake of the first order."[48]

And a major blunder for William Wellman's anointed Air Corps.

The bombing of the monastery comes close to the end of the film. After this, the shell-shocked Sgt. Warnicki finally hears his kids' voices on a portable phonograph record and goes mad; then Captain Walker's body is brought in. Wiseguy Dondaro refuses to stop stroking the dead man's face or holding his hand. As authors Clayton R. Koppes and Gregory D. Black wrote in *Hollywood Goes to War*, "*Story of G.I. Joe* came as close as the movies dared to speaking of male love."[49] (Charles "Buddy" Rogers slobbering over Richard Arlen's corpse in Wellman's Oscar winner *Wings*, pre–Breen Office, was probably closer to what the authors had in mind.)

After the film opened wide on July 13, 1945, Mitchum's underplaying (did he ever *not* look like he was asleep?) was nominated for an Oscar for the only time in his career; the Best Supporting Actor award went to James Dunn for his excellent comeback performance in *A Tree Grows in Brooklyn* (1945). Lauding *The Story of G.I. Joe* to the skies, James Agee called it "an act of heroism" and "a tragic and eternal work of art."[50]

In the film's moving final shot, Pyle and the Infantrymen march into a frame of darkness, lit by a barely rising sun, a startling and poetic shot by Wellman; as if these heroes were marching into Eternity. Tragically, that's exactly the way it turned out. Most of Wellman's 150 soldier-actors died on Okinawa. Also on the casualty list was the man whose work inspired it all, Ernie Pyle, who was shot in the head by a Japanese sniper.

Burgess Meredith's final voice-over as Pyle are the perfect words to express the audience's final farewell to the American war film and its cinematic heroes as World War II was coming to an end (even if it *wasn't* the final war film made during the conflict):

> This is our war. We will carry it with us from one battleground to another. In the end, we will win. I hope we can rejoice in our victory, but humbly.... As for those beneath the wooden crosses, we can murmur, "Thanks, Pal, thanks."

IV

Section 8
1946–1959

> Time has run out of gentlemen. No doubt the troops
> would be happier with another general in command.
> A butcher who would waste their lives to no purpose.
> Well, if they don't perk up, they'll have their butcher.
> —General Cummings, *The Naked and the Dead*

The war was over.

The Nazis, the Imperial Japanese and the Italian fascists were defeated. The Soviet Union, no slouches at imperialism themselves, ultimately moved in and re-conquered much of the territory the defeated Axis had recently abandoned. Few of these Eastern European nations would really taste freedom until the U.S.S.R.'s downfall 46 years later.

The U.S. military had outfought the Japanese in the South Pacific and the Nazis in Western Europe. Among the Allies, especially the British, it was America that had emerged as *the* major superpower in the west, with a military that was unbeatable. Hollywood films would reflect this attitude, with a positive portrayal of war veterans, much as the film industry had done after the First World War. However, this justifiable pride in our fighting men and women did not prompt a rush to produce more war films. In the wake of V-J Day, it seemed that war films were now *verboten*. The failure of John Ford's excellent (if historically inaccurate) *They Were Expendable*, released at the end of 1945, demonstrated to Hollywood that American audiences were now sick of war—off screen *and* on.

In 1949, William Wellman's *Battleground* and Republic's *Sands of Iwo Jima* became exceptions to the rule. Great War veteran Wellman was a genius at making war films depicting both global conflicts (with the possible exception of his last film, the dreadful *Lafeyette Escadrille*, 1958), and it would be the success of *Battleground* that would spark a whole new batch of World War II films even into the new era when North Korean troops stormed south past the 38th Parallel. Both *Battleground* and *Sands of Iwo Jima* were box office smashes that had the full cooperation of the Department of Defense. *Iwo Jima* star John Wayne would always get along famously with the brass-hats of the three main branches of the Armed Forces and went to them for aid in his productions for many years, all the way up to his controversial *The Green Berets* (1968).

Yet the Duke would be smart enough to realize that he couldn't continue to play the same uncomplicated heroes after the war. Like many other intelligent leading actors, he was open to darkening his image, with portrayals that cast him as either tormented or semi-villainous, even while playing the hero (*Red River* [1948], *Wake of the Red Witch* [1948] and most successfully, *The Searchers* [1956]). In *Sands of Iwo Jima*, the Duke portrayed Marine Sgt. John Stryker, who takes a group of new leathernecks and turns them into battle-hardened warriors. Tough yet tormented (there are hints of a broken marriage and an abandoned family in his past), Stryker was a veteran non-com with his own personal demons. Unfortunately, while doing his job, some of his methods at discipline sometimes crossed the line from tutoring to outright psychotic, as he strikes a Marine across the jaw with a rifle butt and points his loaded Browning Automatic Rifle at another during a battle. Believing that another Marine was derelict in duty, he pulls him away from everyone else to beat some discipline into him. Though Stryker's harsh discipline is depicted as necessary in order to mold the novice grunts into tough warriors, he's still a *long* way off from R. Lee Ermey's cruel martinet in *Full Metal Jacket.* Indeed, *Sands of Iwo Jima* went far beyond what veteran ball-busters played by Pat O'Brien or Dick Foran did in Warner service films of the 1930s. World War II had now made military discipline a matter of life and death. Certainly, for a portrayal of the Corps, things had changed radically since the days of *The Unbeliever* and *What Price Glory?*.

Other controversies soon emerged. Marine Captain Leonard Fribourg was *Iwo Jima*'s technical advisor. After seeing a rehearsal featuring the infamous rifle-butt-across-the-jaw moment (reportedly an improvisation worked out by the Duke and director Allan Dwan), Fribourg angrily complained to Marine brass. But the bit stayed in. My older brother Marvin, who had been in the Army, had taught me the same rifle maneuvers, like the horizontal and vertical butt-strokes. In the film, Stryker uses the horizontal butt-stroke to sock Private Choynski (Hal Baylor) in the jaw. It was obvious that the Corps liked both the Duke

LOCK 'N LOAD!: Big John Wayne in his iconic role as Marine Sgt. John Styker in *Sands of Iwo Jima* (1949). Styker's harsh methods turned off some Marine censors, but the Duke's portrayal laid the groundwork for even tougher on-screen Marine sergeants in the years ahead.

and the film itself; to them, a little excessive discipline that ended up protecting a Marine was okay.

But Captain Fribourg wasn't the only leatherneck involved in the production. Captain Harold G. Schrier, the officer who led his platoon up Mount Suribachi on February 23, 1945, played Stryker's platoon leader in the Iwo Jima scenes. In the film, while climbing Mount Suribachi, Stryker is shot dead by a Japanese sniper, who in turn is blown away by one of Stryker's men. However, according to Captain Schrier, there were no casualties on his patrol up the mountain. Republic cast the three surviving Marine heroes who raised the flag at Mount Suribachi: Ira H. Hayes, Rene A. Gagnon and John H. Bradley (father of James Bradley, co-author of *Flags of Our Fathers*). Bradley, the last surviving flag-raiser, looked back on the film decades later and bitterly recalled, "If you think you will see real action like Iwo Jima by seeing the picture, I really think you will be sadly disappointed. Chief Hayes says they have the picture so fucked up, he isn't even going to see the movie."[1]

Bradley's son James recalled that the flag-raisers' two scenes were only bits, with the three heroes huddled around John Wayne as he gives orders and a quick glimpse of them raising the flag. "A total of 30 minutes of filming," noted the younger Bradley.[2] One must also remember that John Bradley, like many combat veterans, rarely if ever spoke about the war. Therefore, James grew up never knowing of his dad's bravery, his raising of the flag, nor his winning the Navy Cross for courage under fire.

Besides the immortal Wayne line "Saddle up, let's get back into the war," *Sands of Iwo Jima* is the first war film that gave us the line, "Lock and load!" Reportedly, an actual order given to World War II Marine platoons before going into battle, it's a movie line that would still be going strong over half a century later.

In 1947, RKO released *Crossfire*, a film noir social problem film featuring Robert Ryan in a chilling portrayal of Sgt. Montgomery, a psychotic anti–Semitic soldier who murders a Jewish war veteran. The film was based on ex-soldier (and future filmmaker) Richard Brooks' bestselling novel about prejudice against homosexuals, African-Americans *and* Jews, leading to a murder. The novel is full of tense and tormented characters obsessed with race and ethnicity and how a postwar melting pot America is ready to boil over. In 1949, Stanley Kramer produced *Home of the Brave*, dealing with racism against an African-American soldier, based on gay Jewish playwright Arthur Laurents' Broadway hit about bigotry against a *Jewish* soldier. The end result of both these film versions was all-too-predictable compromise. In *Crossfire*, Kenneth MacDonald's major announces to all concerned that the U.S. Army does not condone a bigoted character like Sgt. Montgomery; in *Home of the Brave*, it is deduced that James Edwards' black soldier is full of guilt and self-hatred. Both films gave a pass to the military for decades of systematic racism and anti–Semitism.

Still, both productions alluded to something far more sinister among the United States Armed Forces which had previously not been depicted. Instead of teamwork and self-sacrifice, slogans that were promoted to maximum effect during the Hollywood war films of the early 1940s, the American serviceman was now shown fighting his own demons, and sometimes actually surrendering to them. Previously seen as perfect, the American warrior was now starting to be depicted as a bully, bigot and murderer. There would still be cinematic heroes in American war movies, something that would never truly die (nor should it), but now different portrayals would darken the mix. Even officers were no longer off limits, as those in charge were soon to be seen as vain and corrupt, or heartless butchers sending out men to die for the sakes of their own egos and military reputations.

The American military, like so many militaries around the world, would see its share of blunders. From then on, however, the Armed Forces of the movies would reflect this fallible image of imperfect warriors. So, as war films depicting both World War II and the Korean War flooded the screen, Harry Cohn's Columbia had the audacity to film a bestselling war novel of life in a sleepy Army barracks in Hawaii just before the attack on Pearl Harbor.

And though the film version was considerably watered down from the novel, the brass-hats that monitored Hollywood scripts were *still* not pleased.

In 1939, as the world was edging towards war, a young man from Robinson, Illinois, enlisted in the Army. "Jernin' up" at age 17, James Ramon Jones served in the 25th Infantry Division, 27th Infantry Regiment in the peacetime Army and ended up smack in the middle of one the most earthshaking events in American history. Stationed at the Schofield Barracks in Oahu, the 19-year-old private was an eyewitness to the startling sight of Japanese Zeroes swooping over Pearl Harbor. After America's entry into the war, he was sent along with his regiment to Guadalcanal, where he participated in the Battle of Mount Austin. The fighting reopened an old ankle injury that would plague him for many years after. Discharged a month after D-Day, Jones gave some thought to memorializing his wartime experiences into published fiction.

However, in terms of returning combat veterans turning the war into bestselling gold, Jones (like Herman Wouk, for that matter) was a latecomer to the field. In 1948, veterans Norman Mailer published *The Naked and the Dead* and Irwin Shaw *The Young Lions*. The two novels fought each other to attain the #1 spot on the *New York Times* bestseller list.

Jones' *From Here to Eternity* was published by Scribner's in 1951. It quickly won the National Book Award and joined the other two war classics on the bestseller list. And, like the other two novels, *From Here to Eternity* was a searing portrait of an Army that seemed to brutalize its own men almost as much as it sought to defeat the fascist enemy. *The Naked and the Dead* and *The Young Lions* were set, for the most part, on the battlefields of Europe and Asia. *From Here to Eternity* depicted an Army barracks on Hawaiian soil during peacetime. The brutal figures who persecute Privates Prewitt and Maggio can't even use the excuse of disciplining their men to the horrors of war since America had not yet entered the war. Certainly, in Jones' novel, there is no mistaking the author's indictment of the Army, with revelations of officers and enlisted personnel frequenting whorehouses, constant infidelity, depictions of homosexual liaisons, discrimination against Jews and a military stockade whose head sergeant commits acts of torture and brutality that would have delighted Himmler.

And even *these* elements of the novel were retained only after Scribner's draconian edits of the original manuscript, which depicted far more violence and debauchery.

Warner Brothers had an option on the novel, then Fox. The Department of Defense refused them permission to use Army installations and personnel should they attempt to film it. Columbia was the third studio to purchase an option on the book. However, unlike the other moguls, the usually ornery Harry Cohn was not intimidated by government dictates, not even inquiring whether the Department of Defense would give their permission. This harks back to the days of *Devil's*

Playground, when Cohn gave the Navy as good as it got. Screenwriter Daniel Taradash was like practically everyone who knew Harry Cohn—he couldn't stand him—but he later grudgingly admitted that the mogul "was a man with a lot of guts."[3] Taradash also revealed that Cohn had met with "immense pressure" from the studio's New York office. Columbia's Washington representative Raymond Bell read the book prior to filming ("I feel like I spent a weekend in a whorehouse"[4]), and he felt that Jones' supposedly anti-military tract could be used as propaganda by America's Cold War enemies. Starting in March 1951, with ink barely dry on the novel's galleys, treatments were written and discarded. Producer S. Sylvan Simon went to Washington to meet with the Department of Defense, as well as Army brass. The responses were predictably negative:

> The treatment portrays situations which, *even if they ever did exist* [author's italics], were certainly not typical of the Army that most of us know, and could serve only to reflect discredit on the entire service.[5]

Unfortunately, during this studio-to-Washington back-and-forth, no one bothered to ask the brass-hats the all-important question, "Why in the world would a

IT AIN'T YOUR GRANDDADDY'S ARMY: Ernest's Borgnine's "Fatso" (far left) takes on Frank Sinatra's Private Maggio in the groundbreaking film version of James Jones' controversial novel *From Here to Eternity* (1953). The onlookers include Claude Akins (standing behind table), Douglas Henderson (far back of room), Mickey Shaughnessy (glaring at Sinatra) and Burt Lancaster (standing at table behind Sinatra).

basically decent man and brave combat veteran like James Jones make up such things if there wasn't some basis of truth to them?" One does wonder what answer the Department of Defense bureaucrats would have come up with.

Certainly, they couldn't have liked the brutally cynical speech from the novel by a General Sam Slater. Spouting off to his friend Captain Holmes on the trials and tribulations of the U.S. Army of 1941, Slater's comments on "control" and "the majority of men must be subservient to the machine" smack more of George Orwell than Ernie Pyle.

> Of course, we still pay "Honor" lip service in the recruiting posters and the industrial editorials, for the sake of appearances, and they eat it up because they are afraid. But do we depend on recruiting for our manpower? It would be absurd, wouldn't it? No, we have a draft, a peacetime draft, the first in our history. Otherwise, we would not have the men. And we must have the men, and have them ready for this war. We have no other choice; it's either that or defeat. Modern armies, like every other brand of modern society, must be governed and controlled by fear. The lot of modern man has become what I call "perpetual apprehension." It is his destiny for several centuries to come, until control can become stabilized. If you don't believe me, look at our insane asylums and the increase of their patients. Then look at them again when this war is over.[6]

Taradash always maintained that the novel had no political implications of any kind, and was instead just "an honest book."[7] Still, after Columbia hired Jones to write a treatment of his own novel, the screenwriter complained that he had "never read a worse treatment of a first-rate novel."[8] Indeed, Jones, an admitted womanizer who used his Hollywood sojourn to meet a lot of starlets and go to a lot of parties, changed his own book a little *too* much. He had Karen, Captain Holmes' wife, recast as his sister. When Prewitt is given "the Treatment," Holmes asks Sgt. Warden to take it easy on him; instead, some minor non-coms are revealed to be the villains, not the originally corrupt Holmes and the higher-ups who backed him.[9]

With the Army *not* responding positively and producer Sylvan's sudden death, the project went into limbo. Then, in the fall, with war veteran Buddy Adler producing, Taradash went to see Cohn and get *From Here to Eternity* started again. According to Taradash (who had been with the Signal Corps writing training films, not fighting at Guadalcanal like Jones), he suggested making the local whorehouse into "a social club," insisted that Fatso Judson's brutality could be suggested rather than shown, move Private Maggio more center-stage, emphasize his friendship with Prewitt, then have him killed him off by Fatso. Use clever segueing to go from scenes of Sgt. Warden and Karen cheating (doing nothing more than passionate kisses, especially on the beach) to Prewitt's romance with Lorene, prostitute at the previously mentioned "social club." And since it's a social club, Lorene would now go from hooker to "hostess." Karen's hysterectomy, as well as her getting "the clap" from Captain Holmes, vanished. Also gone was the novel's stereotypically neurotic Jewish soldier, Private Isaac Bloom. (This portrayal is quite unlike Irwin Shaw's depiction of Jewish soldiers in his *The Young Lions*, in which the victim of anti–Semitism actively fights back against his *goyish* persecutors.) In fact, Bell called Jones' book "anti–Semitic and anti–Catholic."[10] Captain Holmes is still a rat, but his cheating on Karen is never shown. Also omitted is any mention of homosexuality in the barracks.

It has been written repeatedly that Frank Sinatra had wanted to play Private Maggio ever since he read the book, presumably after it went on sale in 1951. However, Sinatra, a man who *had* championed racial equality and fought anti–Semitism years before the Civil Rights movement, was not the most tolerant of Hollywood celebrities concerning the homosexual community. In the mid–1950s, Sinatra had his *From Here to Eternity* co-star Montgomery Clift tossed out of a party when Clift made a pass at one of the Chairman of the Board's male guests. This alone—as well as the derogatory portrayals of homosexuals in his own later films—causes one to question just *how much* of the book Sinatra had actually read, since Maggio is "a paid companion and (according to a later uncut edition of the novel) partner to homosexuals although he appears to be heterosexual."[11] Presumably reading the edited version of the book, Sinatra might have been taken with Maggio's hot temper and defiant nature, which he obviously saw as himself, and probably skimmed over the character's willingness to take advantage of gay men, something he knew would not be shown on-screen anyway.

Taradash's approach hit the right note with the brass-hats by early 1953 (at least according to Taradash). And though portraying himself in later interviews as tough and uncompromising with the Army, the screenwriter *still* asked the Department of Defense how to punish Captain Holmes. In the novel, the corrupt officer is actually promoted and transferred from Schofield. In the film, Taradash makes a decent senior officer an onlooker as Holmes fails to intercede as a private has a fight with Prewitt. A board of inquiry then kicks Holmes out of the Army. Karen and Warden sadly part, whereas during the Production Code years, Breen would have decreed a harsher punishment for these "sinners." After killing the brutal Fatso, the mortally wounded Prewitt returns to Schofield in the wake of the Japanese attack and is shot dead by MPs. The Army he had always loved has now returned his loyalty by taking his life.

Though accepting the changes, director Fred Zinnemann still grumbled years later that Holmes' dismissal was "the worst moment in the film, resembling a recruiting short. ... It makes me sick every time I see it."[12] The helmsman was also annoyed when the Army insisted that Maggio

"IF A MAN DON'T GO HIS OWN WAY, HE'S NOTHIN'," PART I: *From Here to Eternity* (1953) stars Montgomery Clift in his greatest role as Private Robert E. Lee Prewitt. The character's independent streak is at odds with the Army's demand for obedience.

died from hitting his head after falling out of a truck rather than from blows delivered to his skull by the brutal Fatso. This is quite a change from the book, where Maggio pretends to be crazy and is issued a Section 8 out of the Army.

The Department of Defense had its own complaints. *From Here to Eternity* made over $30 million (one of the most profitable films of the 1950s), and won Academy Awards for Best Picture as well as for Zinnemann, Taradash, Sinatra and Donna Reed, the Army refused to be given credit of any kind in the opening titles. Adding to this hissy fit, the Navy banned the film from being shown to Navy personnel, branding it "derogatory of a sister service."[13]

> I hazard a guess that if Navy veteran Herman Wouk's novel had been titled *The Caine Incident*, minus that inflammatory word *Mutiny*, Navy cooperation would have been obtained speedily.

With the military bureaucracy, perhaps not as "speedily" as Admiral James Shaw admitted years later after the release of Columbia's *The Caine Mutiny*.[14]

Several studios had shown interest in Wouk's bestseller immediately after its publication on March 19, 1951; later that year, it won the Pulitzer Prize. Wouk had served in the South Pacific aboard two destroyer-minesweepers, the *Zane* and the *Southard*, starting as an assistant communications officer, making it to the rank of second lieutenant, then ending up as executive officer on the *Southard*. He was even recommended to captain the *Southard* and take it home at the end of the war. The ship eventually ended up beached at Okinawa, destroying Wouk's chance at a captaincy. Still, Wouk was a Navy man all the way, and did not possess the hostility towards the USN that *From Here to Eternity* author James Jones had for the Army. Wouk's officers were composites of men he had known; with an officer named after the *Southard*, and Captain Queeg referring to a ship that happened to be named after a Columbia University literary professor Wouk had studied under. Wouk had shown his manuscript to naval officers and brass-hats for much-needed technical advice and then, after completion, their opinions. Apparently, no one had a problem with it. There were even officers and enlisted men who totally agreed with Wouk's depiction of a disturbed captain and admitted that they had known men like Queeg in real life. Topping this desire for accuracy, Wouk sought a benevolent point of view concerning the Navy; he said his book was "a mutiny of the mind," not one of 19th century physical insurrection with cutlasses and keelhauling.[15]

The novel was on the *New York Times* bestseller list for 17 weeks, replacing *From Here to Eternity* in the top spot. For those readers who felt uncomfortable with soldiers frequenting whorehouses with the country on the verge of war, or corrupt officers cheating on their emotionally shattered wives, or systematic corruption and sadistic stockade sergeants, Wouk's tome seemed like a breath of fresh air. There was no violence, adultery or profanity. It was as clean and spiffy as a naval officer's uniform. Warner Brothers was quickly scared off by the Navy's loud refusal to see Wouk's novel, the same one applauded as realistic by so many USN officers, turned into yet another film knocking a branch of the Armed Forces.

After the usual complaints of "inaccuracy" and the portrayal of the service as "derogatory," the Navy refused to assist in the making of any film version of the novel.[16] Two main sticking points remained unresolved: the USN's rather neurotic claim that there had never been a mutiny in the Navy (there *had* been), and the insistence that the USN would never put a disturbed man like Captain Queeg in a position of authority—neglecting to check with sailors who had personally informed Wouk that they *had* served under such a man. Also, in their declaration about there never having been a Navy mutiny, they neglected to mention the *Somers* mutiny of 1842, when three seamen were hanged for their planned insurrection. Unfortunately for the captain, one of the men he ordered hanged was Midshipman Philip Spencer, who happened to be the son of the Secretary of War. Tried for murder before a naval tribunal, the captain was eventually found not guilty, with the court believing his claim that he had put down a mutiny. As the Navy would do for at least another century afterwards, it had taken care of its own.

In the spring of 1951, liberal filmmaker Stanley Kramer took an option on *The Caine Mutiny*, and then negotiated with Harry Cohn at Columbia to finance and distribute the film. Kramer had produced the groundbreaking—yet compromised—attack on racism, *Home of the Brave*. His forte was controversy and the exposure of social problems in American society that had yet to be explored. (Actually, they *had*, in different forms and far more subtly, by Warners in the '30s and Fox in the '40s.) Activist filmmaker that he was, Kramer also had an inflated opinion of his ability to be a pain in the butt to the powers-that-be: "I was known as somewhat of a 'rebel' to the military establishment and to the government sources with whom I dealt. If I wasn't a 'rebel,' then I was considered a radical, a man who was dealing in extremes and in bothersome material."[17]

Of course, the Navy enjoyed nothing more than grinding down malcontents and turning them into polished professional officers and obedient crewmen. Hell, every Hollywood movie about the USN basically said the same thing! Kramer's rebel streak may have worked in a postwar America when the film industry was desperate for controversial subject matter, but not with the men who had so recently triumphed over the Japanese juggernaut in the South Pacific. Kramer's obstinacy, neatly matching the Navy's, ended up dragging out negotiations over an acceptable screenplay for the next 18 months. Proof of this bureaucratic stall was revealed by Slade Cutter, director of the Navy's Public Information Division, who admitted that he was ordered by higher-ups to "drag the navy's feet, so to speak, as long as possible to delay the inevitable and to get the script cleaned up as much as I could."[18]

After the smash of *From Here to Eternity*, Kramer, pressured by Harry Cohn, now suddenly sped up negotiations with the Navy. However, the producer still reserved the right to his "rebel" credentials. He hired the recently blacklisted Communist helmsman Edward Dmytryk to direct (Dmytryk had "squealed" on his buds to HUAC, forever triggering their enmity). And then there was the man Kramer chose to write the screenplay. Navy PR maven Cutter claimed that talking to screenwriter Stanley Roberts was like talking to Baby Snooks.[19] Roberts' Communist pedigree didn't help. Said Cutter:

> My pride in the navy was something absolutely impossible for him to comprehend or accept. He thought I was silly, unrealistic, irrational and that possessor of that worst of all impediments to progress—the military mind, whatever that is.[20]

Roberts had been a scenarist of B comedies and Westerns, ultimately sagebrush sagas where the villains turned out to be upper-crust professionals like bankers and lawyers. And, like Kramer's choice of director, Roberts had also squealed to HUAC. Nevertheless, Cutter admitted that Kramer's choice of screenwriter "had no small part in the dragging feet operation."[21] Kramer also angered the Navy by refusing to go through military channels: He went over their heads to confront the Secretary of the Navy. Cohn was getting almost as furious with Kramer as he was with the brass-hats. As a concession, Kramer was willing to hire Herman Wouk to work with Roberts, but the author truly loved the Navy, and told Kramer he was even willing to return his advance so as not to piss off his friends in the USN. In a nasty letter, an infuriated Kramer called Wouk a "jellyfish."[22] It takes a special kind of person to call a man who had served aboard two minesweepers and fought at Okinawa a "jellyfish." And Kramer still had the gall to send Roberts' completed script draft to the Navy. Predictably, Slade Cutter was appalled: "[T]he enlisted men were worse than bums and the admiral was a stuffed-shirt," said the disgusted PR man.[23] Cutter's department practically begged Kramer to portray the *Caine* and Captain Queeg as aberrations, not typical of the Navy.

Kramer enlisted the cooperation of Admiral James Shaw as technical advisor, and also hired left-wing screenwriter Michael Blankfort to go over Roberts' screenplay and bring it more in line with Navy demands. Despite Kramer's self-described "rebelliousness," Admiral Shaw's participation helped immensely. He also arranged shooting on Navy destroyers and minesweepers while they were moored at naval bases in San Francisco and Pearl Harbor.

Still, the Navy did not allow Kramer to give them credit for cooperation with the film, just as the Army denied Columbia the same thing with *From Here to Eternity*. In a move designed to assuage the Navy (and which also happened to be dripping with sarcasm), Kramer added to the credits: "The dedication of this film is simple: To the United States Navy."

Needless to say, the film is far different from the book. In the novel, there are times when 90-day wonder Willis "Willie" Keith takes center stage. A piano player, the soft-living, pampered young man signs up as a midshipman to avoid being drafted into the Army's infantry and being sent to Western Europe battlefields. He loves nightclub singer May Wynn, and has to deal with his snobby mother who disapproves of her. Communist helmsman Dmytryk emphasizes this snobbery in the film—without mentioning her Italian ancestry, that is. Keith joins the *Caine*, an old tub with a slovenly crew. After the captain is relieved, he is replaced by martinet Philip Francis Queeg. Under pressure by the Navy, Kramer was forced to remove Queeg's far more serious derelictions of duty that are in the book: His pressuring his officers to sell the ship's liquor rations to him, then smuggling it off the *Caine*; his blackmailing Keith to pay for it; his attempts to keep his ship *out* of the battle zone; and his panic during a typhoon, among other examples of his cowardice, dishonesty and incompetence.

Lt. Maryk and others relieve Queeg of his command during a typhoon; at trial, Navy flyer and former civilian lawyer Barney Greenwald defends them. Unlike the film, however, Wouk writes of *three* destroyers having gone down due to the storm, making Queeg's commands to his crew life-and-death decisions. Though the captain is declared sane by psychiatrists, the clever Greenwald gets Queeg to crack up on the stand. After the "mutineers" are declared innocent, Maryk is banished to a dead-end command in the Land Craft Infantry; Queeg is assigned to run a naval supply depot in Iowa; and writer/amateur shrink Lt. Keefer gets a book contract. It is during this celebration of his signing and the officers' acquittal when a drunken Greenwald laces into the cowardly writer. In a powerful speech depicting Queeg as the original Nazi-fighter keeping his people from the crematoriums, Greenwald bluntly says,

> See, the Germans aren't kidding about the Jews. They're cooking us down to soap over there. They think we're vermin and should be 'sterminated and our corpses turned into something useful.... So, when all hell broke loose and the Germans started running out of soap and figured, well, time to come over and melt down old Mrs. Greenwald, who's gonna stop 'em? Not her boy Barney. Can't stop a Nazi with a lawbook.[24]

Declaring men like Queeg the ones who "stopped Hermann Goring from washing his fat behind with my mother," Greenwald tosses his yellow-colored drink in Keefer's face, in effect, making Keefer "Old Yellowstain." The attorney had also predicted that Keefer would get his book published and that he'd marry Hedy Lamarr; in the film, Greenwald merely says he'd "marry a movie star," since Lamarr's career was in decline by the mid–1950s. Oh, the irony of the Navy censoring Lamarr's name: During the war, the glamorous actress and inventor had developed a radar system that helped the USN detect torpedoes!

And still, even after the acquittal and Queeg's banishment, the book goes on to detail Keefer's cowardice during a kamikaze attack which results in the death of his brother—a character not in the film. Willie Keith takes command of the *Caine* and continues to try to marry May (whom he had earlier slept with), but she doesn't appear interested.

In October 1953, Wouk's stage version of the novel, depicting only the court-martial, and now called *The Caine Mutiny Court-Martial*, was successful enough to head to Broadway after a Southern California run. Directed by Charles Laughton, it was a hit after it bowed at New York's Plymouth Theater on January 20, 1954, a full six months before the release of the Columbia film starring Humphrey Bogart as Queeg, Van Johnson as Maryk and

"STRAWBERRIES" STATEMENT: Real-life Navy vet Humphrey Bogart in one of his greatest roles as Captain Queeg in the film version of the bestselling novel (and hit play) *The Caine Mutiny* (1953).

Fred MacMurray as Keefer. Bogart was a full 20 years older than Queeg, and Kramer pushed for the aging actor over the already-cast Richard Widmark. The younger actor may have been the right age for Queeg, but Bogart had actually *been* in the Navy, where he fought bravely during World War I. Offscreen, the former Sam Spade and Rick Blaine was a crack seaman with his own boat, the *Santana*, which he named his production company after.

Slamming Queeg and those in command whenever they could, Dmytryk and Roberts depict the *Caine*'s crew as a motley bunch, but they also show its captain as an incompetent and dangerous dictator; alongside Queeg, his lackadaisical crew is sympathetic. Yet Dmytryk the Compromiser, who blabbed about his friends during the blacklist, is also on display. When Greenwald indicts the mutineers on their tendency to approve and disapprove of their superiors, the director is parroting the pro-authority line of a government that plainly had a problem with dissent. According to the film, it was not the crew's job to judge their superiors. This was the same attitude that promoted conformity, not only in America but, ironically, the Soviet Union and other Communist nations (though defying authority in Iron Curtain countries often meant a death sentence).

Bogart was nominated for Best Actor for one of his best performances of the 1950s, and the film was a hit with audiences and critics, justifying all the headaches with the USN behind the scenes.

"Will leave it to you to get three heavy-breasted chickens for the roles of Kathy, Elaine, and Pat," wrote Warner Brothers helmsman Raoul Walsh to studio production chief Steve Trilling.[25] The female roles were for the film version of yet another bestselling war novel, written by yet another author-warrior who had put his wartime experiences down on paper and turned them into literary gold.

Soon after Pearl Harbor, 17-year-old Leon Uris from Baltimore ran off to join the 2nd Battalion, 6th Marines. After a tour of duty in New Zealand, the young radioman fought bravely at Guadalcanal. In 1944, he somehow survived the botched landings at Tarawa. Stricken with several jungle diseases (malaria and dengue fever among them), his hospitalization caused him to miss the 6th Marines' landing at Saipan, a hellhole that almost wiped out Uris' battalion.

By 1953, now a former journalist (even though he had flunked English three times in high school), Uris finally wrote a novel about a Marine battalion which had fought on Guadalcanal and Tarawa, just like its author. Yet these leathernecks also fight on Saipan, a field of battle the author had never seen. Published by G.P. Putnam & Sons, *Battle Cry* shot up to the top of the bestseller lists. In the 1950s, the American reading public couldn't get enough of World War II—except, that is, books about the Holocaust.

The recruits who join up and train at the Marine base at San Diego, and later New Zealand (like Uris), are a cross-section of young men from different ethnicities and social status. So, despite their various prejudices and hidden demons, they must learn to work together as a team, the Marine Way. The book has the usual heart-of-gold hooker, Marines having various affairs, violence, racial prejudice and other such behavior guaranteed to be watered down for the film version; but emphatically *not* containing the brutality or debauchery of *From Here to Eternity* and *The Naked and the Dead*, or a controversial takeover of a ship like *The Caine Mutiny*. With the ink on the galleys barely dry, the book was bought by Warner Brothers; the studio *finally* purchasing a bestselling war novel without the usually crass Jack Warner screwing up the sale. Having testified against Irwin Shaw during the Blacklist, Warner lost the chance to film Shaw's wartime novel, *The Young Lions*; subsequently, the author gleefully sold the rights to Darryl F. Zanuck's 20th Century–Fox.

The casting was, more or less, flawless. Van Heflin was the tough but sensitive Major Sam "Highpockets" Huxley, who, coincidentally, commanded Uris' 2nd Battalion, 6th Marine Regiment. Aldo Ray, soon to be typecast as soldiers in war movies, was love-'em-and-leave-'em, girl-crazy ex-lumberjack Private Andy Hookens. There were also James Whitmore as Master Sergeant "Mac," a tough veteran non-com; soon-to-be studio contract player Tab Hunter as Private (later Corporal) Danny Forrester, Perry Lopez as Spanish Joe, and John Lupton as Private Marion "Sister Mary" Hotchkiss. Walsh's so-called "big-breasted chickens" were the talented Mona Freeman as Kathy (Danny's girl back home), Nancy Olson as Pat, a New Zealand war widow, Anne Francis as a nice hooker, and Walsh favorite, future Oscar-winner Dorothy Malone as Elaine, the "older woman" who seduces Danny. Cast as the platoon clown was a former CBS page who wanted to break into films, a fresh-faced Southern kid named Justus E. McQueen, who took the name of his screen character (just as May Wynn did in *The Caine Mutiny*) and forever onward would be known as L.Q. Jones. Obviously, all of them didn't get cast at once; and despite the fact that shooting had already started, the casting wars went on. On February 15, 1954, Walsh wrote Trilling from the Marine Recruiting Depot at San Diego, suggesting the studio get Gloria Grahame for Pat. After mentioning who he considered the best actors (Whitmore, Lopez, Jones, Hunter and Ray), the helmsman rather dismissively wrote, "The rest are dog meat."[26] Some of the "dog meat" who didn't appear in his film were future Warner contract players James Dean and Paul Newman, Newman's wife Joanne Woodward, the up-and-coming Walter Matthau, Patricia Crowley, Margaret O'Brien and Susan Strasberg (the latter testing for the role of Kathy). According to Tab Hunter, also up for the role of Elaine were Phyllis Thaxter and Meg Myles.

Hunter, soon to become one of Warners' biggest heartthrobs, wrote:

> An advanced crew was scheduled to begin location shooting in Puerto Rico first week of February.... Contracts has been signed with the Department of Defense, allowing Warner Brothers to use actual Marine maneuvers as part of the film. The military wasn't about to postpone its war games to accommodate a bunch of make-believe marines.[27]

"Don't let these actors annoy you," Walsh wired Steve Trilling from San Juan on February 27, 1954. "To me, they are strictly dog meat," he wrote, repeating the insult from his previous cable. "I am here to put on a battle with the Marines, which I am going to do."[28] The director had cut his teeth staging battle scenes, especially ones depicting the USMC, 30 years before, for *What Price Glory?*. Many of the firefights in *Battle Cry* were also to be filmed on the island of Vieques, a training location for the Navy Department, which, of course, commanded the USMC, who also did war maneuvers on the atoll. Vieques was ceded to the U.S. after our victory in the Spanish-American War of 1898; during World War II, the island was to be used to harbor the remnants of the Royal Navy should mainland Britain be conquered by Nazi Germany. However, in early 1954, Walsh had other uses for it: "I am here to photograph D Day [sic] landing's ship maneuvers and naval cannon fire."[29] However, since this was set in the South Pacific, Walsh was *not* filming the actual D-Day landings in

France. In fact, had Walsh attempted to realistically film the Marine landing at Tarawa, with miscalculations by higher-ups, dangerous reefs, turbulent waters, Japanese snipers and undetected booby-traps, all of which resulted in the needless deaths of hundreds of Marines, it was a sure thing the Corps would have denied Warners any assistance with the production. On March 8, Walsh wrote to Jack Warner, "Can you put cameramen front of tank shooting or shooting through gun turret or some other intriguing way having tank bearing down on whatever is on front and have camera vibrate when tank goes off? Steve [Trilling] and I have seen all film. Looks really great. Everybody doing wonderful job."[30]

Despite the cast and crew doing great work (with L.Q. Jones claiming years later that Walsh didn't like working on Saturdays or whenever it rained), and the arduous location shooting, the director was about to run into another problem. Almost as soon as he returned to Burbank, he received a studio memo from story editor Finlay McDermit:

> Welcome home! While you have been fighting the battle of Vieques, the home front has been staging a close-quarter battle with the Breen Office. This has been a nip and tuck affair, but I believe we have successfully defended what the Breen Office describes as the most gutsy (he might have meant *gutty*) script (and they include *From Here to Eternity*) to pass their inspection.... We could still fail to get a Seal unless the following points are handled with extreme caution.[31]

McDermit's "points" were, to Walsh and the studio, predictable:

> Danny and Kathy way too intimate on page 47; intimacy still a problem throughout script; wanted dominant emotion to be tenderness instead of passion; scenes with Dragon's Den [a nightclub] too much sexual innuendo; had to take out mention of "cheap room."[32]

At least a couple controversial plot points hover around Danny Forrester that were disapproved by both the Breen Office and Navy censors. Away from Kathy, Danny has an affair with Dorothy Malone's Elaine; in the book, she's the wife of a naval officer. This particular plot point had *never* been approved by the USMC. Uris, who ultimately did the screenplay, had met with Department of Defense officials in Washington. Though he reported in October 1953 that the Corps "were enthusiastic and loved [the book]," a major topic was the affair between Danny and Elaine. As Uris had written Warner producer Henry Blanke on October 19, 1953, "The Corps feels that Forrester represents an idealistic type of boy ... the type of youth they hope to appeal to. Showing him, as an eighteen year old, humping a married woman twice his age will have many detrimental aftermaths."[33]

Uris wanted to keep the affair in the film, but Harry Cohn's hit film about the Army, like an old albatross, returned to haunt the negotiations. Uris wrote, "There is a deep feeling of bitterness in Washington about *Eternity*. They feel that Yarbrough [Elaine, played by Dorothy Malone] sequences are put in directly as an imitation of that film."

However, in a Breen Office memo dated December 23, the unknown writer (M.V.M.) claimed that Elaine "will be dropped in the re-write, thus eliminating the adulterous affair between Danny and Elaine." Yet by the start of production the following year, Elaine was still in the screenplay, and Walsh had eagerly cast Malone in the role.[34]

Ironically, the relationship between Private Marion "Sister Mary" Hotchkiss, the platoon's would-be novelist (John Lupton), and the hooker, Rae (Anne Francis), didn't bother the Corps, perhaps because Hotchkiss was in love with her and no sex occurred during their time together. In fact, according to Uris, the Corps was not anti-sex, just "merely anti-illicit."[35]

However, soon enough, another "illicit" relationship occurs, again, with Danny. After breaking up with Elaine and returning home to Baltimore for furlough, Danny and Kathy go swimming and stay out all night. Kathy's parents are outraged at the obvious implications. In a letter from Breen to producer Hal McCord, dated July 1, 1954, the censor complained about Danny and Kathy's swim, which "unmistakably suggests a sex affair."[36] In a February 22 letter, Breen even ridiculously suggested that, before a fadeout, "Kathy and Danny be shown in a standing or upright position, rather than prone."[37] Whether standing or lying down, the upshot of the lovers' sex-before-marriage in the novel is changed for the film by having them elope and get married by the time they return home. In the same letter, Breen insisted that "the breasts of women—be fully covered at all times."[38] Enforcing his own memo on casting so-called "big-breasted chickens," Walsh maliciously cast Malone as Elaine; she also never fails to appear before us without wearing the *tightest* tops in Creation.

In their own complaints about the production, the Marines insisted that the film featured far too many deaths of likable characters, with the Corps obviously fearful that such displays of on-screen deaths would affect their recruiting drive. Again, to the Corps brass-hats, screen leathernecks could get all the girls they want; violent, bloody death on far-away atolls was a different matter. Therefore, characters who died in the novel get a reprieve in the film (though not commanding officer Highpockets Huxley). The Corps also complained after a screening that Danny, whose life is spared in the film, still comes home wounded, and that Hookens loses his leg. Indeed, those who read the book and knew of Danny's death, saw in the film version that as soon as he was shot, his wife Kathy wakes up with a horrible foreboding that her young hubby has been killed. However, thanks to the USMC, this display of sixth sense foreboding is found to be ridiculous and Danny returns home in one (wounded) piece. Also dropped from the screenplay at Breen's insistence was Uris' name for Highpockets' men: Huxley's Harlots.

The film's commanding officers have also been whitewashed. "Highpockets" is tough, but tormented, with an implication (more in the novel than the film) of an unhappy marriage. Mac is also very tough, but when he leads his boys into a barroom brawl, it's against thuggish employees who refuse to give up Ski (William Campbell), a drunken Marine who's getting "rolled" by a loose woman. Breen insisted that the woman with Ski *not* be a prostitute, that there be a divan in her room instead of a bed, that her "cheap room" be described as a "sitting room," that they not be lying down, and that she was there to roll Ski and nothing else![39]

The Corps' drill instructor (Gregory Walcott) is tough as well, but he's also a little *too* nice, ultimately laughing it up with his charges; this belies the image of a *real* D.I., as well as R. Lee Ermey's psychotic top-kick from 1987's *Full Metal Jacket*. Predictably, another Corps complaint about the script was an extended argument between Highpockets and Mac, as well as Highpockets and Major General Snipes (Raymond Massey). The USMC emphatically did *not* want subordinates having loud arguments with their superior officers.

One of the Corps' and the Department of Defense's biggest complaints were scenes where ordinary leathernecks display racism. During World War II, the armed

MARINE RECONNAISANCE: Foreground, left to right: Van Heflin, James Whitmore and Carleton Young in the film version of Leon Uris' novel *Battle Cry* (1955).

services were segregated, something you wouldn't know from the film since it was shot on location at Marine bases in the mid–1950s, which showed blacks mingling with whites. Yet, going back to Uris' original novel, there is a character named Mortimer "Speedy" Gray; a loudmouth Texas racist assigned to the radio squad, he delights in persecuting Pedro Rojas, a Pharmacist's Mate. The son of poor Mexican immigrants, the Latino Marine dreams of one day becoming a doctor. "Speedy" also showers hatred on Jake Levin, a Jewish radio man from Brooklyn. Tellingly, Uris, the future author of *Exodus* and *QB VII*, and the author of the final screenplay, had no problem removing all of the novel's Jewish characters for the film version; whether at the behest of the Corps or the usually self-hating Jack Warner is not known.

Yet documentation exists, unearthed by author David L. Robb, detailing Marine disgust with the racism displayed by Speedy and Rojas' later recitation of the horrible poverty a discriminated Mexican-American must endure in a racially polarized Texas. In the film, Speedy is played by the future portrayer of Davy Crockett, Fess Parker, with little-known actor Victor Millan playing Private Rojas. One of the reasons Millan was little-known was due to interference by USMC and Pentagon censors uncomfortable with both Speedy's displays of racism and Private Rojas' memories of racist persecution back home.

"He's no Texan," spits out Speedy to his Latino nemesis, "he's a greaseball." He also points out the "difference between a spic and a real Texan."[40] In fact, after Millan delivered his heartfelt speech about suffering racism back in his hometown, the actors and crew burst into applause. However, on the scripted page that contained the speech (a copy of which is on page 296 of Robb's book *Operation Hollywood*), *someone* from the Department of Defense wrote the word **Terrible** with a double-underline. In the speech, Rojas recites the outrages he suffers and says, "No one here knows what a 'spic' is," a line that actually *praises* the Corps for accepting a man no matter what he is or where he comes from.[41]

Yet Rojas' recitation of poverty and racism existing in one of the most patriotic states in the union disturbed Brigadier General Joseph C. Burger, assistant division commander of the 1st Marine Division. Writing to the Department of Defense's public information office, he griped, "One major objection which has not yet been incorporated is the comment by Pedro on page 93. Suggest modification of the paragraph which starts 'This is why Pedro is sorry he came.' This speech by Pedro would not only be objectionable to Texans, but to Americans as well. It would also be put to good use by Communists who are sure to use it out of context."[42]

Though the Communists *would* use the speech out of context had they known about it, there was no denying the existence of the very racism that Private Rojas was revealing.

And so, in order for Walsh to have all the Marine tanks, planes and hardware he needed, as well as location shooting on Marine bases, Private Rojas' screen time was cut down considerably. Victor Millan and his wife found this out the hard way, on the night of the Los Angeles premiere. And since Rojas' presence was reduced, so was that of his Texas tormentor Speedy; now Fess Parker appears at the beginning of the film and then disappears altogether. However, Caucasian actor Parker didn't have to worry about his career, with TV fame just around the corner; Latino actor Millan's career would never recover. Ironically, in a film removing the mention of systematic racism, it still pays tribute to the contributions of Navajo code-talkers whose radio communications baffled Japanese soldiers. Yet the deletion of Private Rojas' speech would not be revealed for several decades.

"I didn't know about any of this," Uris claimed in 2003, not long before his death. "I was basically off the picture after I wrote the manuscript." Though from Baltimore, the author described himself as a "New York liberal."[43] Yet Uris *had* compromised with the Corps and the Department of Defense about their concerns with his script; with the author obviously having seen the finished film and fully aware of the removal of Millan's scenes at the time of its premiere. In fact, it was obvious that the "New York liberal" author would never lay claim to having cut out an anti-racism speech, or for that matter, had never once complained about the deletion. Uris would do only one other screenplay in his movie career: Paramount's *Gunfight at the O.K. Corral* (1957). He certainly didn't have to worry about jeopardizing his screenwriting career had he spoken out far sooner than just before his death. Instead, Uris blamed a Marine colonel ironically named "Jim Crow." "The Corps wanted to be protected, that's all," said Uris. "So, of course, I'm not going to write anything that is objectionable to the Corps. Period." He also insisted, "Colonel Crow was a big-time Marine hero, and he was technical advisor on the film. Politically, if they wanted to change something, they would give it to Crow, not to me. I had no power."[44]

First of all, the officer's full name was Colonel Henry Pierson Crowe, with a final e; he *was* nicknamed "Jim." He was credited as *Battle Cry's* technical advisor. It is *very* possible that Crowe was the one who insisted on deleting dialogue about Texas racism against Latinos. Yet for Uris to act as if he didn't know about the speech's removal until almost half a century later was a bit hard to believe. Uris had also removed any depiction of Jewish Marines, a deletion the Marine Corps of the 1950s apparently had no problem with; Jewish soldiers in the Army-themed *From Here to Eternity* and Jewish sailors from the Navy-set *The Caine Mutiny* also disappeared from their film versions. The military may have been desegregated but causing Jews and other ethnicities to disappear certainly didn't signal a change in the bigoted thinking of a military bureaucracy.

Despite military censorship, however, *Battle Cry* was a hit, especially with the men in charge of protecting their image. After a preview of the film for the Department of Defense, Walsh received a telegram from them: "This is the best Marine picture ever made."

In a letter to the commandant of the USMC, General Lemuel C. Shepherd, dated December 10, 1954, shortly after the film's premiere at Hollywood's Pantages theater, Walsh enthusiastically wrote, "My compliments to you, and the Marines have landed again."[45] What Walsh didn't mention was all the turbulence that occurred behind the scenes before box office victory was achieved.

As the 1950s progressed, with rock'n'roll, hot rods and rebellious youth on the horizon, the war film, a genre whose usual milieu demanded discipline and obedience of its characters, would continue to be popular.

However, as young thugs started to appear in the juvenile delinquency films, the flip side appeared to be the clean young boys of the war film. And though they sought a spotless image on screen, the military couldn't wipe out off-screen incidents of the past which revealed a far darker image than the brass-hats cared to admit.

On July 20, 1921, General Billy Mitchell commanded a squadron of pilots from the Army's Air Service (years before they became the Army Air Corps) on a bombing run over the Atlantic. It was peacetime, yet the pilots were about to bomb a captured German battleship miles off the Virginia coastline—and not just *any* German battleship, but the feared dreadnought, the *Ostfriesland*. Under Mitchell's leadership, the Air Service had already sunk old German warships in the previous weeks, including the destroyer *G-102* and a light cruiser, the *Frankfurt*.

The *Ostfriesland* was another matter. A huge monstrosity of a ship (22,808 metric tons, 548 feet long), it saw action during the Battle of Jutland, the greatest naval battle of World War I. Now it was to be a big metallic guinea pig at the insistence of this controversial commander of the Air Service.

Mitchell came up through the ranks in the Army the easy way (his father was a Senator from Wisconsin), but there was no doubting his energy, sincerity and can-do work ethic. He enlisted during the Spanish-American War and did occupation duty in Cuba and then the Philippines, where he fought against Filipino guerrillas. Army brass took note, promoting him accordingly. Commanding squads of bombers during the Great War, Mitchell became an early convert to the possibilities of air power. However, the final victory over Imperial Germany prevented him from enacting his new idea: bombing the Germans on their own soil—including civilians—until they sued for peace, a prospect that horrified American Congressmen. The hero general knew the power brokers in Washington, as well as the armed services. Mitchell wanted a modern and separate Air Force—with himself in charge. Airmen sympathized with his quest, constantly complaining about soaring through the air in "flying coffins."

But Mitchell's timing was off: *No one* wanted to put money into new bombers or fighter aircraft. Least of all, the brass-hats of both the Army's air arm or their sister air branch in the Navy. They were barely surviving the fact that the government was cutting loose their service personnel and drastically reducing the budget on new military hardware. It was a time of peace; who needed to re-arm? Or for that matter, re-arm on a massive scale along the always-fantastic lines that Billy Mitchell had in mind?

Another aspect to Mitchell's personality was his *huge* ego, his off-putting talent for self-promotion, and his big mouth. Not always knowing—or caring to know—all the facts, Mitchell routinely ripped apart the Army for refusing to recognize air power's potential. He also endlessly slammed the Navy, claiming that building a warplane was a lot cheaper than a battleship, and that air power would make warships obsolete. This comment alone infuriated the admirals. His insistence on supporting the idea of a separate Air Force angered Army brass, who guarded their own bailiwicks and refused to turn any power over to a new sister service. Conversely, the Navy detested Mitchell for suggesting that sea power was useless against the airplane; which, of course, meant that *they* themselves, meaning the admirals, were to be put out to pasture. Franklin D. Roosevelt, the assistant secretary of the Navy, fairly detested Mitchell, calling his theories "pernicious." At other times, FDR questioned Mitchell's sanity. (But in 1932, the cold-blooded Roosevelt, campaigning for president, had no problem accepting Mitchell's support.)

It took an awful lot of schmoozing with powerful Senators before Mitchell was granted permission to hold his tests to prove that the airplane could successfully sink battleships at sea. Though this might not seem controversial today, students of history are well-aware of the success of air power from Pearl Harbor to Midway and dozens of other World War II battles in which battleships and destroyers rarely saw each other as they fought, but bombers had no problem targeting warships hundreds of feet below.

Mitchell cunningly ordered his squadron to bomb *near* the *Ostfriesland*, not at it. He knew that the shock waves alone would tear open the mammoth ship's hull with a powerful concussive effect. By the time the bombs did their work and the *Ostfriesland* listed to port and started to sink, it is said that admirals watching the tests openly wept.

The success of the tests made Mitchell a national hero, an even bigger one than after he returned from the war. He wrote articles and books on air power, though it was later revealed that parts of his *Winged Defense* was pirated from the works of air power theorists Giulio Douhet and others, especially Douhet's *The Command of the Air*. General Mason Patrick was chosen as head of the air service, with Mitchell appointed his deputy. To keep Mitchell far away from the American press, the Army ordered Patrick to send his vain deputy on a world tour to assess the military capabilities of other nations. During a 1922 trip to Japan, an alarmed Mitchell saw the wartime footing of the Imperial Japanese armed forces. He also suspected that Weimar Germany was secretly rearming in violation of the Versailles Treaty. Keeping his number two away from the Washington press corps, Patrick sent Mitchell to Hawaii in 1924. Slamming the poor defenses on Oahu and the other islands, Mitchell's 324-page report predicted a Japanese attack, including a bombing of Pearl Harbor. However, he thought the attack would come from land-based aircraft from Japanese-held islands in the Pacific. A good point, but the aircraft of the day would not have fuel tanks large enough to enable flying thousands of miles without refueling. But Mitchell was right that innovations in design would eventually correct this problem.

He also dismissed the possibility of aircraft carriers—the vessel that eventually won the war in the Pacific against the Japanese—thinking that they couldn't operate effectively on the high seas, nor hold enough aircraft to make a difference in battle. Again, a good point; from England to Germany to the United States, the primitive aircraft carriers of the 1920s were far smaller and pilots risked their lives far more frequently, either by having their planes go over the side after takeoffs or crashing on-deck on the return flights. Instead, Mitchell put his faith in airships, helium-powered vessels he envisioned as dropping bombs on enemy fortifications.

Mitchell's faith in rigid airships would be sorely tested. Already demoted in rank to colonel after his term as air deputy, already renowned for speaking out against Army incompetence, Mitchell was finally banished to the command of the army post at Fort Sam Houston in San Antonio, Texas.

On September 2, 1925, a helium-powered naval airship, the *Shenandoah*, crashed in Noble County, Ohio. Lt. Commander Zachary Lansdowne was in charge of the ship. Ordered by naval brass to fly over 40 Midwest cities on what was clearly a publicity junket for the Navy, Lansdowne practically begged naval brass to delay the flight so the airship wouldn't run into the area's traditionally violent summer storms. The admirals rather callously dismissed his concerns and insisted he follow their orders. Flying over Caldwell, Ohio, on the morning of September 2, the *Shenandoah* was buffeted about by violent updrafts; it was blown skyward by high winds for over 300 feet and then seconds later abruptly plunged towards the earth. The ship's gas bags couldn't stand the pressure and the dirigible soon lost power to stay in the air. As lightning and high winds tore the ship apart, the control car fell to earth, along with Commander Lansdowne and several helpless crew members. Two crewmen fell through holes in the hull and dropped to their deaths hundreds of feet below; all in all, 14 crew members, including Commander Lansdowne, perished. Twenty-nine surviving crewmen actually rode pieces of the broken ship down to earth.

Within hours of the crash, hundreds of curiosity seekers arrived at the various crash sites and scooped up every item from the ship that they could, including the logbook, something that would have aided naval investigators trying to determine the cause of the crash. Farmers charged "admission" to enter crash sites near their property; they even hawked drinks of water for ten cents apiece. More perniciously, the gawkers also stripped the dead crewmen's bodies of their valuables, including Commander Lansdowne's Annapolis class ring.

And these were the people the Navy was trying so hard to impress.

Enraged by the tragedy, Colonel Mitchell called together a roomful of journalists in his office at Fort Sam Houston and distributed a nine-page, single-spaced condemnation of both the Army and Navy, with words like "criminal negligence" and "treasonable" being the document's most quoted. Mitchell's document also drew attention to another Navy snafu: a mission undertaken by Commander John Rodgers and his crew, to fly from San Francisco to Hawaii. Mitchell felt that the three PB-1 seaplanes they were using for the mission hadn't enough required flying time and, sure enough, Rodgers and his crew inevitably ran out of fuel and were forced down near Hawaii.

On the direct order of the cold-blooded President Calvin Coolidge, who also detested Mitchell, the colonel was charged with violation of the 96th Article of War. The court-martial began in early November and lasted for seven weeks. Defended by feisty Congressman Frank Reid, Mitchell was the victim of dirty pool from beginning to end. His military judges were hardly impartial, while the prosecution, taken over from the low-key Colonel Sherman Moreland by the vindictive Major Allen Gullion, were quietly being aided by Army and Navy officers digging up dirt on the accused. (To hide their perfidy, in the courtroom they fed documentation to prosecutors, not while wearing their uniforms, but in business suits.) The defense had successfully challenged the presence of Major General Charles P. Summerall as president of the Court—he was the officer in charge of Hawaii's defenses that Mitchell had criticized in 1924! Yet even with Mitchell's old pal Douglas MacArthur as one of the judges, the result was never in doubt. After seven grueling weeks, Mitchell was sentenced to a kind of limbo where he would remain in the Army, yet be relieved of all his duties and receive no pay. Though this was later upgraded to half-pay, for a man with expensive tastes like Billy Mitchell, it was a death sentence.

During Christmas season of 1955, Warner Brothers released *The Court-Martial of Billy Mitchell*, a film that turned this iconic and complicated man's ordeal into a cliché-ridden vehicle for two-time Academy Award winner Gary Cooper. It opens just before the general (Cooper) and his crew (including Darren McGavin) bomb the *Ostfriesland*. We are told that the success of the tests makes Mitchell a hero, yet the film conveniently skips over his service in the Philippines and Cuba. All his life, Mitchell was a racist and colonialist, mourning the Spanish abandonment of Cuba to people he considered inferior, and using the N word more than once in various letters to relatives. This aspect of his military career is decidedly *not* part of the non-controversial Milton Sperling-Emmet Lavery screenplay (with contributions by blacklisted Communist screenwriters Dalton Trumbo and Michael Wilson, and some assist by the always cynical Ben Hecht). If the film tried to convey an anti–U.S. military tone courtesy of Trumbo and Wilson (shades of *Devil's Playground*), Sperling and Lavery water down the condemnations considerably. The film is also directed, if one wants to call it that, by an unusually disinterested Otto Preminger.

In the film, Mitchell is close friends with the doomed Commander Lansdowne (Jack Lord) and his lovely wife Margaret (the lovely Elizabeth Montgomery in her film debut and a decade before playing TV's most adorable witch). In reality, it's doubtful that the busy Mitchell had time to visit the Lansdownes with the regularity Cooper does—especially since the doomed commander was a *Navy* flyer, a breed the real Mitchell held in contempt.

To silence Mitchell, Army brass-hats transfer him to Fort Sam Houston. Predictably, the *Shenandoah* crashes, killing Lansdowne and some crew members; the film does *not* mention the sleazy scavengers who robbed the corpses and stole pieces of the fallen ship. Outraged, Mitchell condemns his superiors and is set to be court-martialed by those same men. Charles Bickford plays a mythical General Jimmy Guthrie, an opponent of Mitchell's air power theories who becomes president of the court. Ralph Bellamy is Congressman Frank Reid, an enthusiastic supporter of Mitchell's quest for air power; in reality, Reid took Mitchell's case more for publicity reasons than for his being an air power groupie. Unfortunately, the film never shows us Reid's insulting the court several times by calling the generals "you people" and other terms not displaying proper respect to the military.

The film also removes Mitchell's two wives and various children. Since he has no wife at all in the courtroom or anywhere else in the film, you'd think Mitchell was a bachelor. In fact, his first wife, Caroline, frowned upon her husband's long journeys and, during one bitter argument not long after he returned from wartime France, somehow got herself shot in the chest. Caroline said it was an accident; Mitchell claimed it was a suicide attempt. (He was also fighting for custody of his children and wanted to dismiss her alimony payments.) The Army, on his side for once, hid the shooting from the eyes of the press. His younger second wife, Betty, was far more pliable to the egocentric officer, and it was *she* who was at his side in the makeshift courtroom in Washington's Emery Building practically every day, something the film doesn't ever show.

TRIAL AND PLENTY OF ERRORS: In *The Court-Martial of Billy Mitchell* (1955), Gary Cooper (standing) was miscast as the controversial general. In this shot, he's flanked by James Daly (left) and Ralph Bellamy (right).

Under the aegis of the usually strident Donald E. Baruch, the Department of Defense's motion picture section barred producer Milton Sperling from using the trial's original transcripts, forcing him and his screenwriters to work from old newspaper articles and books on the trial. This didn't satisfy Lt. Colonel H.D. Kight, head of the Army's public relations division. In a memo to Baruch, Kight insisted that the screenwriters have "distorted the facts and history of the court-martial" and "placed the Army in an unfavorable light throughout the script." He also claimed that the screenplay "[created] the impression that Billy Mitchell was the victim of a deliberate sabotaging of justice by those responsible for seeing to it that Mitchell received a fair trial. This was no 'Star Chamber' proceeding."[46]

Then there's the appearance of Margaret Lansdowne. Elizabeth Montgomery gives an extremely convincing performance, especially when she claims that she was visited by a Navy lieutenant who wanted to know what her testimony would be at Mitchell's trial. In reality, Margaret *was* visited by an arrogant Navy lieutenant, but it was just before her testimony before the Court of Inquiry for the crash of the *Shenandoah*. There was also the theft of a letter written by Commander Lansdowne, telling

Margaret of his reservations about his fateful flight. In the film, however, Sperling turns this obvious attempt of the Navy to intimidate a civilian witness into the "concern" of Lansdowne's Navy buddies to see that the late commander is not "embarrassed." Predictably, Baruch accepted the weasly compromise.

The film's entire tone is laudatory to the Army and Navy brass who go against Mitchell. The system is never impugned, nor the selfish egos, turf wars or thick-fingered bureaucracy behind the condemnation of air power and military preparedness. The film says that Mitchell's tormentors are sincere men, but misguided. They *never* do anything callously or give orders that result in the deaths of innocent service personnel.

Ask the crew of the *Shenandoah*.

Rod Steiger gives the best performance as a very chilling Major Gullion. Tired of Cooper's military version of Mr. Deeds, we are galvanized by Steiger's eloquent yet nasty portrayal of an eloquent yet nasty man. With very little effort, the young actor effectively steals the film from Cooper and other veteran actors. Fred Clark, a good comic actor for Warners and other studios, plays Moreland as perpetually being the butt of someone's punchline. In real life, Colonel Moreland was hardly a clown.

In the film, Mitchell pompously states, "Politics and the Army don't mix," making one wonder what planet he's on. Every military in the world deals in politics, with the real-life Mitchell a vain, ambitious and self-promoting glad-hander who had many decades' experience in the sometimes turbulent jungle of the military-industrial complex, rubbing shoulders with movers and shakers in both the Pentagon and the Congressional halls of power. However, in Cooper's hands, Mitchell is a principled idealist who believes in air power and nothing but. And kept secret for many years was the fact that part of the reason for publicly slamming the Army and Navy—as he had written in a letter to his second wife, Betty, that he insisted *not* be made public—was for publicity and helping the sales of his book *Winged Defense*. Doesn't sound like a character played by the actor who personified Marshal Will Kane, does it? In fact, when Billy Mitchell, Jr., met Cooper during filming and asked him whether he could play his father, the actor's response disturbed him: "They pay me to play myself," he said. For this reason alone, Mitchell's family hated the casting, preferring that the controversial officer be played by the more fiery James Cagney. That would have been a distinct improvement, but still not ideal casting.[47]

Ultimately, Billy Mitchell's predictions were not all *that* accurate. Air power did *not* make the Navy's battle fleet obsolete; World War II proved that air power *still* needed a strong Navy, a tenacious infantry on the ground, and tough leathernecks on both land and sea. His support for rigid airships was misguided, as the disasters of the Navy's USS *Macon* and, on a larger scale, a Nazi blimp called the *Hindenburg* proved. He also dismissed the importance of aircraft carriers, believing them to lack maneuverability and the on-deck space to hold more aircraft; "a delusion and a snare," he called them. However, it was the aircraft carrier and the Navy's imaginative use of them that later won the war in the Pacific. The narrow-minded and colonialist airman had also met and liked Benito Mussolini, saying that the creator of the fascist movement "stands as one of the greatest constructive powers for good government that exists in the world today."

However, Mitchell also predicted how a militarily resurgent Germany would use air power to aid them in their conquests, many years before the creation of the

Luftwaffe and its successful bombing campaigns all over Europe. Having met the Japanese from the days of their triumph in the Russo-Japanese war and in subsequent decades, he knew of their expansionist policies. In the 1920s, he accurately predicted a Japanese aerial attack on Hawaii, though he suspected it would come from land bases closer to the islands, not from his hated aircraft carriers. After the Japanese attack on Manchuria in 1931, he also predicted (again) that they would attempt to attack the U.S. with their navies supplied by oil and tin from the conquered Dutch East Indies—a future Japanese target. In the film, Steiger's Gullion mocks Mitchell's prediction that the U.S. will one day be attacked by Japan, a piece of dialogue that clearly puts the 1955 audience in Mitchell's corner.

At the end of the film, Mitchell's actual removal from all Army duties and being denied pay are avoided; nor do we see Mitchell angrily quit the Army not long afterwards. Instead, we see the former general, now dressed in a suit, passing an admiring gauntlet of uniformed airmen and leaving a building where he looks up and sees planes in flight. They then morph into 1950s jets. We don't see the 56-year-old Mitchell die of a heart attack in New York City, leaving his loyal young wife thousands of dollars in debt. Instead, we see an optimistic ending where Mitchell's predictions of progress in air power come true, and we are never told that the Army, even into the 1950s, *still* refused to overturn the verdict of his trial.

Then in 1956, United Artists released an independent production that showed our fighting men under the command of liars and cowards....

> "The battle baitin' bazooka bouncers of company C!"
> "It rips open the hot hell behind the glory!"

Such were the glory-loving taglines of a new film that took the darkest, most cynical look yet at the American military. Directed by new filmmaker Robert Aldrich, *Attack!* broke new ground with its depiction of a dysfunctional officer in charge of an infantry company and the corrupt military bureaucracy that protects him. Based on a Broadway play by Norman Brooks called *Fragile Fox* that lasted less than a month, *Attack!* enraged the military and infuriated traditionalists who wanted uncomplicated, flag-waving tributes to our fighting men, and nothing but.

Aldrich was called "maverick," "iconoclast" and "innovative" by the nation's critics; people who had worked for him or seen some of his films had far different opinions of the auteur. A fiery former assistant director for left-wing and/or Communist filmmakers Charlie Chaplin, Edward Dmytryk, Joseph Losey and Abraham Polonsky, Aldrich soaked up anti–American politics like a sponge. Though he was no doctrinaire Communist, his attacks on American institutions usually crossed the line from legitimate dissent into crude violence, mean-spiritedness and virulent sexism (all of which were elements of films made by mentors Losey, Dmytryk and Polonsky). Certainly, from the perspective of the 21st century, it's hard to take the violence against his female characters or the ridiculous macho posturing in his films.

Yet there was no denying Aldrich's talent, or his quite impressive drive to attack sacred cows that should be attacked. Released in the fall of 1956, *Attack!* was one of his finest films; a work made before the relaxing of the Production Code on-screen allowed Aldrich to aim for gratuitous violence and mindless rage over good dialogue and character development. Originally called *Fragile Fox* (the name of the Army company), the play was renamed *Attack!* in the middle of the war film–loving 1950s for added box office. However, if one ignores Dmytryk's *The Caine Mutiny*, *Attack!* (1956) is the closest film up to that time dealing with the plot of a dysfunctional American commander. However, by the end, Dmytryk backed off from attacking the system that allowed a Captain Queeg to take control; in *Attack!* Aldrich had no compunctions about taking down the Army command structure.

It is 1944 in war-torn Belgium in the shadow of the Battle of the Bulge. Aldrich's first set-piece grabs our attention: Lt. Joe Costa (Jack Palance) and his undermanned platoon are pinned down by a heavy Nazi barrage. Costa screams into his walkie-talkie for his superior, Captain Erskine Cooney, to send in reinforcements to save them. Aldrich then cuts to an officer sitting in a Jeep whose face we never see. Instead of responding to the plea for help, the officer just puts the walkie-talkie on the seat beside him, ignoring the request. Following this, men are either shot up or blown to bits.

Captain Erskine Cooney (Eddie Albert) is the officer in charge of Fragile Fox Company: cowardly, irresponsible, alcoholic, a bully, and obviously unfit for command. He has clashed many times with the far more stalwart Lt. Costa. Willing to risk the lives of his men so he can glory in his position of command, Cooney is less than pleased when he finds that Costa has survived the battle. It seems that Cooney owes his position to Lt. Colonel Clyde Bartlett (the always outstanding Lee Marvin, an ex–Marine wounded at Saipan). Bartlett is a corrupt officer who hopes that his coddling of Cooney will win him the favor of the captain's powerful Senator father, as he counts on a cushy job for himself after the war. Both Cooney and Bartlett are clearly good ol' boys from Down South and Aldrich takes a perverse delight in ripping the culture thoroughly (*without* showing Southern racism).

When Cooney orders Costa and his team to recon a village to see if the Germans have taken it over, the lieutenant directly threatens to kill him if he lets his company down again. Predictably, when the squad is attacked, Cooney refuses to send them backup, resulting in the needless deaths of his men. Costa and his team (which include the always youthful-looking Richard Jaeckel as Private Snowden; *Stalag 17* veteran Robert Strauss as Private Bernstein; and the future Jed Clampett, Buddy Ebsen, as Sgt. Tolliver) take refuge in a bombed-out farmhouse, where they soon capture an SS captain (Peter Van Eyck) and his aging subordinate Otto (Steven Geray). Ultimately, Costa throws the obnoxious SS officer out in the open, where he's riddled by his own men.

With Nazis attacking their town, Cooney guzzles liquor bottles, refuses to face the urgency of the situation, and suffers mental breakdowns; with Aldrich pointing up stereotypes of Cooney's macho good ol' boy father. Back at the now-besieged Fox Company, Costa's arm is ripped off after being crushed under the wheels of a tank. He dies just before he can murder Cooney. Instead, the cowardly officer is shot dead by the honest Lt. Woodruff (William Smithers) while trying to surrender to the Germans.

Unlike previous war movies featuring a besieged American infantry, Aldrich has his soldiers show concern for what the invading SS troops would do to Bernstein once they found him. And though Warner Brothers movies during the war years may show a Jewish soldier once in a while, under the Breen Office and the Roosevelt administration censorship, Nazi anti–Semitism was barely, if ever, mentioned during that period.

AN OFFICER, BUT NO GENTLEMAN: William Smithers (left) alongside real-life war veterans Jack Palance (center) and Eddie Albert (right) in Robert Aldrich's controversial *Attack!* (1956).

Though Woodruff offers to confess to the murder when the Americans show up, the rest of the Cooney-hating company also fire their guns into the dead officer, destroying Woodruff's claims of acting alone. However, when Bartlett arrives with conquering American troops and learns the truth of Cooney's death from Woodruff, the corrupt officer plans to say that the Germans killed him; this would enable him to give the dead Cooney a posthumous medal and bring favor upon himself. However, as the film ends, Woodruff phones a commanding general to give him a full, honest report of what happened to Fragile Fox Company and its screw-up of a commander.

Aldrich said years later of his controversial film, "My main anti-war argument was not the usual 'war is hell,' but the terribly corrupting influence that war can have on the most normal, average human beings, and the terrible things it makes capable of that they wouldn't be capable of otherwise."[48] In an interview with adoring leftist critic George N. Fenin, Aldrich called his film "a sincere plea for peace." At one point, Fenin rather ridiculously compared *Attack!* to director Lewis Milestone's anti-war masterpiece *All Quiet on the Western Front*.[49]

Aldrich's comments about the changes war makes in human beings were all very true. Yet *Attack!* was *not* an anti-war film as much as it was anti–commanding officer. It never attacked enlisted men who went onto the battlefield and did the actual fighting; it attacked the brass-hats in charge. In the person of Cooney and Bartlett alone,

TAKE NO PRISONERS: In *Attack!* (1956), a Tommy-gun-toting Jack Palance manhandles Steven Geray while Richard Jaeckel pats him down and SS officer Peter Van Eyck hovers in the background. The film shows American soldiers facing a ruthless Nazi enemy as well as an uncaring commanding officer.

they were seen as corrupt, deceitful, mercenary and vain, willing to send men out to die to score political points, and, in the case of Cooney, cowardly and self-pitying when things don't go their way. Certainly, the attack on American military commanders is far more evident than Aldrich's claims of attacking the hell of war itself. *All Quiet on the Western Front* justifiably attacked the lunacy of nations getting involved in World War I—though the German-made *Westfront 1918* told an anti-war message far more subtly and with less finger-wagging than Lewis Milestone's Oscar winner.

However, World War II was a fight against genocidal maniacs. With Nazism conquering Europe, was Aldrich saying we should be anti-war and come to some kind of accommodation with their brand of evil? Were we supposed to have "a sincere plea for peace" with the architects of the Final Solution? And though war *was* corrupting and made "normal average human beings" do "terrible things," participation in the Second World War didn't always destroy the fighter who survived it; case in point, war veterans like Lee Marvin, Eddie Albert, Peter Van Eyck and Jack Palance, all of whom gave flawless performances in Aldrich's allegedly "anti-war" movie. In fact, in an ironic counterpoint to his cowardly officer, Albert was a naval hero; he won the Bronze Star rescuing over 70 wounded Marines with his landing craft at the battle of Tarawa (a badly planned military fiasco if there ever was one). However, like many heroes, Albert never spoke of the acts of bravery he performed during the war.

Filled with good dialogue from Norman Brooks' original play (which barely survived 55 performances), Aldrich's low-budget film was successfully "opened up" by screenwriter James Poe, with suspense and good performances throughout. A work which showed, for the first time in the post–World War II years, a seriously disturbed Army commander being responsible for the needless deaths of his men, *Attack!* also triggered a battle between the maverick filmmaker and the not-so-flattered subjects of his film. As the director said years later:

> The Army saw the script and promptly laid down a policy of no cooperation, which not only meant that I couldn't borrow troops and tanks for my picture—I couldn't even look at Signal Corps combat footage. I finally had to buy a tank for $1000 and rent another from 20th Century–Fox.

Aldrich was not only forced to rent equipment and uniforms from Fox, but also very familiar cannon and gunfire sound effects previously heard in Warner Brothers' films.

Denying Shermans and M-1s to Aldrich's company was just the tip of a large contentious iceberg. Three days before filming began, Lt. Colonel H.D. Kight, chief of information of the Department of the Army, called the script

> a distasteful story and derogatory of Army leadership during combat including weak leadership, cowardice, and finally, the murder of the Company Commander. In view of the above, the Department of the Army strongly disapproves subject script for any type of cooperation.[50]

Head of the Department of Defense's Motion Picture Section, the usually stiff-necked Donald E. Baruch, concurred with the Army's condemnation of the film and upheld the ban, which meant that Armed Forces personnel were not allowed to see the film. In a letter to Aldrich's associate producer Walter Blake, the brass-hat wrote, "The story basically is considered to be derogatory to Army leadership during combat and features weakness, cowardice and murder."[51]

Aldrich wrote back, claiming to take the high ground. Calling Baruch's letter "disturbing," the helmsman sarcastically wrote:

> I do not wish to quarrel with experts on morale, recruiting, propaganda, etc., but I do claim a rather authoritative opinion when it comes to dramatically showing a point of view. Theatrically and film-wise, moral values are measured by comparatives; strength is measured against weakness; heroics against cowardice.... To make characters white it is necessary to have a reflective comparison against characters that are not white.[52]

Using phrases like "comparatives" and "reflective comparison" was barely going to make a dent with military brass-hats who were simply protecting their own bailiwick. Whether it was Aldrich's snide and condescending way of explaining his stance, or Baruch's ignorance—or probably a combination of both—H.D. Kight reinforced the rule of non-assistance on the production by barring Army and Air Force personnel from seeing the finished film: "*Attack* may not—repeat not—be approved for showing Army-Air Force circuit in USAREUR [United States Army Europe]."[53] The loss of box office from U.S. military personnel stationed in Europe infuriated Aldrich.

However, unlike other filmmakers cowed by military non-cooperation on their projects, Aldrich went public. The move could have destroyed his career (which wasn't always going well to begin with), but his ego wouldn't let the matter rest. "I don't want them to dictate how to make my picture," he told *Variety*, a sentiment he emphatically did *not* express to Donald Baruch in his January letter.[54] In record time, Congressman Melvin Price of Illinois heard about Aldrich's war with the Army and was incensed by the Department of Defense's attempt at censorship: "I hope the

American people will not let those responsible for the injustice [denying assistance on the film] get away with their attempt to depict all phases of military life through brass-colored glasses," said the righteous Congressman.[55]

Yet for all the *sturm* and *drang* that the production inspired between Price's congressional committee investigating the matter and the Department of Defense, the brass-hats would still retain their power to make or break a Hollywood film by *still* demanding—and getting—script approvals and denying cooperation to maverick filmmakers.

Attack! was filmed on the lot of the dying RKO studios, as well as rented sets at Universal-International for 35 days at a measly budget of $750,000 (the *New York Times* said $850,000). The controversial and powerful film made back $2,000,000.[56] Starting his review in the *New York Times*, Bosley Crowther wrote, "No wonder the Defense Department declined to cooperate in the production of Robert Aldrich's new film *Attack!*—a fact which has been given some minor public attention of late."[57]

Yet to the brass-hats in charge of guarding the image of the military, *Attack!* was a filthy aberration, not symbolic of the usual admiring portrait of our fighting men that Hollywood displayed. However, Warner Brothers never lacked for military cooperation on their war-related productions due to the ass-kissing attitude of the usually craven Jack L. Warner (who had recently turned in many of his former left-wing screenwriters to HUAC).

In the spring of 1957, Warners released another admiring service-oriented film, this time written and directed by the man who created *Dragnet*. But the premise that inspired that project was one of the peacetime military's darkest scandals.

Attack! had pointed in a direction of filmmakers finally being able to take on the military, however, Warner Brothers was never going to jeopardize its good relations with the brass-hats for the sake of art, realism, or any other supposedly high-brow concept.

Case in point: In 1956, Warners had released the innocuously titled (and executed) *The Girl He Left Behind*. Starring Tab Hunter and the up-and-coming Natalie Wood (the studio was trying to promote them as an "item"), the film has the Tabster portraying a pampered rich boy who joins the Army to impress upon the future Maria the fact that he's "responsible." In his autobiography, Hunter wrote of the director, David Miller: "[He was] keeping us on time, under budget, and thoroughly uninspired."[58] Beginning with sophomoric voiceover about how quaint ending up in the military is, the film features talented comic Alan King as a barracks wiseguy, as well as WB contract player Henry Jones as an over-aged recruit. Also in the cast were future Maverick (and Korean war veteran) James Garner, as well as future Fugitive David Janssen.

Yet it was studio contract player Murray Hamilton as the Southern-accented top-kick Sgt. Clyde who stole this dreadful film. Hunter rejects military discipline all through the film—much as Dick Powell or James Cagney had in previous Warner tributes to the Armed Forces—and then is convinced of the Army's moral superiority by being beaten to a pulp by Clyde (after Hunter, of course, strikes the non-com *first*). At the end, we see the formerly defiant rebel become *one of them*, a corporal under Clyde's firm but understanding influence. Viewed from the perspective of the early 21st century, it is the closest correlation to 1950s conformity—in a non-science fiction way—that shows "possession" and "losing one's soul" to the State that we were ever going to get outside of *Invasion of the Body Snatchers* (1956). Unlike Kubrick's later military madmen, including R. Lee Ermey's Marine D.I., Sgt. Clyde only uses his fists when provoked, and though a pain in the ass at times, he does it for the recruit's own good—according to *this* pro-military film, anyway. Based on the novel by the creator of Private Hargrove, *The Girl He Left Behind* (which off-screen pals Hunter and Wood referred to as *The Girl with the Left Behind*) was basically light and fluffy. That is, until Murray Hamilton's brutal beating of the hero and his subsequent capitulation to military discipline and the loss of his individuality.

Released in early June 1957, Warners' *The D.I.* also shows a tough but compassionate top-kick. Yet Jack Webb's version of the Corps and their D.I.s was based on an ugly incident that the USMC preferred to forget.

At 8:00 p.m. on the night of April 8, 1956, at the Marine Corps base on Parris Island, Staff Sgt. Matthew McKeon, a junior drill instructor at the Recruit Depot, marched Platoon 71, his assigned platoon of 74 men, into a nearby boggy swamp known as Ribbon Creek. This was a training exercise for new recruits: whether they could survive a swampland environment, crossing bodies of water with their rifles and backpacks, and carry on against unseen enemies lurking in the surrounding marshes. McKeon reportedly entered the creek first; and after breaking formation, the men followed, with several joking and horsing around as they waded into the thick, sometimes muddy water. The men originally kept along the creek bed, but were then prompted by their D.I. to go deeper into the water. That's when something went tragically wrong.

A Captain Patrick put in an urgent call to Colonel W.B McKean, commanding officer of the Weapons Training Battalion: "We're in trouble. There are a bunch of recruits coming back to building 761 and it seems that the D.I. has been marching them through the swamps. I'm going down to investigate it." Colonel McKean responded, "Lock up the D.I. Send to sickbay those that need it. Get the rest of them policed up and call me back as soon as you know the number of that platoon and the battalion."[59]

The order to lock up the D.I. and send stricken recruits to sickbay wasn't going to fix the situation *this* time. For whether it was their own negligence or the persistent prodding of the D.I., six of the recruits drowned in Ribbon Creek.

The USMC convened a Court of Inquiry on April 9. The panel's goal was to ascertain just what happened. Sgt. McKeon was a combat veteran of both World War II and Korea; and though initially represented by a Marine attorney, three days later, the non-com sent for top New York attorney Thomas P. Costello, who also happened to be his brother-in-law.

There was no restriction against a D.I. using Ribbon Creek as a ground for training exercises, whether for new recruits as in this case, or veterans. However, Sgt. McKeon might have broken another rule that the Corps strictly enforced: He was seen with a drink in his hand the afternoon of the tragedy. As more testimony followed, it was revealed that he had *several* drinks hours before the night march. A strict disciplinarian, with his own men anyway, McKeon, in the not-so-noble tradition of most Corps drill instructors, might have prodded, pushed and outright bullied the new recruits into going deeper, with six men straying too far from shore due to the D.I.'s jibes.

Yet it was alleged by Colonel McKean and other superior officers that during the search for the drowned men, with 18 Marines literally wading into the murky waters of Ribbon Creek, practically all of the searchers admitted that they had trained in the swamps before, without any harm coming to any of them.

Though it was eventually revealed that McKeon habitually bullied his new recruits, the Court, taking into account his previous tours of duty in combat zones, called him "a mature, stable appearing career Marine," and said that his choice of exercises in Ribbon Creek was "correct and adequate."[60]

In the shadow of adverse publicity against the Corps' allegedly brutal training regimen, McKeon was now the subject of court-martial proceedings. However, besides his fellow Marines testifying on his behalf, the sergeant's battery of volunteer attorneys from New York (besides his brother-in-law) also enlisted veteran Marine hero General Lewis "Chesty" Puller to testify on his behalf. The recurring mantra throughout the inquiry was that the recruits desperately needed harsh discipline in order to survive in actual battlefield conditions, with Puller himself strenuously arguing against a court-martial. By the time Corps Commandant General Randolph Pate testified, one reporter sardonically noted that it was "like calling J. Edgar Hoover to testify about a problem within the FBI."[61]

McKeon was acquitted of manslaughter and of oppressing his men, though he *was* found guilty of negligent homicide and drinking on duty. However, Secretary of the Navy Charles S. Thomas threw out the bad conduct charge and allowed McKeon to remain in the Corps, though as a private. McKeon was sentenced to nine months of hard labor and a $270 fine, but Thomas eventually had the fine dropped and reduced his sentence to three months. McKeon remained in the Corps and even made it to the rank of corporal, until he was medically discharged due to a bad back in 1959.

During the inquiry, the Corps was hit with a batch of bad publicity, with even Congress starting an investigation. As the controversy raged, the anthology series *Kraft Television Theater* laid a claim to the events on the night of April 8. With a teleplay by former Marine James Lee Barrett, *Kraft* broadcast a version of the incident called "The Murder of a Sand Flea" on October 10, almost six months after the incident.

No longer restricted in showing positive portrayals of the country's armed services as they had been in years past, several Hollywood producers besieged the USMC with offers to make a film of what happened at Ribbon Creek. Already angered by the bad publicity, the Corps denied most filmmakers cooperation; but then, surprisingly, gave a green light to director-actor Jack Webb to make a film, not about the incident, but about the Marines themselves. However, trumping the allegedly bad press about the Corps and its sometimes brutal training, Webb supposedly made a film version of "The Murder of a Sand Flea" but with a twist: No one got killed, and the Marines were portrayed *positively*. With this new pro–Marine slant, the delighted brass-hats of the Corps bent over backwards to lend Webb precious locations, logistical support and manpower, with *real* grunts making frequent appearances in the film.

With biting, ahead-of-its-time dialogue by Barrett (the future screenwriter for the film version of Robin Moore's *The Green Berets*) and imaginatively directed by Webb, *The D.I.* was the first film to put the Marine D.I. center stage. Webb portrays Technical Sgt. Jim Moore, a rank that was eliminated a year after the film's release. Webb's energetic performance and Barrett's snappy dialogue impressed Marine brass. Well aware of Webb's patriotism, as well as his aim for realism on *Dragnet* and other projects, the Corps supplied grunts as extras and small-part players (like during the

IV. Section 8

audacious "Who's knocking on my door?" introductory sequence). They also allowed Webb to shoot at the Marine Corps Recruit Depot at Parris Island and the USMC base at Camp Pendleton.

Moore is a crack D.I., a tough but caring man pitted against spoiled rich-boy malingerer Private Owens (Don Dubbins). Moore's captain (Lin McCarthy) wants Owens washed out of the Corps, but Moore sees something in the self-pitying, hypochondriac private that will make a great Marine. When Moore takes the grunts out on a training maneuver, much like the one at Ribbon Creek, Moore kills a sand flea on his face, the slap resounding in the silence. This causes the D.I. to chastise the private for risking the lives of his buddies.

Those who are aware of the incident that inspired this film will instantly notice that there is no creek or any other body of water anywhere during training; hence, no drowning, accidental or otherwise. It's not a drunk or power-hungry D.I. who's responsible for a horrible tragedy, but a selfish private precipitates a near-tragedy—that is, if they were doing recon in actual enemy territory.

Later, to teach Owens a lesson—and getting the men to hate him as well—Moore orders a night maneuver where the company is to find the flea Owens killed and bury it! Here, Webb's Jim Moore comes as close as possible to the insanity of Gunnery Sgt. Hartman in *Full Metal Jacket*. Indeed, when Webb praises the M-1 rifle to his men

YOU KNOW THE DRILL: Jack Webb as the tough Marine D.I. in the appropriately titled *The D.I.* (1957). Warners and Webb whitewashed the infamous Ribbon Creek incident, in which a Marine drill exercise ended with the accidental drowning of several new recruits.

and calls it a Marine's best friend, it's awfully hard *not* to picture R. Lee Ermey leading *his* men in the immortal "This is my rifle, this is my gun" chant in the Kubrick film.

However, unlike Hartman, Moore has a heart. Like Sgt. John Stryker, he is also tormented. The Corps is his life; turning maggots into men is his only goal. He has a tempestuous relationship with dress shop manager Annie (Webb's then-wife, Jackie Loughery), who hates his dedication to the Corps. The Breen Office repeatedly warned Webb against any "capricious sex affair" between Moore and the gorgeous Annie.[62]

Owens is hated by the grunts, especially when the D.I. punishes the company for every mistake the private makes. When Moore catches Owens about to go AWOL by swimming off Parris Island, he's able to talk him out of the attempt. Owens' mom was married to a dead Marine hero and her two other two sons died in combat at the Chosin Reservoir. When she visits Moore, she insists that he make her only son a Marine. The captain also shames Owens by mentioning how "proud" his brothers would be of him. In the end, of course, Moore succeeds in turning the confused private into one of the Few and the Proud. At least Moore did not take Owens out back and beat the crap out of him as Murray Hamilton did to Tab Hunter in Warners' previous foray into the military morality play.

The Corps loved Webb's tribute to them, especially since he neglected to mention that little problem that occurred down at Ribbon Creek. At the end, Webb's titles not only thank the Marines for their cooperation, but also for their bravery at Okinawa, Tripoli, Belleau Wood, Guadalcanal, Tarawa, Saipan, Iwo Jima and Korea. Still, despite the *many* times "Halls of Montezuma" is played on the soundtrack, and Webb's attempts at realism in the life of a tough Marine D.I., the film was *not* successful. Though far more gritty than past pro-military films, the plot of the wiseacre being turned into a crack soldier was getting old-hat despite Webb's unconventional approach. Unlike *From Here to Eternity* and *The Caine Mutiny*, *The D.I.* aged very quickly, its patriotism and pro–Marine adherence to discipline and obedience taking a hit by the Swinging '60s—though the Corps continued to play the film for new recruits at Parris Island as late as 1982.

On April 2, 1958, Fox released the film version of Irwin Shaw's 1948 World War II bestseller *The Young Lions*. As directed by *Caine Mutiny* helmsman Edward Dmytryk, the film, much changed from Shaw's novel, succeeded only partially in transferring the author's theme of contrasting Nazi tyranny with American anti–Semitism. And though the young Jewish protagonist Noah Ackerman suffers at the hands of anti–Semites in the film, including a particularly special brand of hate from his fellow soldiers in the Army, it's much watered down from the brutal treatment he receives in Shaw's novel. Bullied, robbed and insulted by his "buddies" in the company, he is also treated with contempt by his superior officers. When former Broadway playboy Michael Whiteacre eventually begs their uncouth, nose-picking captain to stop Ackerman from fighting ten Christian bullies, the officer coldly turns down his request, declaring that fighting among the men is good for them and will end up helping them survive on the battlefield.

In the novel, there is one other Jew in the company, a large soldier named Fein. Noah is seen as small and weak and, worst of all, a book-reader. Singled out for persecution and menial tasks, he is verbally attacked by the drawling Southern non-com, Sgt. Rickett, who is missing front teeth and has a lisp. I will remove Shaw's original, rather simple-minded *th*s to emphasize the lisp in Rickett's speech (with Shaw obviously failing to realize that it distracts from the hatred in Rickett's words). Angrily, the non-com tells Noah, "This isn't a shitty synagogue on the East Side, this is a barracks in the Army of the United States of America." Then he orders the Jewish private to make every window in the barracks "white-man clean."[63] In the bunk next to Noah, a soldier berates him: "You people got us into this war. Now why can't you behave yourselves like human beings?"[64] At other times, the soldiers make loud comments about "Christ killers" and say that Hitler had the right idea.

In the novel, Shaw has Noah go through the meat grinder. His face is pummeled into meat, changing his appearance. Because of these fights, his cheekbones are broken, he loses many teeth, and it is odd that the post dentist actually bothers to put new teeth back into Noah's mouth since everyone in the company hates him. Similarly, the post physician tells him it's none of his business, but he better stop getting himself beaten up; the proud Noah, refusing outside help, tells him to mind his own business. In the film version of *The Young Lions*, Clift battles his now-reduced *five* Christian bullies and only comes up with facial bruises, not the more-realistic knocking-out of teeth or broken bones. Still, there was a frightening reality to Noah's facial battering that chillingly paralleled a recent accident in Clift's own life. In 1956, he attended a party at close friend Elizabeth Taylor's house in the Hollywood Hills. Foolishly giving his chauffeur the night off, the alcoholic actor drove his own car down the twisting curves on the way home. The resulting crash wrecked Monty's car, broke the bones in his face, caused him to lose multiple teeth, and would have scarred him for life. For a handsome film star, the accident would have been a career ender. Surgeons operated on him and restored his face, but the serenity and expressiveness would be gone forever; his features permanently immobile, or at least not as mobile as they used to be. His alcohol consumption increased, as evidenced when he returned to the set of Edward Dmytryk's *Raintree County* (1957). Nevertheless, Clift's facial mutilation added a gruesome reality to the facial beatings his Noah Ackerman suffered at the hands of his Army bunkmates.

If Noah's torment seems familiar, filmgoers will hark back to the film version of James Jones' novel *From Here to Eternity*, made by Columbia five years before. Making this connection between Robert E. Lee Prewitt and Noah Ackerman even stronger is the fact that both stubborn men were played by the same actor (and Clift was brilliant in both performances). Shaw's novel was published in 1949, Jones' in 1951. Therefore, Shaw, *not* Jones, was the first postwar author to show us a proud, defiant soldier up against Army bureaucracy, yet with a savage twist: Shaw's rebel is a Jew, the same faith as the people who were then victims of genocide. In fact, the scenes where Clift gets "the Treatment" in *From Here to Eternity* are eerily similar to the torment he goes through in *The Young Lions*—provocation is piled upon provocation until the victim is forced to fight back. In *From Here to Eternity*, Prewitt has to fight another soldier to maintain his self-respect, with a corrupt captain standing by as he fights his opponent; in *The Young Lions*, he has to fight five anti–Semitic soldiers while another captain refuses to stop it. Strengthening this connection between the two films, not only are both defiant soldiers played by the same actor, but producer Buddy Adler's original plan was to hire Fred Zinnemann, the Oscar-winning director of *From Here to Eternity*, to direct *The Young Lions*. The half-Jewish Clift added to the power of his scenes of abuse at the hands of his fellow soldiers.

However, in the film version of *The Young Lions*, Sgt. Rickett is played by a non-lisping—and non–Southern—Lee Van Cleef, and Rickett's original line about a "shitty synagogue on the East Side" is changed to "a crummy tenement in the Bronx." Also, "white-man clean" was changed to "white-glove clean." Noah's opponents in the fight have been reduced from ten anti–Semitic soldiers to five. And Shaw's Captain Colclough (played in the film by Herbert Rudley as a real cold-blooded SOB) loses his nose-picking. Like Philip Ober's corrupt captain in *From Here to Eternity*, he is seen as an aberration, an exception, not the rule; a mean, bigoted loser not symbolic of the United States Army—though, as quoted above from Rickett's comment, Shaw is clearly saying that these bigots *are* symbolic of the United States Army.

However, it would not be revealed until many years later how displeased Department of Defense brass-hats were with Shaw's expose of systematic

"IF A MAN DON'T GO HIS OWN WAY, HE'S NUTHIN'," PART II: Montgomery Clift as the persecuted Jewish soldier in the screen version of Irwin Shaw's bestselling *The Young Lions* (1958) The film whitewashed systematic anti-Semitism in the Army and reduced the number of the Jewish soldier's tormentors from ten to five.

anti–Semitism and bullying in the Army. Not only were the anti–Semitic bullies cut down from ten to five and Noah's injuries reduced (with former member of the Hollywood Ten, Dmytryk, more than happy to make the changes), but company commanders green-lighting the attacks were removed from the film as well. According to Shaw in a March 3, 1975, interview, "[T]he brutal, fascist-minded captain is disciplined at the end by his superiors." In other words, the same "safety valve" ending the Army forced into the *From Here to Eternity* script. Indeed, in the context of these changes, one must also remember that the first film to reveal anti–Semitism in the Army, *Crossfire*, with its face-saving remarks by Kenneth MacDonald's major that the Army does not tolerate anti–Semitism, was directed by the same man who directed *The Young Lions*: Edward Dmytryk.

Yet the whitewashing of Noah Ackerman's enemies was only the beginning. Marlon Brando would turn Shaw's brutal young Nazi officer, Christian Diestl, into a likable, sincere young man who didn't want war and was stunned at the existence of the concentration camps. Though Brando (decades later revealed to be an anti–Semite himself) approved the portrayal of the Nazi as a hero, Dmytryk also claimed that he wanted this interpretation, seeing the usual depiction of Nazi villainy onscreen as cliché-ridden and old-hat. There were always "bad Nazis," he said, but there were also "good Germans." At press conferences to publicize *The Young Lions*, Brando parroted this claim. At this point in film history, the postwar 1950s, both Hollywood and Germany would rewrite the fact that most Germans who felt no reason to apologize for their supporting Hitler, were now to be falsely portrayed as *always* hating the Nazis. This new portrayal slammed the "fanatical" Nazi, like those in the SS, but not the millions of Germans who ignored the fact that Jews were disappearing and never coming back. These same "good Germans" grabbed up their jobs, robbed them of their property (the so-called Aryanization Program) and later destroyed their Swastika flags just before the Allies showed up. In other words, the "Good German" was a myth.

However, the filmmakers of Germany and Hollywood were cajoled in this direction, not by Dmytryk's supposedly detested clichés of Nazi portrayals, but by the U.S. State Department and the Department of Defense. Former Nazis were now considered allies against Soviet tyranny. Hollywood reflected this whitewash in *The Young Lions* and *The Enemy Below* (1957), another war film depicting good Nazis which was heavily "influenced" by the Department of Defense and the State Department.

Therefore, with the egomaniacal Brando's enthusiastic backing, Shaw's original conception of Nazi killer Christian Diestl was allowed to morph into a kind of tragic hero, a victim of war who never wanted war. He becomes, according to Shaw, "not at the end a man brutalized out of all humanity by the combination of his fundamental philosophic beliefs," but instead "an innocent wanderer, shocked by the realization of where his behavior, and the behavior of his compatriots has finally led him."[65] This interpretation totally ignored, not only the anti–Semitic and racist hatred of "ordinary Germans" which made it easy to wage war and build concentration camps, but Germany's undeniably strong military traditions, a ritual "coming of age" that called for boys as young as 11 to enter strict military schools with the obvious purpose of training them to conquer other nations. Or, as Shaw would say years later, "The influence of the State Department, which was interested in rehabilitating the image of the Germans at that period, might also be discerned."[66]

In 1960, the long arms of

THE REICH STUFF: Marlon Brando as a "good" Nazi officer in *The Young Lions* (1958).

the State Department and the brass-hats of the Pentagon would strike again, with an even more outrageous whitewash of a Nazi war criminal.

In 1958, however, Hollywood would play it "safe" by setting a new war epic on Japanese-held islands. Seeing the impressive box office take of war epics like *Battle Cry*, the moribund RKO finally decided to film Norman Mailer's bestselling novel culled from his own war experiences in the Pacific theater.

However, unlike *The D.I., Battle Cry* or any other love letter to the military, *The Naked and the Dead* was originally conceived as a piece of cinematic hate mail.

In 1949, Burt Lancaster's Norma Productions bought the rights to *The Naked and the Dead*; it was to be released by Warner Brothers, to whom the actor was then under contract. The script was to be written by Communist screenwriters Philip Stevenson and Joseph Mischel.

Then, in October 1950, columnist Louella Parsons reported that Lancaster changed his mind about filming *The Naked and the Dead*, saying that this was not the right time for an anti-war movie.[67] By December, Lancaster and his partners cancelled the project and the rights returned to Mailer. In 1955, Charles Laughton expressed interest in directing the film. It was to be produced by his partner Paul Gregory, and star Robert Mitchum, but the failure of director Laughton's *The Night of the Hunter* killed any enthusiasm for the project and Laughton never again directed a film. With the project still on the boards (Gregory had bought the rights to the novel for a whopping $250,000[68]), the producer was able to make a deal with RKO. Originally, the studio wanted Lloyd Nolan, who had recently played the mad Captain Queeg on Broadway, to play the power-hungry General Cummings in the Mailer film, and even hired John Farrow as the director. But these plans didn't work out either.

Now driven to the verge of bankruptcy by batty billionaire Howard Hughes and his poor instinct for what audiences wanted, the beleaguered studio was now forced to sue for distribution rights to, of all studios, Warner Brothers, who would also co-finance it. Not only would Warners release another film based on a World War II bestseller, they would have it directed by the helmsman of the successful *Battle Cry*. In fact, Raoul Walsh would commence on-location shooting in Panama on December 12, 1957, and end filming on February 10 of the following year.

In a *New York Times* interview, Walsh admitted that several scenes from the more than 700–page novel would be cut, though perhaps the most telling part would be the word "fug." Barred from using the *real* F-word in his novel by his frightened publishers, Mailer had ridiculously substituted a word that rhymed with *pug*. As in other 1950s American war films, actual curse words—or even their silly substitutes— were never uttered.

The action takes place on the fictional South Pacific island of Anopopei, a choice that already dooms the supposedly realistic war novel to contrivance and cliché. One wonders why Mailer never mentioned real battle zones; there were more than enough of them. In an effort to drive the Japanese from the island, the power-mad General Cummings has the idealistic Lt. Hearn lead the platoon; a decision that doesn't sit well with the brutal Sgt. Croft. Psychotic, anti–Semitic, racist, sexist, violent and deceitful, this particular company top-kick makes "Fatso" Judson look like the Good Soldier Schweik. He has no problem with murdering unarmed natives, kills a captured Japanese prisoner, uses anti–Semitism to goad a Jewish soldier to fall to his death, beats women and spits beer at them, allows Lt. Hearn to walk into an ambush and, perhaps most disgusting of all, crushes a soldier's pet bird to death in his bare hand. As played by *Battle Cry*'s Aldo Ray (already typecast in war pictures), Croft was emphatically *not* a figure for movie audiences to identify with. Despite the badly written screenplay, we're instead supposed to like Cliff Robertson's Lt. Hearn, the idealistic officer who believes in the goodness of man, the flip side of the demonic Croft.

However, the maverick director might have had a personal sympathy for the macho, woman-abusing sergeant. According to Marilyn Ann Moss' biography of the helmsman:

> Walsh had great hope that audiences would find some sympathy for Croft, not only as the story's central character, but also as the engine moving the action forward. To Walsh, Croft was an ambivalent man, an excellent soldier who instinctively understands what he has to do in wartime, even if this renders him as unsympathetic as sympathetic. Walsh himself felt an affinity for a man (a director) who needed to get the job done and sometimes angered those who didn't understand that.[69]

Aping Croft's contempt for Lt. Hearn, Walsh fairly detested the artistically inclined Paul Gregory. He refused to use any of his or Laughton's script, and did his own rewrites, centering more scenes on the character he liked the most in the film: Sgt. Croft. Opposite the driven and downright psychotic non-com, nice-guy Lt. Hearn doesn't stand a chance. Walsh started filming in Panama without a completed script. He eventually rewrote it with Terry and Denis Saunders, and basically ordered his cast to improvise as they wrote. Still, while Gregory hated Jack Warner's cost-cutting on the production—as well as Walsh himself—the director hated the fact that his own attempt at an anti-war film was blocked by the censors who refused to consider scenes of extreme violence and the harsh language used by the soldiers in Mailer's book.

In his novel, Mailer also includes a wide-ranging view of the American Jewish military experience—at least, from his point of view. The author gives us the stereotypical Roth, an intellectual believing himself to be superior to his buddies, and generally a depressing man to have in *any* platoon. On the other hand, Goldstein sees himself as equal to his friends in the company, and is a loving and responsible husband; but, typically, according to the portrayal of Jews at the time, Mailer succumbs to the stereotype of the Jew as Coward. Both men are menaced by Christians United, an anti–Semitic gang within the squad. The anti–Semitic Gallagher of the book is *far* more sympathetic in the film version (at one point in the book, he asks Goldstein if he wants *"gefulte* fish").[70] This more compassionate portrayal in the film is helped by the actor playing him, the eternally youthful-looking Richard Jaeckel, another familiar face of the American war film.

Mailer's depiction of brass-hats doesn't fare any better. Played by Raymond Massey in the film, General Cummings loves power, sees the men under him as pawns to his glory, has an unhappy marriage and, something that was *not* going to appear in the film version, develops homosexual feelings towards Lt. Hearn. He constantly refers to himself as God throughout the novel. As a child, Cummings experienced gender-role confusion that forced his father to send him to West Point. The gay subtext in Cummings' character brings an interesting backstory to the scene in the film version when the general orders Hearn to have a bouquet of flowers brought to his tent every morning ("Do you want me to pick them personally, sir?" Hearn asks sarcastically). The novel also emphasizes Cummings' racism ("If anyone is going to sleep with a Negress...") and anti–Semitism ("They're not all noisy, of course, but there's an undue proportion of coarseness in that race, admit it..."), all while the general pretends to be an intellectual.[71]

Mailer's bitterness against the Army command structure was all too obvious, and his constantly referring to the dehumanizing that takes place in the military makes it clear that the foot soldier goes through hell while the officer elite, like Cummings, treat them with contempt. Opposite all this Army dysfunction and neurosis, the Japanese fascists are almost portrayed as "normal."

Towards the end of the novel, the idealist Hearn is killed, yet the brutal Croft survives. RKO and Warners knew that audiences weren't going to stand for that! In the film, though wounded, Hearn survives, yet Croft is killed. Indeed, with the surviving Jew, Goldstein (Jerry Paris), and the Christian "preacher" Rhidges (James Best) carrying the wounded and thirsty Hearn on a stretcher through miles of jungle, we almost see the idealistic lieutenant as a martyred Christ figure. Hence his "faith in the spirit of man" speech to Cummings at the end that Mailer would never have written.

Though Mailer had finished his sprawling book at the tender age of 25, he egotistically believed his work to be "the greatest war novel since *War and Peace*," and also deserved to be a bestseller—though he would grudgingly acknowledge that at times the novel was also "sloppily written."[72] Other authors had a different opinion about Mailer's claim to literary genius. As Gore Vidal wrote:

> My first reaction to *The Naked and the Dead* was: it's a fake. A clever, talented, admirably executed fake. I have not changed my opinion of the book since.... [Yet] every time I got going in the narrative I would find myself stopped cold by a set of made-up, predictable characters taken not from life, but from the same novels all of us had read....[73]

Mailer described Walsh's film version of his work as the worst film he had ever seen. Audiences concurred, staying away in droves. In fact, *The Naked and the Dead* merely added nails to the coffin of the now-dead RKO Pictures. Meanwhile, Jack Warner turned his attention to the successful film version of the Broadway hit *Damn Yankees*, starring the studio's previous portrayer of soldiers and Marines, Tab Hunter.

> Tight as a saddle girth ... a strong, harsh, haunting novel which will outlast most of the season's fiction.... An ironic and revealing study of courage and cowardice.

So proclaimed the uncredited writer of the book review in the *Chicago Tribune* in 1958 as he critiqued Glendon Swarthout's second novel, *They Came to Cordura*. An author who traveled widely, as well as a soldier and journalist for the Third Infantry during World War II, Glendon Fred Swarthout was an artist who never repeated himself in his work. And certainly, if one looks closely at this talented writer, one will see immediately the author's contempt for sequels and copying the works or writing trends of others. Swarthout valued originality. His stories and novels bucked popular trends; his characters went in their own direction; his subject matter was usually for mature adults; the situations his characters got into were sometimes disturbing; seeing no easy way out, his people faced difficult questions and answered them in their own way.

Indeed, with the Western genre constantly showing its heroes as flawless (like the overrated works of Louis L'Amour), who but Swarthout would have shown us (in *The Shootist*) a hero whose body is deteriorating from cancer?

Swarthout set *They Came to Cordura* at the time of Pancho Villa's raid into

Columbus, New Mexico, prior to America's involvement in World War I. In the novel, Swarthout, like his tormented protagonist Major Thomas Thorn, asks the question: "What is courage?"

Unfortunately, as we see through Thorn's tortuous physical and psychological journey, the five men to whom he asks this question end up turning our veneration of heroes into a pathetic lie.

On December 20, 1913, General John J. "Blackjack" Pershing reported to the Presidio in San Francisco to take charge of the 8th Brigade. A month later, he was ordered to take the 8th to Fort Bliss, Texas, and patrol the Mexican border. At the time, far too many border towns (like Juarez) became battlefields between Villistas and Mexican dictator General Huerta's troops, with Pascual Orozco's forces sometimes joining on the side of the Federales. Bullets and artillery could easily fly over the border, something Pancho Villa personally ordered his men to be careful about, since it would trigger intervention by American troops.

Pershing hoped to move his family (wife Helen, three young daughters and six-year-old son) to live with him at Fort Bliss. But that was not to be. A fire started in the Presidio and spread rapidly; tragically, Helen and the daughters died of smoke inhalation. Only Warren survived.

Heartbroken, the general known for having "cracked ice in his veins" was about to go into a severe depression. Then, on March 9, 1916, the formerly pro–American Pancho Villa ordered 400 (some say as many as 1000) of his men across the border to attack the small town of Columbus, New Mexico, murdering 18 American soldiers and civilians in the process. Almost two months before, on January 19, some 70 Villistas stopped a Chihuahua City–bound train near Santa Ysabel. They pulled off the train 18 American workers, including the general manager of the Cusi Mining Company, and shot them dead. Pancho Villa would claim afterwards that the officer in charge, Colonel Pablo López, exceeded his authority, but no one really believed him. This disbelief in Villa's word was reinforced after his surprise attack on Columbus in early March. Furious over President Woodrow Wilson's support of Venustiano Carranza over him, as well as Wilson's order to bar all gun shipments to Villistas, the former bandit now had a gloves-off policy towards his former allies. To this day, it's not known who actually hatched the plan to have Pershing take charge of the Punitive Expedition into Mexico to capture Villa. General Frederick Funston, Pershing's superior, was supposed to lead it, but it's quite possible that strings were pulled in the corridors of power, though this time, the brass-hats did it with some heart. Mourning the horrible deaths of most of his immediate family, and feeling guilty over not being at the Presidio to save them, John J. Pershing needed to be on a mission—fast. Thus, the Punitive Expedition ultimately was not successful in capturing Pancho Villa, but it *was* successful in saving the life and career of an officer who would lead American soldiers to victory in the coming world war.

In *They Came to Cordura*, Glendon Swarthout focuses his story on a American Army officer haunted by the fact that he was not where he thought he should be. He is forced to journey through a hellish Mexican desert to exorcise his demons…

It is the time of the Punitive Expedition into Mexico. Major Tom Thorn (Gary Cooper in his second-to-last film) is the Awards Officer, as his task is to find men worthy of the Congressional Medal of Honor and recommend them to Washington. Former Communist Party member Robert Rossen, the film's co-writer (with Ivan

Moffat) and director, seems to take a particular delight in zinging the American military, though Swarthout's novel carries the same bitter indictments. In fact, Rossen's seemingly anti–American film follows the novel very closely, though there are some differences—especially in casting actors who most definitely do *not* fit the characters in the book, beginning with its star. In the novel, Major Thomas (not Tom) Thorn is 40 years old, short, chunky, with close-cropped dark hair. Like a stereotypical nerd, he wears broken horn-rimmed glasses that he tapes up to keep the lenses in place. Not exactly a carbon copy of tall, rugged (and unfortunately at the time, dying) Gary Cooper. The actor's own company, Baroda Productions, paid $250,000 for the rights to the novel.[74]

One Medal winner is Private Hetherington (Michael Callan), and he is the first one Thorn prods with questions about courage. In the book, Hetherington is from the Bible Belt Midwest and had been abused by his fanatically religious father. As a child, he went on religious tent show tours with his parents and was forced to memorize whole Bible passages. Though Rossen might have wanted to focus on this abuse, he and Moffat had to exclude it from their screenplay. During the Cold War, attacks on religion were *out*.

Villistas are quartered at the fortress-like ranchero of an American woman named Adelaide Geary (the aging Rita Hayworth), the daughter of a Senator whose many scandalous affairs drove her to Mexico. The vain and arrogant Colonel Rogers (Robert Keith, who practically repeated the role of an egomaniacal military officer in the Western *Posse from Hell* two years later) is supposedly "spoiling for a fight"; it is implied that, to soothe his sizable ego, the Army has given this pathetic dinosaur command of storming the ranchero. Unfortunately, with a mechanized Army on the horizon, Rogers sees the attack as a last great charge of a mounted cavalry— he even wants his men to use sabers! This is to be done with horsemen riding abreast in a straight line across the field of battle, something any student of history knows is suicide opposite a force capable of delivering massive firepower (indeed, 19th century cavalrymen probably thanked their lucky stars that Indian tribes never had the use of Gatling guns). Rogers also wants the woman who harbored the rebels to face treason charges for aiding and abetting the enemy of a foreign power, though a Mexican regular points out that, whether Federals or Villistas show up, she has little choice but to give them what they want.

Rogers' troopers charge, cavalry-style, at the ranchero and they are predictably mowed down by concentrated rifle fire from well-protected Villistas. The film tries, but it never comes close to the brutality with which Swarthout imbues the sequence in the novel, especially the agony of the horses, many of whom plunge into dug-up pits and break their legs, forcing their riders to kill them. However, five men are able to do heroic deeds amidst this blundering attack. These men are Sgt. Chawk (a miscast Van Heflin), the ambitious Lt. Fowler (*Battle Cry*'s Tab Hunter), belly-aching malingerer Corporal Trubee (a miscast Richard Conte) and Private Renziehausen (years before *Bewitched*, Dick York). None of these actors look or sound like the characters originated by Swarthout, with Heflin obviously far too intelligent for the hulking, psychopathic Sgt. Chawk in the novel. Despite all their faults, they're able to defy the odds and gun down several Villistas. Despite a head injury, Chawk tosses two of them off a roof.

A meeting with Rogers doesn't go well. When Thorn refuses the arrogant commander's insistence that he write him up for a medal—for essentially getting his men killed for the sake of his ego—Rogers orders him to take these men and escort Geary across the desert, with no other protection, to the base at Cordura. Since these men are to be awarded medals, Thorn wants to keep them alive, so they are being taken out of action.

Throughout their journey, Thorn rather annoyingly queries the five men, wanting to know *exactly* why they performed their heroic deeds. However, tempers are rising, with many believing the persistent rumor that Thorn cowered in a ditch while Villistas stormed Columbus. Blood is also spilled with the formerly cheery Renziehausen turned into a depressed young man due to his ear being shot off; because of this mutilation, he wants to refuse the Medal. However, it seems that the others also want to refuse the Medal; Fowler doesn't want it because of perceived jealousy of his superiors (thus stalling his climb to a higher rank), Trubee would rather have "special privileges," and Chawk actually murdered someone before he fled into the Army to escape the law, with the resulting publicity exposing him for all to see. Eventually, Hetherington is taken down by malaria; in the novel he shouts out passages from the Bible during his fever.

Without food, water or horses, the "heroes" are now showing their worst sides, with the gun-toting, sleep-deprived Thorn forced to stay awake to protect himself from the psychotic Chawk. Then Thorn falls asleep, but to keep Chawk off of him, the

DESERT RATS: Left to right: Van Heflin, Tab Hunter, Gary Cooper, Richard Conte and Rita Hayworth in a publicity still from the film version of Glendon Swarthout's *They Came to Cordura* (1959). Director Robert Rossen's film questioned the bravery of soldiers we revere as "heroes."

now-sympathetic Adelaide says, "I can give you sleep." Loosening her blouse, she goes over to the sergeant as Rossen provides a fadeout.

In the novel, Adelaide's degradation is far more brutal:

> The giant turned his broken head.
> "'Chawk,'" she said, coming closer.
> His mouth opened, he made a strange animal noise, and lunging forward on all fours reached with both arms and seizing her by bare hips hurled her to the ground beneath him.
> Thorn's eyes closed.
> The sound they made was that of a bird being killed, beating its wings in dust and terror.[75]

Now forced to pull a railroad sidecar containing the weak Hetherington (the others refuse to help), the tired Thorn is felled by a rock tossed by Fowler. The officer is dragged down the tracks, though the slight scraping on Gary Cooper's face is nothing compared to the dragging of Thorn in the novel. Critiquing the film for *The New Republic*, Stanley Kauffmann complained about what the aging Cooper had to go through in this scene. In the novel, Swarthout has Thorn literally go through the wringer. Bare-chested, and now without his glasses, the famished officer is dragged *under* the car as it plunges down a grade, tearing off much of the skin on his face. Yet he *still* has the insane drive to point his gun at the men. After Fowler drops a rock on the small of Thorn's back, the others join in, all except Hetherington and Adelaide; thus, these "heroes" murder their commanding officer. Rossen wanted to end the film the same way, but studio officials did not want such a tragic ending, and none of them savored the loss of box office when audiences realized that Cooper was going to be killed off.

In both novel and film, the men find Thorn's book where he wrote of their gallantry. Suddenly realizing the import of their heroic actions, and despite the ravings of Fowler that they'll all be tried for Thorn's murder, the men continue on to Cordura, which just happens to be right over the nearest hill. What will happen to them, Swarthout leaves up in the air. Will there be a swift Army punishment or will

STAND DOWN! Gary Cooper (in his second-to-last film) points his .45 at his fellow soldiers in *They Came to Cordura* (1959), a film portraying Medal of Honor winners as dysfunctional bullies and neurotics.

there be an Army cover-up so they can exploit these renegades receiving the coveted Medal? Both Swarthout and Rossen let us work their fate out for ourselves.

Ivan Moffat said at the time, quite logically, that Swarthout's entire premise was "fairly unlikely." Still, in a meeting with producer William Goetz, he tried to get the executive to green-light the fact that Cooper's character should wear glasses like the Major Thorn of the book. Goetz allegedly asked Moffat: "Do you see that painting on the wall? It's a Picasso. I'd very much like to keep it. That's why Cooper won't wear glasses in the picture."[76]

It's pretty obvious that Cooper himself would have agreed with Goetz. Carefully nurturing a heroic image for himself on screen, the actor was not about to jeopardize it, even a little, by playing a "four-eyes."

The moviemakers shot in Mexico and St. George, Utah.[77] Swarthout's symbolism gets a little obvious. His self-flagellating, self-tormenting lead character is Christ-like in his need to "save" the souls of his heroes for the Medal of Honor, fully realizing that they "know not what they do." Even his name is Thorn, as in Crown of. In the novel, stripped to his waist, his clothes in rags, his hands blistered and bleeding as he pushes the rough handle of the railroad sidecar, Thorn goes through a kind of crucifixion. In the film, despite Kauffmann's protest, Cooper has a walk in a park compared to the tortures the Thorn character puts himself through in the novel. There, Trubee, Chawk and Fowler browbeat and torment Thorn with his past act of cowardice like three smarmy Roman centurions, with the ambitious Fowler turning into a kind of Pontius Pilate in officer's uniform.

Casting choices also worked against the film's success. Van Heflin could handle complicated character studies on screen far better than Cooper, and it was obvious that it was *he* who should have played the tragic Major Thorn; Cooper did not have the range for the part. However, Cooper was also dying of cancer, making his self-torturing scenes, especially with the railroad sidecar, particularly hard to watch. (Kauffmann, who didn't know of Cooper's illness, was obviously affected by the scene's brutality anyway). Though the red-headed Hayworth was not the young black-haired beauty of the novel, the actress expertly brought out the character's jaded bitterness. In fact, the much-married star and long-suffering employee of Harry Cohn had a gone-through-the-mill reality which was perfect for her character.

Thanks to war veteran Swarthout, as well as ex-Communist Rossen, *They Came to Cordura* was a potpourri of military chicanery. Press censorship by the Army is bitterly mentioned by reporters on the Mexican border before the Punitive Expedition; General Rogers is a pompous brass-hat nightmare who sacrifices the lives of his men for his own vainglorious need to reenact a pathetic cavalry charge. He expects the Medal of Honor for the fiasco; when he is refused the medal by Thorn, the general vindictively sends him on a suicide mission with no military assistance. The "heroes" slated to get the medal are *not* noble or even brave, they're dysfunctional losers and parasites who just happened to be at the right place at the right time and do the right thing *despite* their craven personalities. At the end of the novel, they evolve from "heroes" to symbolic Christ-killers when they gang up on Thorn and murder him.

Predictably, even with the watering-down of its most controversial elements and a $4,000,000 budget, *They Came to Cordura* tanked at the box office.

In the next decade, the image of the American military would take another hit.

War films would continue to be box office champions, especially those dealing with World War II in which we were victorious. But other films would emphasize the dark side of the American military experience. Some warned of the dangers of military dictatorship, some showed the American soldier as rapist and murderer. By the end of the decade, with the continuation of the Vietnam War and a wave of political assassinations, pessimism won out; and the image of the American military as dysfunctional, incompetent and even sinister would become the rule, not the exception.

V

Lockdown
1960–1970

> Yes, I know who Judas was. He was a man I worked for
> and admired until he disgraced the four stars on his uniform.
> —Colonel Martin "Jiggs" Casey, *Seven Days in May*

During the 1960s, the tumultuous American political scene began with the Cuban Missile Crisis and the Bay of Pigs, continued with the assassination of President John F. Kennedy and the inauguration of Lyndon B. Johnson, and climaxed with our military involvement in Vietnam. Influenced by the idealistic policies of the Kennedy administration, American films took their cues from the numerous bestsellers written by experienced political correspondents such as Fletcher Knebel and Allen Drury. In fact, never before, certainly not in the era of the Breen Office or at any time during the McCarthy era, had Hollywood focused so much on the American political scene; with its battlin' bastard child, the American military film, not very far behind in growing popularity.

However, before the newly sophisticated military-political films of the Kennedy era took hold, Columbia released an international production shot in England and starring a German actor that cast a not-too-judgmental look at a famous scientist's Nazi past.

With a screen story written by a German, an American and an Englishman, starring Curt Jurgens (world-renowned at the time for portraying Nazis with integrity) and imaginatively directed by the underrated J. Lee Thompson, *I Aim at the Stars* took Nazi rocket scientist and war criminal Wernher von Braun and turned him into the kind of great hero of cinematic bios you'd ordinarily attach to Paul Muni. According to Steve Chibnall, in his J. Lee Thompson biography, "The U.S. Army saw the celebration of von Braun's achievement as a useful promotional and recruiting tool, and producer Charles H. Schneer spent two years researching the project and developing a script with Jay Dratler."[1]

I Aim at the Stars, sarcastically subtitled *But Sometimes I Hit London* by the film's detractors (including a hilariously devastating song by humorist Tom Lehrer), was made with the permission of the governments involved, including the American military-industrial complex, as a way to coerce the audiences of the western democracies into loving America's new star scientist. To the defense establishment, von Braun's efforts launched the Saturn-V moon rocket, thus trumping the Soviets and their 1957 Sputnik. The government had already backed the anti–Semitic Walt Disney into putting von Braun on *The Wonderful World of Disney* to promote the ex–Nazi's brilliance in helping his new adopted country develop their space program. Yet for all the blather about our scientist hero seeking to advance humanity, our Defense Department, as well as those in Germany and England, covered up an ugly truth that was born, not in the stars, but in the pain and starvation of slave labor camps here on Earth.

As the war ended for Nazi Germany, the OSS, under the ruthless Allen Dulles—who was well aware of the Holocaust, but minimized the urgency in his reports to his superiors—secretly smuggled Nazi war criminals and their families into the U.S. to work for the government. This included mass-murdering SS officers, plus some rather brutal and callous scientists, the same ones who experimented on camp survivors and forced them to work in slave labor factories. Of course, the U.S. was not alone in this immoral behavior; the British, French and especially the Soviet Union *also* grabbed up Nazi technicians, guilty of war crimes, to work for their governments, justice be damned. Portrayed by the above governments as an apolitical rocket scientist only interested in aerospace development, von Braun was protected from persecution for being a war criminal and a major contributor to Hitler's war machine.

As Eric Lichtblau wrote in *The Nazis Next Door: How American Became a Safe Haven for Hitler's Men*:

> Military leaders wanted desperately not only to exploit their scientific and medical achievements, but also to prevent the Russians from seizing their work first. They provided the scientists with visas, houses, offices and research assistants. Officially, the top secret program—known as Project

IT AIN'T ROCKET SCIENCE: Curt Jurgens in *I Aim at the Stars* (1960), a whitewashed biography of Nazi rocket scientist Wernher von Braun.

Paperclip—was banned to any "ardent" Nazi who took part in wartime persecution. But this was a fig leaf, a bureaucratic cover that was routinely ignored, as the U.S. government brought in professionals with direct links to Nazi atrocities and helped some of them "cleanse" their war records. The fact that a number of them had built rockets on the backs of slave laborers at concentration camps, or performed hideous medical experiments on concentration camp prisoners, was of little concern.[2]

It would not be revealed until after von Braun's death in 1977 that the smuggling of Nazi war criminals into this country was found to be far more common than first thought. Or that Walt Disney's pal, the alleged apolitical star-aimer, had been a high ranking SS officer (*Obersturnbamfuhrer*, or major) who had his V-1 and V-2 rockets built by concentration camp labor, an idea enthusiastically endorsed by the aerospace genius.

The rockets that terrorized London and Antwerp were built at the Peenemunde rocket site and the underground rocket factory at Dora-Mittelwerk in the German town of Thuringia. Slave laborers worked until they dropped; and when they did, the SS quickly disposed of them. Any slowdown or "sabotage" of the building of the rockets prompted harsh SS reprisals; unspeakable torture and painfully slow death. Most of the time, however, the SS hung starving, slow-working prisoners from the rafters on a crane as an example to the other prisoners. Sometimes secretaries watched their agony for amusement. Prisoners were literally stuffed into tunnels to sleep, hundreds of them, with no room to stand or even sit up. An average of 20 prisoners a day died of starvation and disease, including feces and vermin in the tunnels where the prisoners slept. They were considered cogs in the machinery. The SS wasted little time in procuring even more slave labor from occupied countries to fill the void left by the dying. The Peenemunde rocket scientists, including von Braun, were well aware of the atrocities. In some cases, their involvement went from awareness to demanding that the prisoners pick up the pace—something the SS guards were more than happy to enforce. Twenty thousand prisoners died at Dora-Mittelwerk; besides starvation and disease, a great many of them were also beaten, whipped and hanged for what their overseers, including von Braun, termed "shoddy workmanship."[3]

Liberated by the Allies, surviving prisoners who were eyewitnesses to the horrors of Dora-Mittelwerk openly accused von Braun of being a more-than-willing participant in the atrocities, personally torturing prisoners who didn't contribute to his works of genius. There were also meetings at Peenemunde with high SS officials in which von Braun would demand "18,000 more prisoners" to work on his rockets. With typical callousness, von Braun boasted many years later:

> Working in a dictatorship can have its advantages, if the regime is behind you. I'm convinced that the man in charge of Stalin's atom bomb just has to press a button and he'll be supplied with a whole concentration camp full of labor. We used to have thousands of Russian prisoners of war working for us at Peenemunde.[4]

He would also rave about his erstwhile employer, praising the Fuehrer as "a new Napoleon" who possessed "astounding intellectual capacities, the actually hypnotic influence of his personality."[5]

It was not as if von Braun's involvement with slave labor was a big secret; articles and books had been written about it. However, despite von Braun's statements, even during a memorable interview with *The New Yorker* (almost wishing for the "good ol' days" of the Third Reich to return), as well as the very important postwar testimony of the few survivors of Dora-Mittelwerk, much of this info would be suppressed by Dulles, Disney, our State Department and the Department of Defense. The Soviets were our enemy now and the American public had to be brainwashed into accepting this brilliant but cruel man as a forward-thinking hero. Von Braun himself, in the now-expected tradition of ex–Nazi thugs, either denied or downplayed his participation in war crimes. Even his death in 1977 seemed well-timed, as revelations of our protection of Nazi war criminals (starting with "Butcher of Lyon" Klaus Barbie) began to focus on von Braun's scientist collaborators like Arthur Rudolph. With his own participation in rocket-building slave labor factories, Rudolph's many humanitarian awards were taken away and his name struck from the walls of aerospace institutions. He died a pariah a few years later. Disney's pal did not live to suffer this ignoble fate.

In the beginning of the film, von Braun is a brilliant child launching dangerously effective toy rockets into neighbors' homes. This is portrayed as comedy as well as forcing upon us an image of the young von Braun that, even in his youth, his experiments are what counted, not the extermination of humanity by his inventions. In fact, from all reports, little Wernher was a smug, superior, obnoxious little sadist who tortured squirrels and other small animals to see if they would survive under certain space conditions—including denying the poor creatures oxygen.

As an adult (Curt Jurgens), he is an obsessed, apolitical genius forced to work for the brutes of the SS. And though the film attempts to confront the more controversial elements of his life (von Braun did not want the filmmakers to show his Nazi past *at all*), for his every collaboration with the SS, there is an apology that excuses his behavior. The filmmakers emphasize his arrest by the SS for alleged anti–Nazi remarks he made in private (Himmler planted a spy among the scientists). In reality, it was towards the end of the war and von Braun was making what Himmler considered "defeatist" comments. Hitler (he of the "astounding intellectual capabilities") overruled his Reichfuhrer SS and had von Braun released so he could continue with his missile work.

The film never once mentions or shows any slave labor working on the hero-scientist's missiles. In fact, von Braun's real-life SS collaborators are portrayed as his enemies. Politics mean nothing to him, he loudly pronounces; he just wants to build his rockets. In fact, as one can tell from his postwar remarks about Hitler and dictatorships, von Braun had certainly been a far more enthusiastic supporter of National Socialism than the powers-that-be in America cared to admit. The film's blatant censoring of von Braun's *real* role working for the Third Reich—by the very same government that was then employing him—had opened with the acknowledgment: "To the Department of Defense and particularly the Department of the Army of the United States our sincere appreciation for their cooperation and assistance during the making of the film." In reality, it was the filmmakers who were cooperating with the Army, *not* the other way around. Considering all the Nazi war criminals who cheated the hangman through our government's Operation Paperclip, the filmmaker's "dedication," approved by a vain Department of Defense, is more than a little obscene.

In fact, *I Aim at the Stars* producer Charles H. Schneer had produced most of Ray Harryhausen's films throughout the 1950s and early '60s (like *Earth vs. the Flying Saucers*). Ironically, despite Harryhausen's many wonderful stop-motion dragons, ogres, cyclopses, aliens, living skeletons, dinosaurs and giant octopuses, *I Aim*

V. Lockdown 127

GUEST OF THE S.S.: Under U.S. government and Pentagon pressure, the *I Aim at the Stars* (1960) filmmakers turned cold-blooded Wernher von Braun (Curt Jurgens, seen here with unidentified actors) into a hero and ignored his many war crimes.

at the Stars had to be Schneer's first experience producing a film featuring a *real* monster.

Besides the military's insistence on covering up von Braun's war crimes, an added controversy is James Daly's Major Taggert, an embittered American officer who lost his wife and child in London thanks to our "hero's" V-2 rockets. In fact, the propaganda is brilliant, if not downright unfair and insulting to victims of Nazi terror. Taggert browbeats the supposedly apolitical scientist and keeps reminding him what his rockets did to his family. He threatens von Braun with a hangman's rope, and then is shocked that his brass-hat superiors want to have the now-*ex*–Nazi work for the American government—what the intelligence community would call "turning" a member of the opposition. The major is portrayed as the *only* Allied officer who openly hates von Braun. We never see any American military officer with even a fraction of the bitterness that Taggert expresses; this portrayal, of course, makes the tormented officer look like a beating-a-dead-horse loony. (A Navy Intelligence captain named Bosquet Wev referred to an acknowledgment of war crimes as "beating a dead Nazi horse.") Indeed, had the filmmakers chosen to defy the military's dictates on the film and shown von Braun's *true* service to the Nazi State, including Dora-Mittelwerk, then Taggert would not have been portrayed as such an unreasonable stuffed-shirt. However, at the end of the film, with the successful launching of the *Explorer-1*, the embittered major, now a TV and print journalist, calls von Braun "my friend" and wishes him luck.

The filmmakers, backed by the image-makers in the international political and military leadership, are clearly saying that if the embittered Taggert, whose own wife and child were victims of von Braun's handiwork, can forgive him, why can't we?

The depiction of the compassionate American officer was not lost on *New York Times* critic Bosley Crowther:

> In Germany and later in America, [Major Taggert] badgers Dr. von Braun until the latter assists in launching our first *Explorer* satellite into space. Then he generously hails the scientist as a faultless hero he has been made to appear. Obviously, this making a "heavy" of a character who loudly articulates the understandable emotional attitude of many Americans and British towards Nazi scientists will not assist in changing whatever feeling the resentful may have about Dr. von Braun.[6]

Crowther didn't have to worry on that score. Hundreds of protesters, refusing to swallow all the bilge, greeted the film's opening in England and America with loud accusations about ignoring history and insulting the memories of von Braun's many victims. The film also falsely equates Nazi missile-launching to the Allies bombing raids, with no one in the film bothering to mention the Final Solution or the fact that conquering Allied Armies (that is, the non–Soviet ones) did not subject the German people to mass incarcerations, slave labor to build their weapons, or ethnic cleansing.

Curt Jurgens was a good actor, an anti–Nazi, and a man who almost always played the mythical Good German on screen. Three years before, he had played the good Nazi submarine captain in *The Enemy Below*, a film whose benign portrayal of the German Navy was backed by the Department of Defense. Like Thompson & Co., Jurgens was a major asset in the government's whitewashing of the scientist–war criminal.

Insisting that the way the Allies waged war was no different from that of Hitler's Germany, von Braun attempted to answer his accusers by issuing a statement justifying his service to the Third Reich: "I have deep and sincere regrets for the victims of the V-2 rockets, but there were victims on both sides. A war is a war, and when my country is at war, my duty is to help win that war."[7]

With the Allied and German governments refusing to discuss von Braun's activities at the Dora-Mittelwerk factory, and the American military's refusal to see the protests as legitimate rage, media reports on the film's opening never seriously attempted to rebut von Braun's rather infuriating comparisons. This allowed him to lamely answer for the V-2 attacks on London, not his stewardship of the Dora-Mittelwerk factory. The bodies of the poor souls who died building his rockets rot somewhere outside the village of Thuringia; never acknowledged, eternally forgotten.

For the man who aided in their murders, however, there would be hero worship, enormous wealth and instant celebrity.

With much of this injustice aided and abetted by the higher-ups in the United States military.

Released in 1961 by United Artists, *Town Without Pity* was set in postwar West Germany. The plot deals with four American soldiers accused of raping a young German woman from a small village. Kirk Douglas had produced and starred in the controversial anti-war masterpiece *Paths of Glory*, in which he played the attorney defending three soldiers accused of cowardice (they were framed by an ambitious French general). In *Town Without Pity*, Douglas is back at the defense table, this time defending GIs accused of rape.

Predictably, producer Walter Mirisch had to deal with a grumbling Production Code office, now headed by Geoffrey M. Shurlock. In an April 21, 1961, letter to Mirisch, Shurlock detailed why the film should not be made: "The basic story—a multiple rape of a German girl by four American soldiers—seems to us to carry the subject of rape much further than we have hitherto felt to be approvable."[8] After complaining that the opening sequences are "overly lustful," plus the skimpiness of the girl's bikini, Shurlock also lowered the boom on the G.I.'s dialogue, which he insisted was "unacceptably sexually gross."[9]

The film is based on the German novel *The Verdict* by Manfred Gregor (real name: Gregor Dorfmeister). He had been a young German soldier in the *Wehrmacht* in the last days of the war. He was ordered to guard an unimportant bridge as Americans stormed Berlin; his experiences became the basis for his anti-war novel *The Bridge*, made into the classic German anti-war film of the same name by director Bernhard Wicki. Here, in a screenplay featuring an uncredited contribution by the blacklisted Dalton Trumbo, Gregor continued to express mixed feelings towards Nazi Germany's American conquerors.

Karin Steinhof (Christine Kaufmann aka Mrs. Tony Curtis) apparently wants more from her mama's-boy boyfriend, Frank (Gerhard Lippert), than the occasional peck on the cheek. After a fight with Frank, she angrily swims across a river and is accosted by four off-duty American soldiers: Sgt. Chuck Snyder (future *Gomer Pyle* sergeant Frank Sutton), Corporal Jim Larkin (Robert Blake, who was later accused of real-life murder), the prematurely bald Private Jim Haines (Mal Sondock, an American deejay residing in Germany), and a World War II hero, Corporal Birdwell Scott (veteran of many military films, the always youthful-looking Richard Jaeckel). Thoroughly disgusted by the soldiers he's ordered to defend, Major Steve Garrett (Douglas) is forced to attack the rape victim on the stand in order to save the four felons. Karin's thick-headed and prejudiced banker father (Hans Nielsen) wants the four Americans to hang—even Corporal Larkin, who, it is implied, *didn't* participate in the rape. Garrett begs the stubborn old man *not* to have him cross-examine his daughter. But Garrett is finally forced to tear her apart on the stand, revealing her to be *not* quite as innocent as first thought.

CHAMPION: *Town Without Pity* (1961) **starred the great Kirk Douglas as an Army colonel defending four soldiers charged with rape in postwar Germany.**

The four soldiers are certainly a potpourri of extremes in Gregor's ambivalent depiction of Germany's American military occupiers. Snyder is a brutal psychopath; Haines is basically bland and doesn't seem to know right from wrong; Larkin is revealed to be impotent and neurotic. The most interesting of them all (played by an actor who started in the 1940s) is Corporal Scott. A hero on the battlefield, Scott doesn't seem like the type who would commit such a violent and cowardly act. As played by Jaeckel, Scott sardonically "dismisses" the act by telling Garrett that it was a sunny day, the mood was right, and the situation presented itself. This is a far different response than that of the brutal Sgt. Snyder who basically recites the usual defense of a rapist who's been caught: She *wanted* it.

Scott knows what he did was indefensible (his drunkenness being no excuse), but instead of blaming the victim or suddenly begging mercy, he's flippant when giving an excuse. Still, his refusal to say he was framed hardly excuses him either. To Garrett, the corporal is not only a hero who once fought bravely in battle, but a predator who should be ashamed of his medals. None of the four accused men makes the United States Army look good, but ultimately the film shows that the American military justice system is not impugned. (Fearful of how badly the film would portray the military, an unknown censor suggested that Karin be raped by just *one* soldier.) The officers in charge are angered and disgusted by the four men, and want to show the people they conquered that they are fair.

Perhaps more symbolic of American fairness is Major Garrett. Though Douglas gives his usual intense performance, he also skillfully conveys moments of doubt and introspection. You see the wheels turning in Garrett's mind, especially in non-verbal moments. With looks and silent responses, he shows his inner battle.

Expertly directed by Gottfried Reinhardt, the film benefits from actual Bavarian and Swiss locations, with sharp performances all around—especially those of the native German actors, even in the smallest roles as townspeople or witnesses. Also outstanding is Barbara Rutting as muckracking journalist Inge, and Ingrid van Bergen as jaded bargirl Trude, who hates "town girls" (well-bred women who judge "low-class" women like Trude, but are actually hypocrites). Brunette and blonde, respectively, these women are two sides of the same coin that Garrett has to deal with.

Dedicated to his job as a military attorney, Garrett is twice-divorced, and there is lots of sexual tension in his encounters with Inge. When he enters his hotel and Inge sees him, she removes her horn-rimmed glasses before she accosts him. Full of humor and generally unrestrained, Trude does not flirt with Garrett, but she loyally helps him get evidence so he can bring down Karin. When Garrett investigates the scene of the rape and suggests that Inge play the victim to reenact the crime, the reporter curtly tells him that her clothes will remain on; Garrett later jokes that she should dress up or she'll catch cold. When the persistent Inge (who follows Garrett around all through the film) interrupts his barroom conversation with Trude, the major introduces her as a "town girl"; predictably, the blonde snubs the journalist and cattily leaves the table. Inge calls the rapists "monsters," but to Trude, it's the "town girls" who are the real monsters. Rutting and van Bergen's fine performances help the film, giving Garrett two attractive females who have their own takes on the innocence of the accuser.

Reinhardt falters in showing the vindictiveness of the townspeople. We hear an awful lot about Karin and her family receiving hate letters, but we never actually see anyone openly attack her or anyone else (Frank's brief failed attack on Garrett notwithstanding). Already tormented by her own conscience after the trial's conclusion reveals her less-than-sterling character, Karin is terrified by young people hanging out in the street derisively calling her name. But none of them chases or physically attacks her; Reinhardt makes their taunts sound like good-natured ribbing, something to be shrugged off (they forget about her as soon as she flees). Also, there are several unintentionally laughable moments, especially when it seems that Gene Pitney's "Town Without Pity" is the *only* song playing from the many jukeboxes and beer gardens the protagonists pass throughout the film. Fantastic song that it is, one of Pitney's

COLLECTIVE GUILT: Kirk Douglas and Barbara Rutting go over the scene of the crime in *Town Without Pity* (1960). The film depicted four American soldiers as rapists, and also focused a harsh light on their not-so-innocent victim.

greatest, its constant repetition and the lightly badgering way the townspeople treat Karin, makes one wonder whether the film should have been called *Town Without Decorum*. Another big mistake is Rutting's intrusive voice-over narration telling us what the various German characters in the film have said or are feeling, when subtitles at the bottom of the screen would have sufficed.

At the end, Karin drowns herself off-screen and the accused do *not* get the death penalty. Predictably, however, the sentencing is given according to the men's characters: psycho Snyder gets the longest sentence, Larkin the least. Garrett checks out of his room and takes his Army limo out of town, *not* ending up with Inge. This was indeed a predictable ending. According to an undated synopsis of the film, Garrett is "shunned by his fellow officers...." In fact, Garrett may be alone when he drives off, but he is never shown being shunned.[10] Case closed, Garrett has done his job; what exactly was proved? Throughout the film, it seems that only Karin's father wants a hanging; German citizens *not* wanting foreigners punished, especially members of the Army that conquered them just 15 years before, is unusual to say the least. Also unusual is the fact that not one character mentions Nazism, or the way their brutal criminal justice system treated foreigners. Herr Steinhof, a banker who lived through the Third Reich and had to have supported them, is obviously prejudiced against Americans, but is never once allowed to long for "the good old days" before his conquered nation was split in two. Indeed, Nazi Germany was a whole nation of "towns without pity." One wonders why Reinhardt and his screenwriters didn't once contrast the Germany of the Nazi era with the refusal of older Germans to face their pro–Nazi pasts in 1961.

Another film from the early 1960s with a dark view of the American military was the little-known *War Is Hell*, made by independent filmmaker Burt Topper in 1961. It was released in the fall of '61 in Japan and West Germany, but not in the U.S. until a few years later. It was always suspected (especially by actors who worked in the film, like Tony Russel) that its depiction of a psychopathic, glory-hungry American sergeant who murdered both fellow soldiers and unarmed Communist prisoners, held up its release. Written and directed by Topper, a naval veteran of World War II, the film splits the image of the American soldier between the cowardly, vain homicidal top-kick and another sergeant, an honest, upright hero who wants to expose the killer (much as the later *Platoon* would split the image of the American military between "good" and "bad" sergeants). Archly titled *War Hero* in Europe, the film might have been saved by the filmmakers' decision to have the most decorated hero of World War II provide a two-minute introduction. And so, with the supposed endorsement of Audie Murphy putting into perspective our involvement in Korea, *War Is Hell* was finally released in the United States in October 1963. And it was still playing at the Texas Theater in Oak Cliff, Texas, where an ex–Marine named Lee Harvey Oswald was arrested by Dallas police for the murder of Police Officer J.D. Tippit; he was soon charged with the assassination of President John F. Kennedy. It was the supreme irony that a psychotic ex-serviceman should be arrested while watching a war film that depicted the dual personality of the American soldier in wartime.

In 1958, an author named Peter Bryan George, published a novel dealing with a coming nuclear war. An RAF fighter pilot in World War II, George started writing not long after he returned to England. His literary output consisted of military-themed thrillers at a time when ex–MI-5 commander Ian Fleming was only *starting* to conceive of an espionage novel depicting the adventures of a Cold War–era British secret agent.

An alcoholic tormented by depression, George also kept changing the titles of his thrillers once they crossed the Atlantic—and even changed his pen name several times. Peter George and Peter Bryant seemed to be the ones most used.

Published in England as *Two Hours to Doom*, the 1958 novel depicted a paranoid U.S. Air Force general named Quinten ordering three nuclear-armed bombers from his SAC base in Sonora, Texas, to make a pre-emptive strike on the Soviet Union. The president and his cabinet attempt to stop the bombers by alerting the Soviets. Unlike the wonderful dialogue that heralded the famous scene in the film version ("Think of how *I* feel, Dmitry..."), the U.S. president has no trouble getting the Russians to collaborate in attempting to shoot down the bombers. Though the government has regained control of the Sonora SAC base, Quinten, the only man who knows the recall code, commits suicide. However, the SAC executive officer is able to decipher the mad general's doodles on a desk pad and come up with the Code. Two of the bombers receive the recall code and return to base a few minutes before they would have arrived at their Soviet targets. The third bomber, the *Alabama Angel*, has a broken radio and does not receive the recall code. Yet the *Angel* is already damaged and fails to destroy its target. At one point, the American president offers the Soviets a chance to annihilate Atlantic City if the errant bombers reach their targets. Still, note that George, the former RAF officer, did not depict a renegade *British* general ordering an atomic attack.

It is said that Stanley Kubrick had always been obsessed with the threat of nuclear war. After becoming a money-making director, he even considered moving his family to Australia, which, according to the novel and film version of *On the Beach*, was going to survive a nuclear strike, thanks to the many caves where residents could seek shelter. A ridiculous theory if ever there was one!

Kubrick could count several nuclear physicists, scientists, theorists and authors as his friends; he consulted with them often. To get a little pre-shooting publicity, he and his flacks released the story that the busy filmmaker actually had time to read over 70 books on the subject of nuclear war—a hell of a trick for *any* cinematic genius on the verge of a productive peak. In March 1959, *Two Hours to Doom* was published in America as *Red Alert*. (To the top bananas at Ace Books, *Two Hours to Doom* sounded like a murder mystery.) Around the same time, another tale of nuclear madness, the short story "Abraham '59, A Nuclear Fantasy" by Harvey Wheeler, was published in *Dissent*. Soon Wheeler would collaborate with another writer, Eugene Burdick, and expand the story into the novel *Fail-Safe*. Meanwhile, in October 1961, Kubrick and his producing partner, James B. Harris, read the Ace copy of *Red Alert* and on November 4, contacted Peter George. By the end of the year, they owned the rights to the novel.

In January, George flew to New York to co-write (with Kubrick) the screenplay of the new project, *Edge of Doom*. After a while, George noticed that the tone of the screenplay was starting to change (Kubrick had already worked on a treatment with Harris). Nightmare melodrama was slowly becoming nightmare comedy. Before George knew it, his deadly serious military characters dealing with a nuclear crisis started to have names like Mufley, Turgidson, Kissoff, Strangelove, King Kong and Jack D. Ripper. George did accept this radical change and he gladly co-wrote the screenplay. However, his discomfort over the direction of his nuclear thriller never really left him, though the added paycheck didn't stop George from writing a novelization of the released film. In another telling, it was *Harris* who didn't want the helmsman to make it a comedy, claiming Kubrick's decision to turn the nuclear thriller into a comedy would "flush his career down the toilet!" Ultimately, the helmsman's creative choice killed a production deal with Seven Arts, which was willing to back the film as long as it was a thriller.

Aware that his collaborator was an alcoholic suffering from severe depression—and not exactly experienced at comedy—Kubrick decided to let the Texas-born satirist Terry Southern, who had been doing an article on Kubrick for *Esquire*, help with the screenplay. It must have been hard for an ex-military man like Peter George to wholeheartedly rip the defense establishment that he had been a part of for so many years (he was *still* in the RAF reserves when *Red Alert* was published)—even if said defense establishment was in another country. By May 1962, the property which had been known as *Two Hours to Doom*, *Red Alert*, *Edge of Doom* and even *The Delicate Balance of Terror*, would now forever be known as *Dr. Strangelove*—and that awful subtitle which no one ever uses when discussing the film. Coincidentally, on December 26, 1961, the same day George's agents finalized the sale of *Red

Alert to Kubrick and Harris, Eugene Burdick sent the team an outline of the as yet unpublished *Fail-Safe*. According to Wheeler, Kubrick said he would consider it after talking with their literary agent. There was a reason for Wheeler's later self-serving claim: Kubrick, George and Harris, claiming copyright infringement, sued Burdick, Wheeler and producer Robert Youngstein to stop, or at least delay, the release of a film version of *Fail-Safe*.[11]

Kubrick's *Lolita* was a recent box office and critical hit, and Kubrick and Harris had no problem getting a distribution deal for *Dr. Strangelove* with Columbia. But the producers would have far less luck with the United States Air Force and the Department of Defense. Permission to use real military aircraft was denied. With military precision, the USAF, fully backed by Don Baruch and the Department of Defense, denied Kubrick all military facilities, armed service personnel, and even shots of bomber and fighter aircraft.[12] Forced to go back to his memories of World War II newsreels and war films, Kubrick and his art directors had to improvise. Ultimately, they not only built a more-than-acceptable B-52 cockpit, but a fully operational War Room with no basis on what it looked like, since the Department of Defense never *admitted* there was such a place. Yet for all Kubrick's alleged claims to nuclear accuracy, and all the books he allegedly had read, his theories, even in a dark comedy, were full of hot air. SAC commanders *cannot* unilaterally order B-52s carrying nuclear warheads into the air. Nor are they cavalier with the Recall Codes, including doodling them onto desk blotters! The president is in charge of the codes, and safeguards *do* ensure that there won't be any crazy orders given by maverick commanders. And if a B-52's radio is busted or communication with SAC is disabled, the plane is supposed to return to base. Did Kubrick read those 70 books on nuclear war for nothing?

Still, the finished film contains attacks on the same military bureaucracy that arrogantly denied him permission to use their facilities and logistical support—starting from the very first shots. Under Kubrick's cameras, it seemed like *every* military aircraft had sexual imagery attached to it; the elongated, pointed nose of a B-52; the opening shots of one bomber being fueled in the sky by another. And though Peter Sellers was a genius who deserved *every* bit of praise for his largely improvised performances of three very different characters, also praiseworthy is Kubrick's razor-sharp takedowns of the military bureaucracy. Far from the gentle burlesque of the prewar *Buck Privates* and *Caught in the Draft*, Kubrick had no Breen Office restricting his choices; the director used recent events (as well as the Air Force's rejection of his work) to fuel his rage. The Cold War was getting hotter; a few years after the Korean War, the Berlin Wall went up and the Soviets threatened nuclear war if they weren't allowed to put A-bombs in Communist Cuba in October 1962. Thanks to President Kennedy's standing tall and defying the Soviets, a madman like Fidel Castro (with Soviet backing) was denied the chance to turn America into a radioactive wasteland. To Kubrick, the political leaders of both superpowers, as well as the American military, were attractive targets. "War should not be left to politicians," laments General Buck Turgidson (future portrayer of General Patton, George C. Scott), implying there would be a better system under a military dictatorship. Still, though a lunatic American general has launched the bombers, the Soviets are equally insane; they've kept secret the existence of a Doomsday device which apparently no one's been told about ("Our leader likes surprises," the Soviet ambassador explains lamely).

Turgidson, the callous warmonger ("We'll lose 10, 20 million, tops!"), is only *one* of the military lunatics Kubrick throws at us. There is Colonel "Bat" Guano (Keenan Wynn), an American officer who points a loaded weapon at a commander of an Allied nation and refuses to let him use a hotline to stop the bombers from nuking Russia, yet is shocked at the thought of breaking into a Coke machine to get change ("That's private property!"). After SAC General Jack D. Ripper (Sterling Hayden) unilaterally sends out the bombers and is aware that soldiers are on their way to capture him, he orders his men to fire at them, claiming they're Communist troops in American uniforms. One does wonder what Don Baruch and the rest of the brass-hats who oversaw cooperation with Hollywood (as well the brass-hats in Washington proper) must have thought of the scene where American military personnel, in unquestioning blind obedience and total ignorance of Ripper's madness, open fire on each other not far from a sign proclaiming **Peace Is Our Profession** (supposedly, an actual phrase used by SAC).

Ripper takes the cake in showing American military force literally gone mad; this portrayal came five years before the rampage of Lt. William Calley and Company C at My Lai. As portrayed by former OSS man and pro–Tito partisan Sterling Hayden, Ripper is a right-wing nightmare. A reactionary hawk still spouting the clichés of Senator Joseph McCarthy, but with a savage, almost cartoonish twist, Ripper plays by his own sick rules. According to the general, the Reds are not only interested in conquering America, but destroying our sexual potency by dumping fluoride into our water supply ("sapping America's vital fluids!"). With these fantasies, Ripper has sent warhead-carrying bombers to Russia, not caring whether this starts a nuclear war. It is debatable just *who* Ripper was based on. Some say it was war hero Air Corps commander General Curtis LeMay, who came up with the idea to napalm the Japanese homeland to get them to surrender in 1945. The ploy failed, but not before thousands of Japanese civilians died and their wood and paper dwellings caught fire across the country. Still, LeMay was a brave and gung ho commander of the kind we needed to win the war; a General Patton of the air, if you will. By the 1960s, however, as an advisor to Presidents Kennedy and Johnson, he was one of the government's most prominent hawks, more than willing to start a world war with the Soviets and bomb North Vietnam into the Stone Age. However, with a mentality still stuck in World War II, LeMay's strategic bombing campaigns against the Viet Cong did *not* have the same level of success they had against the Japanese in 1945. LeMay had also wanted to deliver a "Sunday Punch" to the Soviets; and, in 1954, allegedly ordered nuclear-armed bombers to fly over the U.S.S.R. to provoke a confrontation. Justifying this "order," he supposedly declared to his aides, "Well, if we get this over flight done right, we can get World War III started." However, as SAC commander, he also ordered that all 50,000 airmen with access to nuclear weapons be screened for a "human reliability certificate."[13]

His reckless and controversial statements openly advocating nuclear attack on Cuba and the Soviet Union (during the Cuban Missile Crisis), as well as his unrestrained desire to use nuclear weapons against Vietnam, Laos and Cambodia, infuriated more stable military figures in the Kennedy and Johnson administrations, eventually forcing his retirement in 1965. As a vice presidential running mate for white supremacist candidate George Wallace in the late 1960s, LeMay's loose talk of nuclear war against Russia and Southeast Asia effectively killed the segregationist's campaign. General Ripper he wasn't, but there might have been more than a little of Turgidson in the former SAC commander—and vice versa.

The arrogant and mercurial General Douglas MacArthur might have also been a Ripper "inspiration." Also on the list was a LeMay protégé, General Thomas S. Power, the head of SAC during the Cuban Missile Crisis. The heroic commander of World War II became, like all too many American generals in the 1960s, the *total* warmongering hawk who refused to adapt to the new realities of war. During the Cuban Missile Crisis, he ordered a radio message announcing the readiness of nuclear bombers to hit the Soviet Union. Sent "in the clear," that is, on open radio communications without code of any kind, the message was transmitted mainly so it would rattle eavesdropping Soviet intelligence officers. Whether the unauthorized message (not ordered by JFK, Robert McNamara or the Joint Chiefs) actually worked is uncertain but, inevitably, the Soviets did back down. Yet far more chilling was a remark Power made to a RAND company executive around this time. The general said that if there was nuclear war and the Russians were left with one person alive and the U.S. ended up with two, "then we win!" The RAND exec replied that those two people better be a male and a female.[14]

Though Power does seem like a good bet for being the inspiration for *Strangelove*'s psycho SAC commander, there might be a good case for yet another "kill 'em all and let God sort 'em out" American officer. Born in Texas in 1909 (Texas being the original location of the SAC base where General Quinten launches his bombers), General Edwin Walker had served in both World War II and the Korean War. He had commanded artillery batteries and other units as the U.S. Army fought its way through Sicily and Rome, landed at Anzio and then liberated France. But his over-the-top reactionary opinions infuriated conservative President Dwight D. Eisenhower. While he was commander of the Arkansas Military District, Walker reportedly argued with Eisenhower in 1957 when the president ordered him to guard black students seeking to integrate schools in Little Rock. He bitterly complained to Eisenhower that using federal troops to integrate schools was against his conscience. Hooking up with paranoid Southern reactionary Dan Smoot, Walker solidified his pro-segregationist views. After meeting publisher Robert Welch, founder of the John Birch Society, the general began to parrot the paranoid views of that organization, which routinely saw all presidents, from FDR to Ike, as Communist agents.

Believing Ike to be "one of them," Walker offered his resignation, but the president refused. Instead, Eisenhower sent his errant general thousands of miles out of the country to Augsburg, West Germany to command 10,000 troops. Even there, far from America, Walker couldn't leave well enough alone. He promoted his "Pro–Blue" (as in "anti–Red") agenda to the men at his new command, just as he had to the men under him during the Korean War. However, this time he was also promoting the racist ideology of the John Birch Society and other reactionary groups. By now, Eisenhower was gone and new president John F. Kennedy, well-aware of Walker's pathetic proselytizing antics (including calling Truman, Eleanor Roosevelt and Secretary of State Dean Acheson "definitely pink"), wasn't going to be as nice as his predecessor. After having the general shuttled from one backwater command to another, the president and Defense Secretary Robert McNamara finally accepted his resignation. Said Walker, "It will be my purpose now, as a civilian, to attempt to do what I have found no longer possible to do in uniform."[15]

What he did was what he couldn't do as a military officer in a democracy. Five years after protecting students at Central High in Little Rock, he organized protests against Army veteran James Meredith and his efforts to integrate the University of Mississippi in the town of Oxford. Backed by Texas billionaire H.L. Hunt and other reactionaries, Walker ran for governor of Texas, but lost to John B. Connally (the choice of then–Vice President Lyndon B. Johnson). When journalist Thomas V. Kelly asked Walker to respond to praise from George Lincoln Rockwell, head of the American Nazi Party, the former World War II hero reacted like an SS officer and punched the reporter in the eye. Continuing to spread the bad word, the ex-general gave inflammatory speeches on Southern radio stations slamming the "anti–Christ conspirators of the Supreme Court" who had struck down segregation. He also proclaimed that when he enforced integration in 1957, he "was on the wrong side!"[16] In February 1963, Walker joined racist demagogue Billy Hargis in a speaking tour chillingly named Operation Midnight Ride. Walker and his John Birch allies even printed handbills declaring "Wanted for Treason: JFK!" They were still being handed out in Dallas on November 22, 1963, when the president was murdered in his prime. Walker himself had been the victim of an assassination attempt (allegedly by Lee Harvey Oswald) and filed a plethora of lawsuits against various media outlets whose opinions of his reactionary speeches he didn't care for, though his respondents in court got it easy (witness Thomas Kelly's black eye). He had already been arrested for sedition and insurrection while he and his supporters attempted to physically thwart federal troops from enforcing integration in Southern schools. Walker also promoted another familiar falsehood from the John Birchers: that Communists were pouring fluoride into our water supply to make us impotent. With some glee, Attorney General Robert F. Kennedy ordered that Walker undergo a 90-day psychiatric evaluation. Challenged by the ACLU, the government had to drop its prosecution and the former general spent just five days in the asylum.

However, as the nation changed and proto-fascist organizations like the John Birchers became a memory, the former macho general faced another dilemma. On June 23, 1976, the 66-year-old reactionary who hoped to "purify" America both racially and politically, was arrested for public lewdness in a men's room in a Dallas park: He was accused of fondling and propositioning a male undercover police officer. He was arrested again in Dallas for public lewdness on March 16, 1977. Both arrests were misdemeanors that ended in suspended sentences and fines, but the exposure (pun intended) must have embarrassed the former gubernatorial candidate. Talk about sapping "precious bodily fluids"!

Walker loudly proclaimed that he didn't want the government's pension, but as he got older and more infirm (and no one would hire him for racist speeches any more), he ended up begging that same "pinko" government for his pension, which they finally gave him in 1982. Having never married or had any children, Walker died in 1993, three days before his 84th birthday.

In *Dr. Strangelove*, Kubrick shoots Sterling Hayden from below and close-up as he delivers his monologue about "purification" and the insidious Communist plot of "sapping the nation of bodily fluids." Ripper is a madman; a caricature of an already caricatured Edwin Walker and other warmongering generals. However, Peter George is *still* able to put in plot elements from his book. Like General Quinten, Ripper kills himself, leaving those who wish to stop the bombers empty-handed. However, as in the novel, our heroes, in this case, RAF Group Leader Mandrake (also Sellers), is able to figure out the Recall Codes from the doodling on Ripper's desk blotter.

Sellers deserves much praise for his various performances. He always said that Dr. Strangelove's voice was based on that of famous New York City crime photographer Arthur "Weegie" Fellig, the production's still photographer. The Ukrainian-Jewish Fellig (real first name: Ascher) came to New York at age nine; and while Sellers does a dead-on impression of Fellig's deep voice, he leaves out the photographer's strong New York accent. For Strangelove's scary persona *and* his German accent, Sellers had to find another source of inspiration. It's a good bet that that the actor-comedian might also have been imitating the most famous ex–Nazi of the early

DOOMSDAY MAVEN: Peter Sellers in his iconic title role in Stanley Kubrick's classic "nightmare comedy" *Dr. Strangelove* (1964). Its portrayal of power-crazed military officers seemed to be based on *real* American generals.

1960s, former German missile expert Wernher von Braun. At the time, von Braun was being lionized by our government. Both Kubrick and Sellers (Jewish and half–Jewish, respectively) were too knowledgeable of von Braun's fame or the controversy of his Nazi past *not* to have it figure in their depiction of Strangelove; Sellers was in the British Army while von Braun's V-2 rockets were raining down on London. Certainly, the actor's use of the von Braun image of rocket maven was no rewriting of history like Curt Jurgens' principled Nazi in *I Aim at the Stars*. Like Strangelove, von Braun was a scientist and munitions expert in a powerful position with the U.S. government; and though he wasn't wheelchair-bound or wearing a black glove, the scientist was also playing a dual role in his dealings with his American hosts. On one hand, a revered aerospace expert for NASA involved even then with our space program, von Braun also worked strenuously to conceal his past as a Nazi war criminal from the American public. Sellers gives us a searing portrayal of a respected émigré now working for the U.S., but every once in a while the murderous Nazi creeps out in the form of a gloved hand trying to strangle the part of him that accepted democracy. You don't need to be a rocket scientist to figure out that one. For the filmmakers, it was the perfect euphemistic middle finger to the former missile-builder and, perhaps indirectly, the U.S. military's protection of him.

Despite the complaints of some critics and the brass-hats, *Dr. Strangelove* was a hit, a classic dark comedy from one of our greatest filmmakers. Kubrick was able to convince Columbia, now officially the same studio set to produce *Fail*-Safe, to release that nuclear drama in April 1964, several months *after* the release of *Strangelove*. Kubrick's film was set to be released in November 1963, but President Kennedy's assassination put the kibosh on that idea. In a slapstick pie-fight at the end, President Mufley is floored by a pie, causing Turgidson to cry out, "The president has fallen!" The timing was too close for comfort. Similarly, B-52 commander King Kong's (Slim Pickens) line about having a good time in Dallas was changed to Vegas. Added to this controversy, there was even behind-the-scenes credit-hogging between Kubrick and George against third-billed scenarist Terry Southern, with the director constantly minimizing Southern's satirical contributions to the script.[17]

With the added revenue that probably would have gone to *Fail-Safe* (which ultimately bombed—pun intended), *Strangelove* stayed in circulation for years. However, any rewards due him for the film's success didn't last very long for Peter George. Though he returned to England and continued to write military-themed thrillers, his drinking and his depression got worse. It soon got to the point where the writer was now answering the door of his cottage with a loaded double-barreled shotgun. On June 1, 1966, two and a half years after *Dr. Strangelove*'s release, George used that shotgun to blow his brains out. He was 42.

With *Strangelove* still raking in the money, Hollywood became bolder in its choices of military-themed movies. General Ripper had showed the industry that depicting madmen in charge of our Armed Forces could be profitable at the box office.

In 1964, Don Baruch and the motion picture section of the Department of Defense were still up to their old tricks. They insisted that Columbia insert a title card at the beginning of *Dr. Strangelove* stating that a nuclear accident could not possibly happen, and they made sure that every library or other distributor of documentary footage denied the producers of *Fail-Safe* the use of military films depicting its aircraft in flight. Now anti-nuclear producer Robert Youngston knew how Kubrick felt when *he* tried to get footage from the USAF.

Similarly, other artists involved in making controversial projects that cast the U.S. military in a sinister light were going to have their own problems with Baruch and the Department of Defense.

In the summer of 1962, while Kubrick was just starting to turn Peter George's thriller about nuclear war into a madcap comedy, Kirk Douglas sent Burt Lancaster a copy of *Seven Days in May*, a new novel by seasoned Washington newsmen Fletcher Knebel and Charles Bailey II. The political thriller dealt with an attempted coup of the United States by patriotic but fanatical reactionary Army general James Muldoon Scott. His motivation: right-wing rage at the president's pending nuclear arms treaty with the Soviet Union. "If the whole point of the functioning of democracy is to have weight and merit," wrote Lancaster to Douglas in late September, then it was important for the film version to show that the generals, "however misguided, are more than just power-hungry.... In fact, a strong case should be made for them." In an October 8 response, Douglas agreed. "They believe in what they are doing—completely," wrote the former Spartacus, "therein lies the danger."[18]

Therein *did* lie the danger. The film's director, political thriller maven John Frankenheimer, said that General James Muldoon Scott was a combination of Douglas

MacArthur and Curtis LeMay. (Co-author Fletcher Knebel said that Scott was based on the disgraced Edwin Walker.) Whether General Scott was based on MacArthur, Walker, Power, LeMay or even the late take-no-prisoners warrior George S. Patton, *all* these men believed in what they were doing; profit and cynicism had very little to do with their motivations. The world in which these men lived contributed to their super-patriotic zeal. On October 22, two weeks after Douglas' reply letter, President Kennedy went on national TV and announced that the government had evidence of Soviet-supplied missile sites in Cuba. This announcement was risky for the young president; his reputation had already taken a hit with the failed Bay of Pigs invasion. However, this was no example of Black Ops gone wrong, but Soviet imperialism once again showing its increasingly ugly head. The world literally held its breath in that last week in October '62 until Nikita Khrushchev grudgingly ordered the sites dismantled. To sweeten this deal, Kennedy ordered the removal of the nuclear arsenals at bases in Turkey and Iran. If anything, Kirk Douglas' timing in his call to his old pal Lancaster couldn't have been any better. Douglas was on the spot when Columbia, who had an option on the novel, cancelled the project due to opposition from the military—but that didn't stop the former Wyatt Earp and Doc Holliday.

Produced by Douglas' company and Paramount, *Seven Days in May* may have been based on a bestseller but hovering in the background was the recent nail-biting *Six Days in October*. However, instead of standing up to the Soviets, as Kennedy had, *Seven Days in May* called for compromise. It's set in the year 1973 (some say 1970); instead of talking about ending our involvement in Vietnam, or even discussing the genius of Martin Scorsese, the characters playing military personnel are all basically happy campers, seemingly glad to be a part of a nation run by the wise and principled President Jordan Lyman (Fredric March). However, not everyone agrees with Lyman's anti-nuclear treaty with the Soviets. Had Scott been a lone loony in the Army who was supplying pamphlets from the John Birch Society to his men, there probably wouldn't have been a book *or* movie (despite Knebel's claim). Instead, General Scott has many co-conspirators in the government, both military and civilian, all seeking to overthrow Jordan and put the nation on a wartime footing. The conspirators have even built a secret military base in Texas.

The plot deals with isolating the president from his civilian aides during a military alert and seizing the government in a bloodless coup; then declaring a military dictatorship. In fact, everything in General Scott's plan actually did happen not too long before in Turkey and many countries in the Middle East and Latin America, though one couldn't say they were in any way bloodless. In fact, *Seven Days in May* was banned outright in Brazil, then run by a military dictatorship, because the junta felt that it would remind the public of the not-too-lenient "gentlemen" then running the country into the ground.

The coup is exposed by Marine Colonel Martin "Jiggs" Casey (Douglas), Scott's aide, who accidently discovers cryptic messages pointing to the plot, as well as the existence of that base in Texas—a base whose existence is denied by the Pentagon. Disturbed by all the weird code words about the Preakness, and the secret base, Jiggs is able to take his concerns to President Jordan (one does wonder how a Marine colonel is able to see the busy commander-in-chief so easily over those in higher authority). Jiggs gets incriminating letters about the general from Scott's former mistress Eleanor Holbrook (the alcoholic and rapidly declining Ava Gardner), going so far as to sleep with her to do so. In fact, Holbrook was supposedly based on General Douglas MacArthur's mistress, Isabel Rosario Cooper, a Eurasian woman who was having an affair with the general. In 1934, MacArthur sued journalists Drew Pearson and Robert Allen for libel—that is, until the newsmen made it clear they intended to use Cooper's testimony in a public trial. Uncharacteristically, MacArthur called a tactical retreat from his lawsuit.

Lyman sends the alcoholic southern Senator Raymond Clark (Edmond O'Brien) on a search for the Texas base, a quest that will revive the Senator's sense of duty and save his soul. On TV, Lyman publicly announces the attempted coup. With the public behind him, the president is able to call for the resignation of Scott and his associates, many of whom are in the Joint Chiefs of Staff. At the end, after a verbal showdown between Scott and Jordan in the Oval Office, the now-vanquished general goes out to his car and is driven away, presumably to MacArthur-like oblivion and obscurity. However, this is not the way scenarist Rod Serling had ended the film. Years later, Douglas wrote in his autobiography that originally General Scott "goes off in his sports car and dies in a wreck."

Backing up the actor's assertion, there still exists an undated synopsis by Rod Serling that ends with: "Listening to the announcement over his car radio, Scott swerves off the road and is killed."[19]

(OVAL) OFFICE POLITICS: Left to right: Martin Balsam (back of head, seated), George Macready, Kirk Douglas, Fredric March and Edmond O'Brien in *Seven Days in May* (1964), one of several film versions of political novels filmed in the early 1960s. This one depicts a military takeover of the United States.

At the bottom of the synopsis, either Serling or a Paramount executive crossed out the words "swerves off the road and is killed," and replaces it with "orders his driver to take him home." Douglas added, "Was it an accident or suicide? Coming up out of the wreckage is the car's radio is President Jordan Lyman's speech about the sanctity of the Constitution."[20] This supported both Douglas and Lancaster's sincere message about protecting the Constitution from anti-democratic forces. However, both actors probably didn't realize how close the ending was to the death of General George S. Patton, another hawkish "loose cannon" who desired war with the Soviets. The general's death from his injuries 11 days after his crash robbed the coming Cold War of one its more hawkish disciples.

Surprisingly, though the Department of Defense frowned on the production due its controversial plot, Douglas and Frankenheimer had no trouble enlisting Kennedy administration support. A huge fan of both military and political literature and films of that time, the president insisted to Kirk Douglas at a Washington banquet that the movie should be made. According to presidential aide Ted Sorenson, Kennedy mused out loud that he knew a couple generals who "might wish" to take over the country.[21] One wonders if the president had visions of Generals LeMay, Power or Walker on his mind. Subsequently, on JFK's orders, Press Secretary Pierre Salinger allowed the production crew to copy the design of the Oval Office for use in the film. Cunningly, the president made sure he was away at Hyannisport as D.C. police cleared the front of the White House of anti-administration protesters (who were, ironically, protesting the 1963 Nuclear Test Ban Treaty); Frankenheimer replaced them with extras posing as protesters against President Lyman's nuclear treaty with the Soviets. And though the Department of Defense banned all filming around the Pentagon, Frankenheimer shot a scene from a concealed van of Douglas entering the Pentagon. Seeing Douglas in a Marine colonel's uniform, leathernecks immediately saluted the actor as he entered.

For Hollywood, the murder of President Kennedy in November 1963 started to become as inconvenient as it was tragic. With *Seven Days in May* set to be released in December, Douglas and Lancaster insisted that its premiere be delayed. Ultimately, the film opened in Washington D.C. on February 12, 1964.

Douglas grew to detest Fletcher Knebel and Charles Bailey II, claiming they looked down their noses at the production ("I resented their pompous attitude"), and he told them that he'd make a much better film out of "your goddamned book."[22] Years later, Douglas wrote, the Johnson administration expressed its displeasure with another film project based on Knebel's book *A Night at Camp David*, because it depicted an unbalanced president. Needless to say, with the far more thin-skinned LBJ in the White House, the film was never made.[23]

Arthur Knight in the *Saturday Review* thought that it was exciting to see Hollywood, "the sleeping giant ... waking up again" after the non-controversial (and, implicitly, pro-military) films of the 1950s.[24] *The New York Times'* Bosley Crowther liked *Seven Days in May* because it proved that democracy worked.[25] A hit with critics and the public, it's still one of the best films to come out of a Hollywood already drowning in heavy political film fare.

Train them! Excite them! Arm them! Then turn them loose on the Nazis!

This tagline was for one of 1967's biggest box office smashes. Filmed at a time when World War II films were still profitable, and the cynicism of the Vietnam War was just then starting to creep into the genre, said box office smash was controversial, dark, biting satirical, violent and over-the-top, and it delivered all the requisite action goods in spades. And, like many good war movies, it was originated by real-life warriors.

In 1959, a New York magazine writer–copy editor, Erwin Michael "Mick" Nathanson, otherwise known as E.M., did a director friend of his a favor and appeared in a few bit parts in the independent production *The Immoral Mr. Teas*. The director, Russ Meyer, told Nathanson a story he had heard years before. Meyer had been a World War II combat cameraman, putting his life on the line at Normandy and other battlegrounds; he was even a staff sergeant for Patton, and the old battle footage Meyer had shot was actually used in *Patton*. Already a member of the Army's 166th Signal Photographic Company, Meyer was assigned to the London division of the U.S. Army Pictorial Service. In May 1944, he was ordered to film a small group of Army prisoners being trained in a Southampton stockade. They had been convicted of crimes like rape and murder, and all of them faced death sentences. Meyer was aghast to learn that these men were going to be parachuted into France before D-Day on a top-secret suicide mission. Reportedly, all of them refused to bathe and shave until their mission was accomplished and, if they survived, were finally set free.

Military police guards started to refer to them as "the Dirty Dozen."

No one knows what happened to Meyer's footage, but what was certain was that none of these men were ever heard from again. Were they killed in battle, or did they survive and escape to freedom after accomplishing their mission? Whether it was true or not, Nathanson was intrigued by Meyer's story, and started a novel on the event—if indeed it was an event, since Army files did not contain any reports on these 12 men *or* their suicide mission. Filmmaker Robert Aldrich tried to buy the novel while it was in galleys, but lost out to MGM. But Aldrich was hired to put Nathanson's now runaway bestseller on film.

It was now the 1960s, more than ten years after Aldrich angered the Army with his depiction of a corrupt military and cowardly officers in *Attack!* The Department of Defense was still powerful enough to pressure filmmakers, but Hollywood and its audiences had most definitely changed. Gradually, Americans started to feel cynical about both war and war movies, rejecting the predictable flag-waving of the conformist 1950s. Vietnam also started to alter their views. Though filmed before the My Lai massacre, Aldrich emphasized the "dirty" in the title. Not the fact that the men didn't bathe, but that they didn't fight by the rules.

The cast was a potpourris of Hollywood's macho men, a great many of them World War II veterans, making this "hip" film a production starring men who were, for the most part, well into their 40s: Lee Marvin, Ernest Borgnine, Charles Bronson, Richard Jaeckel, Robert Ryan, George Kennedy, Telly Savalas, Ralph Meeker, Clint Walker, Donald Sutherland, Jim Brown and John Cassavetes in his only Oscar-nominated performance. The Dozen's Mission: Invade a chateau occupied by high *Wehrmacht* officers, kill them all, and blow the place to smithereens. Simple. Marvin's Major Raisman tells Borgnine's tough General Worden that only a raving lunatic could have thought up such a plan; and in the real world, it's extremely unlikely *any* American commanders would actually send a group of rapists and psychopaths on a commando mission, especially if they were told that they'd probably not come back! Major Reisman was a captain in the novel, and Jewish as well (his first name was Jacob), giving this American officer an added dimension as he leads a death squad against the Nazis. However, just like Department of Defense–influenced films of the past that erased Jewish fighting men from the screen, Aldrich and his screenwriters cut out Reisman's ethnicity.

The Dirty Dozen was originally scripted by former Fox scenarist Nunnally Johnson. The material certainly wasn't the kind of work the witty writer, a product of Hollywood screenwriting from the 1930s to the '50s, would tackle. Predictably, Aldrich, who never filmed a thug he didn't like, didn't like Nunnally's more classy, G-rated screenplay:

> [MGM] had about four or five scripts, the last one written by Nunnally Johnson. This would have made a very good, very acceptable 1945 war picture. But I don't think that a 1945 war picture is necessarily a good 1967 war picture. So I brought in Lukas Heller.[26]

Though claiming that audiences were "fascinated by the anarchy of the picture's first two-thirds and were excited and/or stimulated and/or entertained by the last third," Aldrich *did* have his critics. And they were emphatically *not* excited and/or stimulated and/or entertained.

In his June 16, 1967, *New York Times* review, the always formidable Bosley Crowther wrote:

> [T]o have this bunch of felons, a totally incorriglble lot, some of them psychopathic, and to try to make us believe that they would be committed by any American general to carry out an exceedingly important raid that a regular commando group could do with equal efficiency—and certainly with greater dependability—is downright preposterous.
> And then to bathe these rascals in a specious heroic light—to make their hoodlum bravado and defiance of discipline, and their nasty kind of gutter solidarity, seem exhilarating and admirable—is encouraging a spirit of hooliganism that is brazenly antisocial, to say the least.[27]

Bragging "If Crowther knocks you, you're in very good company," Aldrich added that he "would much rather have a spirit of 'brazen hooliganism' than what passes for patriotism nowadays."[28] Emphasizing the fact that he was expressing admiration for rapists and murderers, the misogynist helmsman also called women "a pain in the ass" and expressed doubt that men and women could ever live harmoniously.[29]

Predictably, the Department of Defense did *not* give assistance to the production. One of the major reasons for this was the type of things the Dozen did to their Nazi enemies, which went beyond merely shooting them.

After the Dozen, some dressed as *Wehrmacht* officers, shed their disguises and launch their attack, the senior German high command and their concubines head for the basement bomb shelter. After blowing away every enemy soldier in their way, the Dozen decides to incinerate the Nazi officers and their tarts in their "impenetrable" basement fortress. In his July 26 *Chicago Tribune* review, Roger Ebert described what happened next:

> Then they screw off the tops of the air vents and drop unexploded grenades down into the shelter. But the Germans grab the grenades and get them away from the airshaft. There's some great footage of all these Germans going berserk and grabbing the grenades while the women run around screaming. Now you might ask, why not pull the pin on one grenade and lob it down into the airshaft? The explosion would clear away the Germans near the shaft, and then you could drop in more grenades without any trouble. Naw, too simple. Instead, pour gallons of gasoline down into the airshaft and *then* toss in a grenade.[30]

TAKING STOCKADE: Left to right: John Cassavetes, Lee Marvin and Richard Jaeckel in the film version of E.M. Nathanson's *The Dirty Dozen* (1967), director Robert Aldrich's triumphant—and controversial—return to the war movie. It angered traditionalists who hated the *Dozen*'s murderous tactics.

The climax enraged many critics who felt that Aldrich's usual anti–American and anti-military passions had gone too far. In this scene alone, American soldiers were now being put on the same level as their Nazi enemy, with the Dozen's murder of non-combatant women being seen by many as a war crime. On another level, Aldrich not only showed that *any* army could be guilty of such cold-blooded acts, but that the Nazis and their aiders and abettors (their female companions) were now the ones being incinerated in a basement crematorium of their own making.

The brutal imagery was not lost on the unknown reviewer of the *Hollywood Reporter*:

> The action is heady, but many will be offended that it includes an act by the U.S. team in which they pour grenades and gasoline through the air vents onto officers and women trapped in a bomb shelter, incinerating them Buchenwald-style.[31]

For the first time in an American film set during World War II, U.S. Army soldiers were treating Nazis and their supporters the way *they* treated their victims, with the Dirty Dozen delivering their own "final solution." In West Germany, censors allowed the scene of Jim Brown dropping grenades into the air shafts, but cut out the pouring of the gasoline, the grenades landing in the shelter, the panic of the generals, and the women screaming. At the time, the German government was still supporting its Nazi veterans, including SS war criminals, with comfortable pensions and protection from extradition.

Soon, the previously hostile generals visit the surviving trio (Marvin, Bronson and Jaeckel) in their hospital room and praise them for the mission's success. But after they leave, Bronson's Wladislaw remarks, "Killing generals could get to be a habit with me." Though he had participated in the killing of Nazi generals, Wladislaw's crack chillingly implied he'd like to murder *American* generals as well, a sentiment that the film's left-wing director seemed far too comfortable with. *The Hollywood Reporter* took notice:

> Is that line supposed to ring pacifistically? The only general we have met is Borgnine, who seems to be one of the most reasonable men of them all. Aside from the top brass who conceived the plan but are never seen, the worst excesses are committed by the lower hierarchy of the officers and by the Dozen, with whom we are frequently encouraged to identify. What was [Bronson's] implication?[32]

Aldrich would return with even more violent, misogynist and anti–American movies—or, as he liked to say, "anti-war" movies—in the next 13 years he had left as a filmmaker.

But he would never again make a film that was as big a box-office success—or as much fun—as *The Dirty Dozen*.

Sometime in early 1939, as war clouds gathered over Europe, young Carson McKullers wrote a short novel she called *Army Post*. Set in a sleepy Army camp down south, the story deals with a host of dysfunctional Army officers and their equally screwed-up spouses, as well as one Army private who appeared to be heavily into voyeurism, all giving in to their hidden desires as Europe and Asia were about to burn.

After two months of steady writing at her Fayetteville, North Carolina, home, McKullers allegedly put the novel away in a dresser drawer and forgot about it. Then her *The Heart is a Lonely Hunter* was published in 1940 and McKullers was justifiably hailed as one of the literary world's newest finds. She was just 23. With little trouble, she returned to her novella about the hidden desires and passions within a peacetime Army post, and it was sold to *Harper's Bazaar* in August for $500 and eventually published in the magazine in two parts in October and November. It was said that *The Heart Is a Lonely Hunter*, a novel which showed compassion for physically and mentally challenged people, had an anti-fascist message. Yet *Army Post*, soon to be retitled *Reflections in a Golden Eye*, was far more personal for McKullers. Devoid of politics, both international and domestic, it's a tale of a married, sexually repressed Army captain who has a fixation on a monosyllabic handsome young private. Not to be outdone in oddball behavior, the private sneaks into the captain's bedroom and spies on his sexy wife as she sleeps. Meanwhile, the wife, realizing she's not going to get any with her sexually repressed husband, cheats on him with another officer, a man whose wife miscarried years before and mutilated herself in despair. This was emphatically *not* the Army of Eisenhower, Patton and MacArthur! It boggles the mind that Carson had the courage to write such a story at the same time the Roosevelt administration and Hollywood were heralding the courage and manliness of our Armed Forces.

There exists a synopsis with a Paramount Pictures logo, indicating that McKullers' agents had peddled a prospective film version to the studio, and it was read by a story reader there in January 1941. Under the subject Theme, this was his description: "A series of strange events at an army post, involving a few men and two women, their minds distorted, twisted into unhealthy shapes, lead to the murder of a soldier."[33]

That someone actually thought that the Hollywood of the day would be interested in filming such a story—or that the Breen Office would allow it—revealed a certain naiveté on the part of whomever sent it to the studio of Hope and Crosby, DeMille and Veronica Lake. Way ahead of its time, *Reflections in a Golden Eye* accurately captured an era in which being "in the closet" was multiplied a thousandfold because its story was set at an Army camp, a place where *machismo* was not only welcomed, but encouraged. Yet the author herself, one of the most groundbreaking literary minds of her century, had her own tragic life story.

The daughter of a man who committed suicide when she was little, Carson was a sickly child who became a sickly adult, constantly plagued with heart problems; when she was 31, her entire left side was paralyzed by a stroke. Married at a young age to Reeves, a bisexual ex-soldier, she eventually divorced him and developed many unrequited lesbian relationships. She dedicated *Reflections of a Golden Eye* to Swiss journalist Annemarie Schwarzenbach, on whom it is said she had a powerful crush. (A *New Yorker* profile once described Carson as "a dreamer who was attracted to big, capable women."[34]) When writing *Reflections*, Carson admitted, "I am immersed in my characters that their motives are my own. When I write about a thief, I become one; when I write about a Captain Penderton, I become a homosexual man."[35]

A frustrated gay woman forced to keep her desires in the shadows, Carson knew quite well the bottled-up, unrequited passions of a Captain Penderton.

Inspiration for the story came to her when she recalled a visit to Fort Benning, Georgia, when she was a teenager. However, the story really germinated when her bisexual husband Reeves mentioned to her the arrest of a Fort Bragg soldier caught peeping inside a married officer's quarters. Penderton is married to lively, but not-too-bright, Army brat, Leonora. *She* is having an affair with Penderton's charismatic superior, Major Langdon; *he* is married to the sickly and self-mutilating Allison, who happens to have a loyal and sexually ambivalent houseboy named Anacieto. Meanwhile, Penderton has a crush on Private Ellgee Williams, following and browbeating him, giving him menial tasks and verbally abusing him, yet never getting a rise out of the monosyllabic soldier. Ellgee is a man who likes riding horses in the nude and breaking into Leonora's bedroom to watch her sleep. Not until *From Here to Eternity* and *The Naked and the Dead* did another novel dealing with the U.S. Army have such a plethora of dysfunctional misfits.

In 1966, closeted gay star Montgomery Clift was set to play Penderton in Warner Brothers' film version of the novel. But Clift's many years of alcohol and chemical abuse caught up with him and he was dead of a heart attack at age 45 in July 1966 while the project was still on the boards. Director John Huston cast the bisexual Marlon Brando, himself in serious decline, as Penderton. Elizabeth Taylor was cast as Leonora; ex–Marine Brian Keith was Langdon; Julie Harris as Allison; Robert Forster as Private "L.G." Williams, and an amateur, Zorro David, was cast as Anacieto. (As the homophobic Huston said to an aide, "Find us a Filipino fag."[36]) In the film, promotions were in order; Captain Penderton became a major and Major Langdon became a lieutenant colonel. Huston had tried to convince McKullers to do the screenplay, but she declined due to illness. Months after the film started shooting, her condition worsened. The correspondence between McKullers and Huston reveals that, though she was ill and facing the amputation of her legs, she sounded positive and was hoping to make it to the film's premiere. But the 50-year-old writer was dead of a heart attack just two months after *Reflection* wrapped.

Huston shot on a barely used barracks on the campus of Nassau Community College in the fall of 1966, though at Liz Taylor's insistence, much of the filming was done in Rome. Huston shot the film in a yellow tint (golden eye, get it?), but was pressured by Warners to release the film in normal color prints when critics ridiculed the pretentiousness of the process (which also hurt the eyes of the viewer). According to the film's producer Ray Stark, the distributor called the process "arty-farty."[37]

As in McKullers' novel, Penderton is obsessed with the unnaturally quiet Private Williams, the man in charge of the stables, including Leonora's horse. Williams' idea of caring for the animal is to ride him in the woods while nude. Frustrated by not getting a rise out of Williams, as well as rage at his wife, Penderton uses his riding prop to beat the poor horse about the head in a scene that's painful to watch. The pompous officer (played by a pompous actor) is then whipped in the face by Leonora during a party with officers and their wives. Penderton's frustration is noted by Huston when Leonora strips before the trembling major as he orders "Don't do it!" in a voice that

IN AND OUT: Marlon Brando as the closeted homosexual officer and Elizabeth Taylor as his straight wife in the film version of Carson McKullers' *Reflections in a Golden Eye* **(1967). Attacks by the film's critics revealed the anti-gay prejudices of the day.**

sounds like an Asian stereotype. (Brando used the same voice during his racist performance in 1956's *The Teahouse of the August Moon*.)

The only actor to get almost universal praise for his performance was the only actor in the cast to actually have been in the military in wartime, Brian Keith, a performer who refined underplaying and naturalistic acting to a fine art. The ex–Marine hero of World War II also makes a mockery of Brando's ego-driven performance as Huston goes in for some unflattering close-ups of the flabby actor. Even McKullers' agent, Robert Lantz, had written to Huston that Keith seemed "to accomplish a sense of truth and reality with absolute ease."[38]

Huston begins the film with a McKullers quote about a murder at a Georgia Army base; and indeed, in real life, it is said that the publication of her novel made officers at Fort Benning uncomfortable. The film ends the same way as the novel, with a jealous Penderton catching Williams in Leonora's bedroom and gunning him down with his service pistol. Of course, the question remains unspoken, as McKullers meant it to be: Did Penderton kill Williams as a jealous husband or as a jilted lover? Typically, Huston praised himself by announcing that "it was the first film to deal with homosexuality in an intelligent way."[39] He didn't bother mentioning his blacklisting of Montgomery Clift after discovering his homosexuality during the filming of *Freud*, nor the epithet he used when talking about the casting of Anacieto.

Huston also didn't brag about the laughs that greeted much of his film, particularly during Brando's showy performance. Though praising Brando, Roger Ebert took issue with "matrons, who found it necessary to shriek loudly, and giggle hideously through three-quarters of it, and their husbands who delivered obligatory guffaws in counterpoint." At one point, Penderton primps himself up before a mirror when he knows that Williams will show up, apparently prompting a reaction the filmmakers did *not* expect. According to Ebert, the audience "had never seen anything so funny in their lives." However, Ebert showed some intolerance of his own when he insisted that the audience "should have been taken out and shot."[40]

Other critics, however, would show the prejudices of the day.

Brando biographer Gary Carey praised the film and called the actor's performance brilliant. However, after labeling the book "McCullers' horror chamber of perversity," he referred to Penderton's mirror scene as "sick secrets we really don't care to know."[41] Warner Brothers didn't help matters. An over-the-top blurb from the film's pressbook proclaimed, "It's dirty! A combination of lust, impotency, vulgarity, nudity, neurosis, brutality, voyeurism, hatred and insanity that results in murder."[42] *The Cleveland Press* said, "There is nothing terribly subtle about Huston's handling of his themes of lust and perversion...."[43] Predictably, the U.S. Conference of Catholic Bishops gave the film an O rating (Morally Offensive) and said that McKullers' novel was about "the twisted relationships and abnormal inclinations of a homosexual Army officer...."[44] *Time* referred to Huston's film as "a gallery of grotesques."[45] *Variety* said that Brando "struts about and mugs as the stuffy officer, whose Dixie dialect is often incoherent,"[46] and commended "the most outstanding and satisfying performance" of Brian Keith. Major curmudgeon John Simon proclaimed the film "distasteful ... pedestrian, crass and uninvolving to the point of repellence."[47]

Needless to say, the Department of Defense did *not* back the film—nor did they have to. And they were probably amused at the film's total failure at the box office. Warners again delved into the subject of gays in the Army with *The Sergeant*, starring

Rod Steiger as a repressed homosexual master sergeant and John Philip Law as the private who's the object of his obsession. Like *Reflections*, *The Sergeant* bombed at the box office.

In August 1965, John Wayne and his secretary Mary St. John were strolling on the campus of his old alma mater, the University of Southern California, when the Duke saw some commotion in front of the Doheny Library. A student anti-war group had set up tables and hung posters protesting the Vietnam War. When a young Marine bedecked with medals strode past them, the students maliciously hooted and showered him with curses. The young leatherneck stoically refused to respond and just kept walking. He had been on the campus to ask administrators about the G.I. Bill. Something about the young Marine veteran had sent chills through Wayne. He was missing an arm.

Enraged, Wayne marched up to one of the tables, slammed down his big fists and told the stunned protesters, "You stupid bastards! Blame Johnson if you must; blame that son of a bitch Kennedy! Blame Eisenhower or Truman or goddamn fucking Roosevelt, but don't blame that kid. Not any of those kids. They served! Jesus, the kid's arm is gone!"[48]

Not long after this incident, the Duke decided to pay tribute to those who served, like that young one-armed Marine. When he discovered Robin Moore's novel *The Green Berets*, he authorized Batjac, his production company, to purchase the rights while he contacted President Lyndon B. Johnson on December 28, 1966, and told him of his plans to make a film version. He also asked the president if he could have Department of Defense and Army assistance. Special White House Assistant (and former Army Air Corps bomber pilot) Jack Valenti reportedly told LBJ, "Wayne's politics are wrong, but insofar as Vietnam is concerned, his views are right. If he made the picture, he would be saying the things we want said."[49]

Wayne also corresponded with White House Special Assistant Bill Moyers about the project. Certainly, no branch of the Armed Forces had a problem with John Wayne, one of the few Hollywood performers they genuinely liked. His films could always be counted on to be patriotic and pro-military. *The Green Berets* was to be the second production in a two-film deal with Universal, the first being a version of Clair Huffaker's western novel *The War Wagon*. A *Green Berets* script was written by longtime Wayne scenarist James Lee Barrett, an ex–Marine (and scenarist for *The D.I.*). Shooting was to start in late spring 1967. But Wayne smelled a rat when the studio kept stalling him on a definite start date. Wayne's son and Batjac producer Michael Wayne was originally told by the studio that they were concerned about the budget. But then Michael met with Universal execs and learned that their *real* problem was the script, which one producer said was the worst he had ever read.[50] In record time, Michael said goodbye to Universal and he and his father took the property to Warners, where the pro-war Jack L. Warner approved the project. As a "make-up" picture for Universal, the Duke did *Hellfighters* (1969), where Wayne and war veteran Clair Huffaker had no problem inserting Communist villains into the screenplay.

On April 4, 1966, the Duke, Michael and Barrett met with Assistant Secretary of Defense Arthur Sylvester about Department of Defense assistance on *The Green Berets*. On the 12th, however, the director for Security Review at the Department of Defense, Charles W. Hinkle, sent a memo to Don Baruch that was full of reservations.

Especially controversial to the brass-hats was the parts of the script dealing with the tacit approval of the torture of prisoners.

> The script should be amended beginning at page 78 to delete the incident of brutality shown toward a prisoner by the Vietnamese officer and the approval of it by the Americans, including Colonel Kirby. This is grist for the opponents of U.S. policy in Vietnam. Such an act of brutality is in violation of the policy of the Department of Defense.[51]

Two days later, Baruch sent Sylvester a memo warning the assistant secretary not to discuss Robin Moore with the Waynes in subsequent meetings. There was a good reason for this: The Department of Defense *hated* the author. To Baruch and the Department of Defense brass-hats, Moore had betrayed them by revealing in his book the quite frequent torture of prisoners by actual Green Beret units. The accounts were so frighteningly detailed that they angrily interrogated the author to find out where he had obtained his information.

After reading the first draft of Barrett's script and calling it a "disappointment," Don Baruch wrote:

> We failed somehow in getting over the mission of the Green Berets in Vietnam, as the basic story now involves an OSS type [mission] into North Vietnam to blow up a bridge, a power plant and to snatch a high-ranking commie, but before this is carried out, our boys participate in a combat action to prevent a new camp from being taken by the VC.[52]

One can almost agree with this assessment if only for the fact that the Vietnam War was a far different animal than World War II, or even Korea. Certainly the Green Berets pulling Black Ops in the jungles of Southeast Asia was not the same as the OSS infiltrating Nazi-occupied France. And for this fact alone, the film would be considered a sad joke, not only to actual soldiers and Marines who had been "in country" at the time, but to filmgoers to this very day. Wayne (co-directing with former combat photographer Ray Kellogg), Barrett and even Jack Warner tried to foist on the public a 1960s war film which had all the clichés of the Hollywood war films of World War II, with the possible lack of a Donna Reed or Phyliss Thaxter leading lady. The film is gung ho macho all the way. The only female "lead" is Irene Tsu as a double agent for the Americans (she sleeps with the evil VC general before setting him up for the kidnapping).

After perusing the script, State Department honcho Francis W. Tully, Jr., insisted that Barrett had to make changes. One sequence that angered Tully was the implication that Kirby's men could cross the border into Laos with impunity for military operations against the VC. Perhaps Tully didn't realize it, but in this sequence, Wayne's Kirby is replicating the actions of Wayne's cavalry commander, also named Kirby, in John Ford's *Rio Grande* for Republic way back in 1950. In this classic Western, Kirby is a stand-in for the real cavalry officer Ranald "Bad Hand" McKenzie, who crossed the Mexican border and risked an international incident to pursue and destroy Kickapoo Apache marauders who fled to safety south of the Rio Grande after murdering Americans along the Texas border settlements. (Despite Mexican outrage, Mackenzie's mission was accomplished and the raids ceased.)

Wayne's co-star David Janssen, TV's *The Fugitive*, himself anti–Vietnam War, sometimes had furious arguments with Wayne on the set. Janssen plays cynical anti-war reporter George Beckworth. Going in-country with Kirby's men (both the Duke and co-star Bruce Cabot, 60 and 63, respectively, were too old for their roles) and witnessing Cong atrocities, Beckworth starts to agree with Kirby's pro-war point of view. However, in Barrett's script, Beckworth does a little more than just alter his political stance. According to Tully's memo:

> The incident in which the newsman, Beckworth, shifts his position to one supporting the U.S. policies in Vietnam is a distasteful one. When he reaches his decision that he has been wrong in the past, he seizes a gun and becomes a combatant. This violates the rules under which he operates as a news correspondent, and to the extent that the incident is considered realistic by those who might see a film based on this script, might indicate that it would not be unusual for a newsman to perform such violations. Also to be noted is the pleasure with which the soldiers accept and approve Beckworth's asking for weapons.[53]

In fact, had he known of the original sequence, it would have been a foregone conclusion that Janssen would have refused to do the scene. Ironically, when *Star Trek*'s George Takei, playing a South Vietnamese Army captain, openly admitted to Wayne that he was against the war, the Duke frankly replied that so was half his cast and crew.

Tully also spotlighted the scene of the beating of a Cong prisoner by a South Vietnamese officer, an act which meets with the approval of Kirby and his team. "It supports some of the accusations of these opponents against the U.S.," wrote Tully, "and is of course a clear violation of the Articles of War."[54] Very true, and despite actual mistreatment of prisoners by the South Vietnamese Army, Tully could have also pointed out that the Articles of War never stopped the North Vietnamese from torturing or murdering American soldiers who fell into their hands.

Barrett and the Waynes made all the changes insisted upon by the Department of Defense. Yet despite these controversies within the script, there was also the inescapable conclusion that *The Green Berets* was a late 1960s version of a cliché-ridden World War II film. In fact, the unbelievably harmonious teamwork between the Americans and the South Vietnamese Army, one of the more corrupt and incompetent armies in all of Asia, is an obvious throwback to the usual Breen Office and OWI-sponsored World War II

THE SUN SETS IN THE *EAST*, PILGRIM: John Wayne as the American colonel allying his forces with the South Vietnamese Army in *The Green Berets* (1968). It was a box office hit, though Wayne and the film were furiously attacked by critics.

blather promoting harmony between us and our Allies (despite some very *real* acrimony between Americans, British and Soviets in how to fight the Axis).

In the film, American troops are there for the villagers victimized by the Cong, and *not once* is any American soldier or officer allowed to complain about the arrogance and corruption of their supposed allies, the South Vietnamese, much less call any of these people "gooks" or any other racist term. This is despite the fact that American soldiers actually *were* kindly to Vietnamese villagers, at least at first, before their numbers were decimated by the VC. Filmed at Fort Benning, Georgia, and other Southern locales, and featuring American soldiers as extras and Japanese actors as the Vietnamese, both North and South, *The Green Berets* exists in a never-never land where the sun sets in the east, none of the South Vietnamese use the Americans as cannon fodder, and all the villagers hate the Viet Cong and have no problem welcoming a foreign non–Asian army into their midst.

In fact, it was pretty obvious after a while that Wayne and Barrett were harking back to the clichés of Wayne's 1945 RKO war film *Back to Bataan*. Directed, ironically, by Communist Edward Dmytryk, the film features Anthony Quinn as a character tormented by his Filipino girlfriend becoming a Tokyo Rose type and broadcasting propaganda for the Japanese. In *The Green Berets*, there is some controversy about Irene Tsu's double agent sleeping with the VC general. In *Back to Bataan*, Ducky Louie is the little Filipino boy kidnapped and beaten by Japanese soldiers; he sacrifices his life by taking them with him over a cliff in a runaway truck. In *The Green Berets*, little Craig Jue is South Vietnamese orphan Hamchunk, who tags after Jim Hutton's likable malingerer-turned-dedicated-soldier Sgt. Peterson. However, unlike the World War II film, it is Peterson who sacrifices himself by insisting on taking point and then getting gruesomely impaled against a tree by a Cong booby trap. When I saw that scene in a Times Square movie house, way back in 1968, I was *extremely* upset. In fact, it is truly ironic that the conservative Wayne slyly inverted Communist Dmytryk's propaganda of the enemy murdering a likable character to demonstrate Red-sponsored villainy. Still, despite the clichés of the typical war film sacrifice, there is nothing cliché-ridden or dismissive about Hamchunk's very real anguish when he painfully realizes that his American soldier–big-brother figure will never return. Here, Wayne expertly shows his own agony as he watches the little boy go from one landing helicopter to another only to find that Peterson is not on any of them.

Yet the Duke also tells the boy—as, for that matter, he could have been telling Ducky Louie had he survived his bout with the Japanese—that he (and, by extension, the South Vietnamese people) are what this war is all about. And this is, again, by extension, the reason the Americans are there. However, this claim also omits the Johnson administration's desire to prop up the anti–Communist leaders of the South Vietnamese government and their chief enforcers, the South Vietnamese Army. The fall of South Vietnam culminated in the so-called "Domino Theory" promoted by LBJ's hawk-like generals.

The production had its problems. Besides trouble with Janssen, Wayne had to deal with Aldo Ray, long past his prime in the 1950s war films *Battle Cry* and *The Naked and the Dead*. An alcoholic for many years, Ray fell off the wagon midway through the shoot, forcing Wayne to give his lines to Batjac regulars Bruce Cabot, Mike Henry and Ed Faulkner. For years after Wayne's death, Ray continued to attack him without once mentioning his alcoholism or his boozy condition causing him to blow numerous takes.

Wayne was honest enough to tell the press that *The Green Berets* was "propaganda," a cowboys-and-Indians movie masquerading as a war film. However, the nation's critics had other names for the film—and they weren't pretty.

In her *New York Times* review (June 20, 1968), Renata Adler called the film

> so unspeakable, so stupid, so rotten and false in every detail that it passes through being fun, through being funny, through being camp, through everything and becomes an invitation to grieve, not for our soldiers, or for Vietnam (the film could not be more false or do a greater disservice to either of them) but for what has happened to the fantasy-making apparatus in this country.... It is vile and insane. On top of that, it is dull.[55]

It isn't every day you find something that's vile and insane, but also dull.

The Hollywood Reporter called it "clumsily scripted, blandly directed and performed with disinterest."[56] Michael Korda, writing in *Glamour*, pegged it as "immoral in the deepest sense." Continuing his hysterical rant, he added that the film was a simple-minded tract in praise of killing, brutality and American superiority over Asians, and racist in the tradition of Rudyard Kipling.[57] One wonders if Korda had actually seen the film since Wayne's colonel and the men under him have absolutely no problem dealing respectfully with their Asian allies who are fighting the North Vietnamese Army.

In *Life*, Richard Schickel criticized the film for ignoring "the realities of Vietnam," and complained that Wayne "has wasted my time, but he is incapable of poisoning my mind or anyone else's."[58] *Cinema Magazine* called the film "so wretched and so childishly sleazy that it is embarrassing to criticize its pretentiousness and banality."[59]

These reviews, many of them attacking Wayne's film for its politics rather than in terms of entertainment value, were subtle compared to Roger Ebert's assault in the June 26 *Chicago Sun-Times*, a "review" that attacked American involvement in Vietnam far more than the film itself. After calling *The Green Berets* "offensive," Ebert declared,

> [W]hat we certainly do not need is a movie depicting Vietnam in terms of cowboys and Indians. That is cruel and dishonest and unworthy of the thousands who have died there....
>
> What is our policy? The film doesn't make it clear. Judging by *The Green Berets*, we seem to be fighting a war for no particular purpose against a semi-anonymous enemy. There is no word about democracy or freedom, nationalism or self-destruction. It appears that the war has been caused entirely by the enemy and that the enemy commits atrocities because he enjoys them. There seems to be no other issue.[60]

Wayne was well aware that "liberal critics," as he called them, would trash the film, though the vehemence with which they did so surprised him. Instead of film criticism, Schickel, Ebert *et al.* became military experts bringing up phrases like "the reality of Vietnam," casting scorn on the nation's foreign policy, accused the producers of racist condensation, and claiming that the film was an insult to "every man in uniform on *both* sides of the war" (Korda). It would certainly have been interesting had anyone in the North Vietnamese Army seen the film and had a chance to be "insulted" by it, though it's highly doubtful it would have passed muster with Ho Chi Minh's censors.

The critics' hysterical reaction hit a roadblock with the nation's working-class audiences who usually flocked to Wayne's films—and didn't bother to read *The New York Times, Cinema Magazine* or *Glamour*. They made it one of Warner Brothers' biggest hits of the year, a fact even *The New York Times* was forced to acknowledge ("*Green Berets* triumphant at the box office!" screamed the headline in their Arts and Entertainment section[61]). The film allowed Wayne and Batjac to laugh their way to the bank as the critics fumed. Also, unlike his critics, Wayne *had* gone to Vietnam, meeting with American soldiers and even indigenous Montagnard tribesmen fighting the Communists.

However, at the time *The Green Berets* premiered on July 4, 1968, in Atlanta, Wayne and his collaborators could not have known that four months earlier, under the command of Captain Ernest Medina, his senior CO, Lt. John W. Calley, led the men of Charlie Company, 1st Battalion, 20th Infantry Regiment, into committing atrocities at My Lai, previously known to Army Intel as Pinkville. Some members of the American Armed Forces—beaten down, exhausted, witnesses to the killings of many of their buddies by Viet Cong, frustrated by the reluctance of villagers to talk to them, became mass murderers—in effect, acting like the Communist enemy they were there to defeat. Body counts range from 300 to 500 villagers, mostly women and children. Faulty intel targeted Pinkville as a Cong stronghold, yet even after facing little or no resistance, Calley and his men opened fire on helpless families, eventually tossing hundreds of them into pits of the kind used to dispose of bodies in places like Baba Yar and the Katyrn Forest.

The Army tried to cover it up, but some guilt-ridden soldiers, as well as leaked photographs of the pits, found their way to journalists such as Seymour Hersh. By the time the news of the massacre came out in November 1969, Wayne's film had made all the millions it could and was out of circulation. One wonders what the reaction to the film would have been if it had been released *after* My Lai. We can make a good guess.

The tragedy known as the Vietnam War ended just the way Wayne and the hawks said it would. After so-called peace talks between the U.S. and the North Vietnamese governments in Paris, our armed forces and diplomatic personnel left the country. Despite having pledged to leave South Vietnam alone, the North Vietnamese Army quickly invaded the South in 1975 and established their rule in typically brutal fashion. They executed thousands of South Vietnamese men, women and children, and consigned millions more to concentration camps; few made it out alive. It was said that during the roundup of the citizenry, the North Vietnamese Army made no distinction between friend and foe.

Also, predictably, there was no response to these atrocities from Schickel, Ebert, Adler or Korda.

Batjac and Warner Brothers had produced a film about the Vietnam War that was, in essence, a clichéd B-grade fantasy; or, if you will, an action-packed adventure movie filled with good guys and bad guys, and totally devoid of the real-life complications and controversy of a military quagmire without end. Topping off this blunder was the fact that our commanders were still living in World War II mode and never once adapted to the cruel tactics of an enemy who could blend into an already victimized and angry populace.

Hollywood followed the lead of Universal, the studio that originally turned down *The Green Berets,* and stayed far away from depictions of the Vietnam War for the next ten years. And when they *did* finally focus on the war in the late 1970s, repudiating Wayne and the hawks, and ignoring the genocidal acts of the North Vietnamese Army, the Americans in these films were seen as the villains, depicted as either hedonistic druggies or psychotic madmen (*Coming Home, Apocalypse Now*, etc.). For in the subsequent decades, with few exceptions, the viewpoint of a John Wayne would give way to the ghosts of My Lai. And films depicting the evil of Viet Cong torturers, like *Hanoi Hilton*, would be few and far between.

> I was pleased by the realization that, through our comic tale of a war that a nation had begun to forget, we could illuminate something about the military mindset and cultural arrogance of the war that was on every American's mind—the one we were waging in Vietnam.[62]

Such were the self-serving words of former blacklisted Communist, Ring Lardner, in his predictably self-serving memoir *I'd Hate Myself in the Morning*. After admitting that he was completely accepted for employment at 20th Century–Fox, the same studio that gave him his last assignment before his blacklist in the late 1940s, the screenwriter-humorist goes on to detail his involvement in adapting and writing the screenplay for one of the studio's biggest hits of the decade.

In 1968, Richard Hooker—real name: Hiester Richard Hornberger, Jr.—wrote *MASH: A Novel About Three Army Doctors*, based on his experiences as a physician surgeon in the U.S. Army Medical Corps during the Korean War, working at the 8055th Mobile Army Surgical Hospital. Those familiar only with Fox's 1970 film version might be surprised to learn that Hornberger wrote *many* MASH novels, and that the studio only filmed the first one. However, even this almost didn't see the light of day, having been turned down by numerous publishers until William Morrow & Company took a chance.

Lardner continued:

> For about two minutes Ingo [Preminger, producer brother of Otto] and I weighed the idea of transferring *MASH* from Korea to Vietnam. But the current war was too close to be funny or irreverent about it. By keeping our story at a safe distance in years and miles, we could safely look askance at an American military adventure in Asia, and let people draw their own parallels.[63]

Filmed from April 14 to June 11, 1969, and released early in the war-hot year of 1970, *MASH* was a controversial way to begin a new decade in cinema; by the end of the '70s, moviegoers were quite familiar with films that featured military villains, and "safely looking askance" would not be necessary. But in 1969, not many directors relished the thought of attacking the brass-hats, especially during the Vietnam War, even if the film *was* set in Korea. According to Lardner, "Most of a dozen directors turned it down before Ingo sold the rest of us on the almost unknown [Robert] Altman, whose accomplishments at the time consisted of a large body of TV work and a couple little-noticed feature films."[64]

Altman seemed the perfect director for Hornberger's tale, consisting of the misadventures of Army field surgeons Hawkeye Pierce (Donald Sutherland, the not-too-bright felon of *The Dirty Dozen*) and Trapper John McIntyre (new actor Elliott Gould). With characters constantly underplaying and even the smallest bit player allowed their own sequences, *MASH* laid the groundwork for Altman's future vignette-fueled ensemble comedies (unlike *Countdown*, 1967, and *That Cold Day in the Park*, 1969, the two "little-noticed feature films" Lardner neglected to mention Altman had recently directed). Ultimately, Hawkeye, Trapper John and, to a smaller degree, Hawkeye's new pal Duke Forest (Tom Skerritt) go about their lives in the MASH unit, operating on wounded soldiers; but what they *really* enjoy is sticking it to the (Military) Man. In fact, looking at the finished film, it's hard to believe the studio actually wanted to cast Walter Matthau and Jack Lemmon in the leads, a casting choice that would have made the film into *The Odd Couple Goes to Korea*.

Instead, Altman, then 44, endeavored to make an extremely angry film that would appeal to an audience half his age. Though *MASH* has often been called "irreverent," perhaps "mean-spirited" and "sadistic" might be better descriptions. Abbott & Costello and other comics had made fun of the military, but Nat Pendleton's hard-nosed sergeant (in *Buck Privates*, 1941, and *Buck Privates Come Home*, 1947) or Dick Foran (in *In the Navy*, 1941) or, for that matter, the officers in *Sgt. Bilko* or *McHale's Navy*, were never attacked with the hostility that Hawkeye and Trapper John have for "Hot Lips" Houlihan and other symbols of military authority. Later admitting that *MASH* was "a cruel film," Altman added, "Certainly that time and that situation breeds that."[65] Yet "cruel" or not, Altman would never have attempted such an attack on the military if not for the non-conformist time in history in which it was made. "An animated cartoon, with the cartoon figures played by real people," was how the critic of the *Hollywood Citizen News* described the film.[66]

Altman had help moving in that direction from his screenwriter, a blacklisted Communist who delighted in ripping the American military, in this case, the Army, a new one. Altman later claimed credit for Lardner's Oscar-winning screenplay (he was furious that he didn't win for Best Director, and that Lardner took far too much credit for what he felt were *his* innovations); other sources report that Lardner's work was hardly changed, bad taste and all. This would mean that the leftist writer was fully responsible for the infamous scene where Major Frank Burns (played by Robert Duvall) prays to Jesus while Hawkeye and Duke laugh and make fun of him; with Forest wondering aloud whether Burns was "this way" back home or whether he "cracked up" here in Korea. The scene is not merely cynical, it crosses the line from irreverence to anti–Christian bigotry, something that, unfortunately, screenwriter Lardner had no problem with. Later, when Major Houlihan and Burns make love, Hawkeye and the others hook up their tent to the camp's PA system, humiliating both of them, especially the sensitive Houlihan, now rechristened "Hot Lips" by the unit. The morning after, Hawkeye, going into infantile nine-year-old mode, baits Frank into attacking him with sexually explicit language concerning Houlihan. Frank is taken away in a straitjacket.

And though the original novel also contains elements of ignorance and misogyny, Lardner's treatment of one particular character deserves a special kind of scorn. With poise and dignity (well, as much as the film allowed), the beautiful Sally Kellerman portrays Major Houlihan, the main butt of the "pranks" perpetrated by our noble rebel heroes. About midway through the film, Hawkeye, Trapper John and the rest of the male unit get together and make bets on whether Houlihan is a real blonde. In Lardner's original script, Hawkeye, Trapper John and Duke are the *only* ones watching when the outdoor shower curtain is ripped away, showing Houlihan in the altogether. Yet even Lardner claimed he was put off when Altman changed the scene, having *everyone* in the camp present. Still, Lardner had no excuse; whether she was embarrassed by three infantile males or the whole camp wasn't the point. Altman also included the nurses as witnesses; apparently, since they have no self-respect at all, and are a party to another woman's humiliation, these women are "approved" by our sexist rogues. It's certainly obvious, then, that the nurses are also considered sexual objects who are there *only* to get laid by the male members of the MASH team. Even when Houlihan complains to their superior, Lt. Colonel Henry Blake (Roger Bowen), he's in bed with a nurse! Even in those supposedly socially enlightened days of the late 1960s, Altman and Lardner are saying, "Boys will be boys." When feminists justifiably complained, Altman lamely tried to deflect the blame:

> The precise point of that character [Major Houlihan] was that women *were* and *are* treated as sex objects. They can't blame me for the condition because I report it. We're dealing with a society in which most of the significant activity until now has been initiated by males. If you make a Western or a sports story or a story about big business or gangsters, it's automatically going to reflect the secondary positions women hold.[67]

It should be obvious to anyone who's seen the film, if not its director, that Altman wasn't *reporting* on the stigma of sexism, he was promoting it. Later, when Hawkeye and Trapper John go to a military hospital in Japan, they needlessly embarrass a middle-aged head nurse and terrorize a short African-American female officer (Trapper John brandishes an umbrella at her as if he's in a swashbuckler film). When Captain "Painless" Waldowski (John Schuck) tells them he can't "get it up," the officer automatically assumes he's a homosexual and *must* commit suicide, thus leading to a valid charge of homophobia in Altman and Lardner's "anti-establishment" masterpiece. To "cure" Waldowski, the MASH unit holds a Last Supper party while the suicidal man is in his coffin. Afterwards, Hawkeye will convince Lt. "Dish" (Jo Ann Pflug) to sleep with Waldowski, thereby "curing" him. Not only do our anarchist heroes treat this woman like a hooker, but Lardner's script, for no reason at all, has them catching a previously "stuck-up" Houlihan making love to Duke. Later, during the interminable football game—in which our amateur football heroes beat the more experienced team with a combination of drugs and other forms of cheating—Houlihan is suddenly treated as an accepted member of the team. In other words, now that this woman has "put out" for one of them, they accept her.

Defending all the mean-spiritedness, the *Chicago Tribune*'s Roger Ebert referred to "Gould and Sutherland and the members of their merry band of pranksters [who are] offended that the Army regulars don't feel deeply enough." He added:

> "Hot Lips" is concerned with protocol, but not with war. And so the surgeons, dancing on the brink of crack-ups, dedicate themselves to making her feel something. Her façade offends them; no one could be unaffected by the work at the hospital, but she is. And so, if they can crack her defenses and reduce her to their own level of dedicated cynicism, the number of suffering human beings in the camp will go up by one. And even if they fail, they can have a hell of a lot of fun trying.[68]

Yet, if anything, the personnel of the branches of the Armed Forces all have their jobs to do, and for the most part, they've performed their duties like professionals; it wasn't their job to question their orders, or let personal feelings cloud their judgment. Neither Hawkeye, Trapper John, Duke or any of their "merry band of pranksters" had a right to approve or disapprove how someone else is affected by the war, or anything else. They're supposed to be doing their jobs, not judging their co-workers. To exhibit infantile sexist behavior because an apparently strong woman or any other character isn't "one of them" smacks of the kind of chauvinism leftists like Altman and Lardner were pretending to be against. In today's workplace, the antics of the male members of the 8055th would be called sexual harassment; to Altman and Lardner, these guys are the heroes. Between Hawkeye and Trapper John's assaulting and drugging an officer (who happens to be shorter than they are) and taking pictures of him in bed with a naked woman, down to their getting rid of Frank Burns by having him taken away in a straitjacket, one is almost sorry that Murray Hamilton's Sgt. Clyde wasn't around to teach our "heroes" a lesson. Hornberger's novel was based on his experiences in the 8055th MASH unit, but according to my late father-in-law, Korean War veteran James Hayden, Sr., the *MASH* characters would *never* have gotten away with even a single infraction; and they would have been kicked out immediately had they pulled off just *one* of their so-called pranks.

"Half the budget was raw meat," George C. Scott said in reference to the surgical scenes in *MASH*. "Every time [Robert Altman] got in trouble, he got back to the operating room with the blood. Cheap tricks. To me, the worst sin of all is cheapness and shoddiness."[69]

When the actor said these words a year after the release of *MASH*, he was doing an on-set interview between camera setups for Paddy Chayefsky's Oscar-winning *The Hospital* (hence the comparison in operating scenes). By then, he had finally won the Oscar for Best Actor—even though he didn't bother showing up to claim it.

And the role he had won it for was that of the most controversial American general—in a field of far too many controversial American generals—that any actor had the privilege to play.

George S. Patton, Jr., was born on what would later become Veterans Day, November 11, in 1885 in San Gabriel, California. The son of attorney George S Patton, Sr., and his wife Ruth, the future general grew up in the lap of luxury, with George Sr. being a political and economic mover and shaker in both his native Virginia and later, Southern California; it is said that the wealthy Pattons helped found much of the San Gabriel Valley. The young Patton also grew up in a military family (except for his dad, who never "jerned up"), with his grandparents and other relations who had fought for the Confederacy regaling the wide-eyed youngster with a Moonlights and Magnolia version of their slave state. They also instilled in him a belief in the glory of war and the excitement of battle; stirring tales of Rebel heroism totally divorced from the reality of missing body parts and painful death. Dyslexic young George applied himself to his studies, forcing himself to read and write properly, and making himself memorize entire poems and chapters of the Bible. He also reveled in the Greek classics, especially tales of ancient conquest.

His family's influence got him into the Virginia Military Institute in 1903, and a Senator friend of his father's later nominated him for West Point. It was slow going at first (Patton failed at math and had to repeat a year), but it was obvious that he loved the discipline and military routines, drowning himself in study, and impressing his instructors with his ideas for military maneuvers. He enthusiastically wrote term papers and articles dealing with plans of battle and deployment of forces in combat zones. He also excelled as an athlete, becoming an expert swordsman, football player and equestrian. He went to Stockholm for the 1912 Summer Olympics.

Patton decided on cultivating an "image" by giving his underlings his "mean face," knowing full well that an officer with an image got people talking about him. It also helped bury the young man's crushing insecurity and self-doubt, things he had to the day he died, despite his success as a military tactician. Toward the end of World War I, after just a couple days on the field of battle, tank commander Patton got a non-fatal wound; his orderly Joe Angelo and a Jewish soldier from Brooklyn, Sgt. Reuben Schemitz, pulled him out of the line of fire and saved his life. Patton didn't have to physically be there urging his tanks on, but it *looked* good to his men and, more importantly, to his superiors and the press.

Due to the Army's doubt about the feasibility of mass-producing tanks (which would turn out to be an important weapon in the *next* world war), Patton switched over to the Cavalry. However, his new command could hardly relieve his feelings of frustration at leading a life of anonymity in a peacetime Army. Patton would thirst for war all his life, the better to gain fame and glory in battle; he seemed not to care that war might not be as beneficial to the millions of others who had to suffer through it. His frustration was alleviated somewhat when Army Chief of Staff General Douglas MacArthur chose him to lead his tanks against war veterans and their families in the Bonus Army on the grounds of the Capitol. Though claiming to agree with the veterans, Patton had no qualms about overpowering his civilian opponents at the points of Army bayonets. When one of the beaten veterans, Joe Angelo, wanted to meet with him afterwards, the ungrateful Patton angrily refused.

During the 1930s, Patton continued to write in Army journals, command numerous brigades and regiments, take charge of tank schools and, most important of all, raise his profile in the eyes of General Staff officers. A rich boy from way back, he rubbed shoulders with the nation's aristocracy, becoming friends with Army Chief of Staff George C. Marshall and continuing his lifelong friendship with the brilliant up-and-coming staff officer, Dwight D. Eisenhower. Sent to Europe to observe the militaries of postwar allies and report on their progress, Patton enjoyed his meetings with top military and civilian leaders, being quite at home among the rich and powerful. It is said that on a fact-finding mission to Hawaii, the future war commander expressed a distrust of the growing power of the Japanese military and predicted a possible attack on Pearl Harbor—as did the controversial General Billy Mitchell.

Out of the horror and fury that the nation felt when the Japanese actually *did* bomb Pearl Harbor on December 7, 1941, Patton was one of the few commanders who was thrilled. For him, peace had been a prison of frustration and self-doubt; *now* he could follow his destiny.

He became one of our greatest generals ever. Though it was perhaps a natural part of the package of being a brilliant war commander, he was also one of the most neurotic. Controversy followed him all through the war, and even after victory, until his death in the aftermath of a traffic accident in Mannheim, Germany, on December 21, 1945, at age 60.

Frank McCarthy was once an aide to George C. Marshall. He had a talent for public relations (as well as contacts with Hollywood power brokers), and always wanted to make a film bio on Patton's life. So did studios like Columbia, Fox and Warner Brothers. Yet they hit a buzzsaw when the project was halted by the late general's longtime wife Beatrice. (Another child of Southern California aristocracy, she had married him in 1910.) The Patton family fairly detested the media, feeling that a hostile press had always had it in for George. According to the late general's daughter Ruth Totten:

> The publicity that the press gave him for years was so disgusting and so unfair that we could not imagine a media as vulgar as the movies giving him any kind of a break at all. We had a mental block that they would picture him as a coarse, cursing, nose-picking, belching gorilla of a man, none of which things he was.[70]

The family's major concerns were how the studios would portray the two infamous slapping incidents, and to a lesser degree, his arrogance, ego, paranoia, rivalries with his fellow commanders, and his barely concealed thrill when he was in the midst of armed combat. Never volunteered by Ruth or the family, however, was the controversial love affair "Old Blood and Guts" had with his attractive niece by marriage, Red Cross nurse Jean Gordon. Apparently, it never occurred to the family that their old man *did* actually say and do most of the off-the-wall things the press accused him of. Still, they hated journalists of any kind, especially Hollywood with its pretensions of filming a bio. Well aware of the family's displeasure with such a project, the Department of Defense insisted that any picture on Patton's life *not* insult his memory; if the family didn't want a film made, then the Army would honor their wishes. Actually, since Patton was a public figure, the studios really didn't need the family's permission, but the Army insisted on the filmmakers obtaining at least their good will. Fat chance! Columbia, even under the cantankerous Harry Cohn, backed off, leaving Fox and Warners to find a way to get the Pattons to drop their opposition to the project.

Then fate took a twisted turn in late September 1953 when Beatrice died, having a fatal heart attack while falling from a horse. Jack Warner, with the tact, grace and good taste for which he was known, decided to have his people contact the Patton family after Beatrice died, yet before the day of the funeral. This was according to new Fox executive—and later *Patton* producer—Frank McCarthy, a man who had no love for the brothers Warner, who were trying to hijack what he felt was *his* project. In fact, Warners *had* exploited the timing of the tragedy to request a priority for a Patton project with the Department of Defense's Office of Public Information just days after the widow's death, and it was quickly registered on October 1, thereby beating Fox to the punch.

Disputing McCarthy's claim, W.L. Guthrie, Warners' liaison to the Department of Defense, wrote in an October 6 memo to studio honcho Steve Trilling that he held off contacting the family since he "figured it would be very bad to call them before, I might say, the body was cold."[71]

Whenever Warners contacted the Patton children, they angrily refused to meet with them. The studio sent Guthrie to meet with family friend General Harry Semmes, to whom Beatrice had given the Patton diaries so he could write a Patton bio. The Patton children maintained their obstinate no-filming stance for another decade and a half, whether the studios were run by crude moguls like Warner and Cohn, or sincere former colleagues like Frank McCarthy. However, McCarthy found a powerful backer in Darryl F. Zanuck, and in the 1950s the former officer–PR maven became a Fox producer. The maker of serious World War II films such as *Twelve O'Clock High*, *Decision Before Dawn*, *The Desert Fox*, *The Young Lions* and *The Longest Day*, Zanuck immediately green-lighted the project. Even after Zanuck had a power struggle over the running of the studio, his son Richard also expressed enthusiasm for the Patton project.

By the mid–1960s, McCarthy had increased his contacts with the Department of Defense's Office of Public Information, and when the brass-hats mysteriously granted a new priority to Fox, the charge was quickly made by the Pattons' attorneys that favoritism was given to the former aide to George Marshall to make the Patton film over the family's furious objections. Now, the new dictates from the Department of Defense were: a film on Patton that was respectful to the military, but still honest enough to show the great man's flaws—in other words, a work that would *never* have been made in the pro-military 1950s. Despite the now-typical bellicose threats from Patton's family, and with the brass-hats desperately needing a film that lionized war heroes during the Vietnam War era, McCarthy's dream became a reality in 1969.

Starring George C. Scott, with a screenplay by the up-and-coming Francis Ford Coppola and Edmund North and direction by *Planet of the Apes* helmsman Franklin J. Schaffner, *Patton* (originally subtitled *Portrait of a Rebel*) basically ignored the general's life pre–World War II and focused solely on his successful command on the battlefield and his sometimes controversial statements off it. This approach also basically ignored any indication that the great general even *had* a family.

The casting of the charismatic but tempestuous Scott complimented the role of the volatile Patton. Though Scott was immensely talented, off-screen he was a violent drunk and woman-beater, as his belting around of former paramour Ava Gardner on the set of *The Bible* proved. Much was made of the fact that Scott was an ex–Marine, despite the fact that he had been a leatherneck during peacetime and he would develop a drinking problem, not as a result of any experiences on the battlefield, but while he on burial detail.

Patton also had his dysfunctional side. A skilled tactician with tanks, cavalry and infantry, he plowed his way across Nazi-occupied Europe where more timid commanders restrained themselves. Patton couldn't help making controversial, even inflammatory statements that angered his superiors (like Eisenhower, who protected him for years) and infuriated the American people (that is, when they weren't praising him for his many victories). Eisenhower, George C. Marshall, General Bedell Smith and many others had already made comments on his penchant for letting his mouth go off without using his brain beforehand. The film exaggerates the rivalry between Patton and General Sir Bernard Law Montgomery, though Old Blood and Guts certainly had no problem trumping him by taking Messina while the pompous British commander moved his forces north a little *too* cautiously. (This was symbolic of the neurotic caution exhibited by Churchill and other British commanders all through the war.) Schaffner and his screenwriters also turned the two infamous slapping incidents into one. On August 3, Patton slapped and verbally abused Private Charles H. Kuhl at an evacuation hospital in Nicosia; a week later, on August 10, he slapped Private Paul G. Bennett. Both soldiers were suffering from battle fatigue, a fact which meant nothing to an angry Patton, who ridiculously accused them of cowardice. He also used his thick gloves to do the slapping and even pointed his pearl-handled pistol at their heads, conduct more appropriate to an SS officer than a U.S. Army commander.

In the film, Scott's Patton shoots dead a stubborn mule blocking his tanks from crossing a bridge on the way to taking Messina. In *Patton: The Man Behind the Legend, 1885–1945*, a far too gentle pro–Patton biography, Martin Blumenson wrote that Patton "had the animal killed," not that he did it himself with one of his pearl-handled pistols. This is something you see in the film, though the book *does* mention him "breaking his walking stick over the mule driver."[72]

Patton was paranoid to a fault, and his diary is full of unsubstantiated charges and unproven accusations against his officer-class rivals Omar Bradley, Bedell Smith and Mark Clark. He even turned against his close friend Ike, accusing the Supreme Commander of giving in too much to the British and harboring ambitions to be president (both true, as it turned out). Yet he was also ignorant on the *many* times Eisenhower had saved his (Patton's) butt. Though he was not assigned to be one of the D-Day commanders on the beaches, Patton believed that Eisenhower kept him out of the loop due to the slapping incidents, even though the decision not to use Patton was made months before. As it turned out, Patton had a major role as a decoy in Operation Fortitude, a clever plot to make the German High Command think that he was in Dover when he was really training the Third Army to attack Nazi forces as they fled Normandy.

Ordered not to cross the Rhine, Patton and the Third Army did exactly that, again trumping his British rival, whom Ike allowed to cross first. However, something that *wasn't* in the film was the fact that both Patton and Winston Churchill unzipped their flies and showed contempt for their enemy's country by urinating in the Rhine. Fully realizing that the British were advancing their own foreign policy interests at the expense of American lives—much as they had done in World War I—the controversial general believed that the Empire had no trouble twisting Ike around their imperialist fingers. "The British have won over Abilene," he would say—Abilene, Kansas, being Eisenhower's place of birth.[73] Head of the Imperial British General Staff, General Sir Alan Brooke returned the contempt with a backhanded compliment:

> I did not form any high opinion of him, nor had I any reason to alter this view at a later date. A dashing, courageous, wild and unbalanced leader, good for operations requiring thrust and push, but at a loss in operations requiring skill and judgment.[74]

But if the controversial general had contempt for the British ("All of us think that if there were ever any pretty women in England, they must have died"), Patton roundly detested our Soviet "allies." Again, like his hatred for the British, Patton was certainly justified in this, as he believed his old friend had given Stalin far too much. Another one of Ike's faults came to a tragic conclusion when he decided to "let the Russians have Berlin." The result: a non-stop orgy of rape and mass murder committed by Red Army troops onto the Berlin populace. Again, *Patton* never shows this; in the film, his hatred of the Soviets seems to be just the old cliché-ridden Red-baiting, not anything based on actual Russian atrocities or proof of their obvious two-faced behavior.

Scott as the general blows away everyone who has the misfortune of sharing screen time with him, like Karl Malden as his superior, General Omar Bradley; in fact, Scott easily blows away Malden like Patton himself overshadowed the more bureaucratic and colorless Bradley (who, along with his young wife, also insisted on a positive portrayal in the film[75]). We also see a grudging respect and admiration for Patton from the German High Command which was based on fact, with German officers openly admitting that out of all the American commanders they were reluctant to face on the battlefield, they feared Patton the most. However, the film shows *Wehrmacht* officers giving Patton this respect, not the madmen of the SS. We might also be a little shocked that the real Patton did *not* have Scott's distinctive face or tough, gravelly voice. In fact, the real Patton had a high-pitched, screechy voice, which must have made his insistence on cursing a blue streak doubly laughable. The real-life general also looked like overweight Warner Brothers character actor Guy Kibbee, though perhaps a foot taller. Yet Scott's portrayal was so iconic that to this day, many envision Patton as looking and sounding like *him*.

However, Patton's hatred for the Russians (he would curse them by using racial epithets like "Mongols") paled in comparison to his hatred of another group. *Patton* ends after victory over the Nazis, with the implication that the hero general would be sidelined because of his hatred for the Soviets. The war was now over, and with no armed conflict to fight in, it is implied that Patton would be a forgotten man; even Walter Bedell Smith (played by Edward Binns) calls him

"GOD, HELP ME I DO LOVE IT SO...": George C. Scott won the Best Actor Oscar for *Patton* (1970).

"mad" for calling for a war with the Russians. Yet Patton, the man, could not sit quietly and rest on his laurels—or keep his big mouth shut.

In reality, there might have been a medical reason for Patton's mood swings and schizoid behavior. For decades, from his youngest days as a West Point cadet to the war years, Patton the sportsman had played football, fenced, sailed boats and rode horses, hundreds of them through the years. In the days before safety helmets, Patton was not only thrown from horses literally dozens of times, but also kicked in the head quite often. There had always been the theory, never proven since he wouldn't submit to a mental evaluation by trained doctors, that the general had bleeding in the brain, leading to moods of enthusiasm one moment and bursting into tears the next. This might also explain his penchant for making totally absurd statements before actually thinking about them.

However, Frank McCarthy's *Patton* not only keeps the focus on the war and ignoring his colorful pre-war past, but it removes the general's private life as well. In real life, his longtime wife Beatrice constantly boosted the ego of her always insecure husband; she appears nowhere in the film. Nor do we see his affair with his niece Jean Gordon. Though both Beatrice and Jean appear in *The Last Days of Patton*, played by Eve Marie Saint and Kathryn Leigh Scott, respectively, McCarthy apparently didn't want anything that would distract from Patton's greatness in war ... like, for instance, depictions of his cheating on his loving wife. Despite the fact that many historians scoff at an affair with Gordon, the young woman killed herself on January 8, 1946, two and a half weeks after Patton died of an embolism at a Heidelberg military hospital, and only a few days after Beatrice Patton visited her in New York and told her off. Gordon also killed herself surrounded by pictures of the general, an odd way to die if indeed there wasn't an affair. It was also rumored that Jean's suicide note said, "I will be with Uncle Georgie in Heaven before Beatrice arrives." In late September 1953, Beatrice "arrived" after she died of an aneurysm after falling from a horse; ironically, her husband's frequent form of recreation. Of course, another reason Jean killed herself could have been that she was heartbroken that the married officer she was having an affair with decided to go back to his wife; something that happened very close to the time of Patton's death.

Also shut out of McCarthy's *Patton* was the general's controversial postwar appointment as military governor of Bavaria. Claiming to want experienced personnel running things in a defeated Germany, Patton allowed former Nazis, even SS officers and political figures, to have control of Bavaria. A still vicious enemy, surviving SS and *Wehrmacht* soldiers were more than happy to remain in power under a friendly American commander. He also allowed imprisoned Nazi soldiers—again, including the SS—to perform drills and maneuvers as if they would once again go on a blitzkrieg. In the TV-movie sequel, the badly paced but mostly accurate *The Last Days of Patton*, based on biographer Ladislas Farago's book, director Delbert Mann and his writers explore this part of Patton's postwar duties. Yet even with a tie-in to the previous Oscar-winning film (Scott again played Patton), the sequel never mentions another reason the general treated the conquered Nazis with respect: George Patton was a vicious anti–Semite.

Ike was horrified when told of piles of bodies discovered by General Walton H. Walker's XX Corps when they burst into Buchenwald. "[It's] beyond the American mind to comprehend,"[76] exclaimed the future president. (The liberated concentration camp was also visited by Patton aide General "Hap" Gay and by Colonel Frank McCarthy.) Horrified upon viewing the work of the Third Reich, Patton cried, "This is yet another evidence as to the unbelievable brutality of the Germans."[77] Patton's visiting the concentration camps would have been a good scene in both *Patton* and *Last Days*. Yet even with McCarthy himself having visited the camps and witnessing Man's Inhumanity to Man, this episode doesn't appear in the Oscar-winning film or its TV-movie sequel. However, documentary footage of Eisenhower and Patton visiting Buchenwald actually appears in the low-budget *Operation Eichmann* (1962).

Despite Patton's initial disgust, the general quickly reverted to irrational form. In Farago's book, the author lays it on the line:

> Nowhere in this record so impressively recorded by Patton and Gay were the camps described by their true names as *Vernichtungslager*, or extermination camps, but rather as camps for political prisoners or slave labor camps.
> Yet never was a single explicit reference made to the Jewish victims of the holocaust—not until much later, when General Patton equated them with the people General Gay had described as animals.[78]

At another point, Farago writes:

> [Patton] was filled with bitter, violent and completely irrational anti–Jewish sentiments—provoked in equal measure by the aesthetic indignation at the sight of that "stinking bunch" of Jews in the DP camps and his new political and social views. He now hated Jews—all Jews—personified by those his armies had saved from certain death.[79]

Long forgotten was the fact that one of the two soldiers who pulled him out of the line of fire after he was wounded in World War I was Jewish. In fact, in later interviews, he would only mention the *Christian* soldier who saved him (not remembering that he snubbed Joe Angelo after the Bonus Army riots). Sounding very much like Hitler or Goebbels, he had written, "Should the German people rise from the state of utter degradation to which they have now been reduced, there will be the greatest pogrom of the Jews in the history of the world." Visiting a German military hospital now filled with dying Jews from the camps, Patton ranted how filthy the Jews had made the place until Ike shouted for him to shut up. Another visitor was a woman from the United Nations Relief and Rehabilitation Administration—"the most talkative Jewish lady," sneered Patton. At one point, he turned to Eisenhower and said that he knew of a deserted German village that he "was going to turn into a concentration camp for these goddamn Jews!"[80]

Though the press had been, sometimes justifiably, hung out to dry for luring the erratic general into making controversial statements, they had nothing to do with private ramblings in his diary and letters to other anti–Semitic American officers, nor his policy of favoring Nazi murderers over their Jewish victims. To him, Jews were "a subhuman species without any of the cultural or social refinements of our time."[81] Oddly, *The Last Days* has Patton making an anti–Semitic remark, but only when he also attacks the Soviets, thus minimizing the impact of the epithet; this, despite the fact that Ladislas Farago revealed dozens of examples of Patton's anti–Semitic behavior in his book. Seeing that his old friend refused to take the Denazification program seriously, Eisenhower fired him as military governor of Bavaria and transferred him to head the 15th Army, "the paper army" responsible for recording the history of the war. It was soon obvious that, had he the chance to finish this "history," as he perceived it anyway, Patton would have ignored the mass murder of Jews and other victims of the Holocaust and probably praised their murderers.

There was a crash of Army vehicles in Mannheim and Patton was seriously injured. He died not in the "glory" of battle or while fighting for his country, but coughing piteously in a lonely hospital bed as an embolism in his right lung killed him.

His genius as a commander and gung ho attitude sped up the conclusion of the war. Yet once victory was achieved, his usefulness was over. His frustration with postwar peace didn't create his anti–Semitism, but it did bring it out into the open. He saw the perfidy of the Soviets years before the beginning of the Cold War, with "hawks" like Generals Curtis LeMay, Edwin Walker and others more than willing to continue where Old Blood and Guts left off and start a war with the Soviets.

But democracies don't have generals in charge of the political scene; they have duly elected civilian leadership. The experience of an anti–Semitic Patton in Bavaria was a good example of what happens when a war-hungry and bigoted military officer is put in charge. Just as Patton showered himself with glory in war, Frank McCarthy's *Patton* also saw just one side of the man, the one that won wars; not the one who, if we aren't constantly vigilant, could also start them.

VI

CEASEFIRE
A Quick Look at the 1970s and Beyond

>Old soldiers never die. They just fade away....
>—General Douglas MacArthur

>[Hollywood was] really not very good at depicting reality.
>—Colonel Donald Gilliland, Air Force Public Affairs Office

In the decade after General MacArthur's death in 1964, the image of the American military, whether soldier, sailor or Marine, emphatically did *not* fade away—nor was he remembered in the respectful way MacArthur would have preferred; certainly not as Hollywood ended up portraying him.

If anything about the image of the military man faded away, it was his being looked upon as a valiant and heroic figure, a professional warrior upholding American values on foreign and domestic soil. However, the specter of Vietnam hovered over the war film years before Hollywood actually did focus on the conflict in the late 1970s. The anti–Vietnam coda entered practically every film genre of the late 1960s all the way up to the release of *The Boys of Company C, The Deer Hunter* and *Apocalypse Now* (excepting, that is, the pro–Vietnam *The Green Berets*). According to the smart set in the print media (its film critics and writers), every conceivable film classic of the day, no matter what genre, was an anti–Vietnam War film. According to that era's self-proclaimed observers of the scene, the film about a blood'n'guts warrior, *Patton*, was an anti–Vietnam film. So was the World War II–set (and very bizarre) film version of Joseph Heller's *Catch-22*—a bestselling novel, *not* a hit film or classic by any means. So was the classic Western of *Americano* outlaws in Revolutionary Mexico, *The Wild Bunch*. So was the overrated low-budget black-and-white gorefest *Night of the Living Dead*. So was the British-made World War I–set *Oh, What a Lovely War!* Even the ridiculous fantasy–Western *Little Big Man* was about Vietnam. Every other film of the time seemed to be a pointed euphemism on Vietnam—except that Hollywood was not making any films that focused solely on Vietnam.

Needless to say, with the brutal realities of Vietnam broadcast on the news every night, the darkening image of the American military carried over into practically *any* service film made at the time that was *not* set in Vietnam. The Navy characters in the film version of Darryl Ponicsan's classic novel *The Last Detail* were emphatically *not* the Navy men under Lewis Stone in *Shipmates Forever*. Navy MPs "Badass" Buddusky (Jack Nicholson) and his buddy Mulhall (Otis Young) were jaded, cynical, foul-mouthed examples of naval flotsam who both love the service yet hate their superiors. They escort a young prisoner named Meadows (Randy Quaid) to the naval stockade, where he'll serve eight years for attempting to steal a measly $40 from a charity sponsored by the wife of an admiral. The film practically blew the meter on the number of curse words spouted in an American film up to that time. Columbia producer Gerald Ayres tried—multiple times—to get the Navy's cooperation, but to no avail. Don Baruch advised Ayres that he'd get nowhere with the admirals. Even the Navy's motion picture division bluntly told him not to bother flying to Washington to discuss the film. The director of the Navy's Production Services Division, Jack Garrow, wrote to Ayres on October 19, 1972, and explained that Bob Manning of the Navy Office of Information "was very correct in informing you that it is very unlikely we could arrive at a mutually agreeable script without emasculating the premise of your story."[1]

Anyone who lived in the real world would have to be blind and deaf not to realize that Navy men (and Army and Marines and USAF, etc.) cursed like ... well, sailors! And that they were resentful of the petty bureaucrats who were their superiors (even when they were *not* being petty bureaucrats). "Badass" Buddusky and his ilk were not an exception, but the rule. Yet he and Mulhall talk to each other like human beings who also come to the sad realization that they're lifers, Navy men who have no other future. Despite their contempt for the brass-hats, they truly love the Navy in their own dirty, foul-mouthed way. They are also professionals. They sympathize with the naïve Meadows and give him a good time in New York, including liberal amounts of drinking, getting into fights (Buddusky's challenging some Marines in a Port Authority rest room is a highlight), and his losing virginity at some midtown whorehouse. But these two Navy rebels *still* grudgingly bring Meadows to the Portsmouth Naval Base for incarceration (where they go up against Michael Moriarty's by-the-book Marine officer). In the novel, the two disgusted MPs go AWOL. But screenwriter Robert Towne (who had to deal with erratic helmsman Hal Ashby) changed Ponicsan's ending and had the two men stay in the Navy. Explaining why he changed the ending, Towne made the euphemistic comparison to the recent conflict that probably thrilled the Every-Film-Was-About-Vietnam crowd: "I wanted to imply that we're all lifers in the Navy, and everybody hides behind doing a job, whether it's massacring at My Lai or taking a kid to jail."[2]

Despite this interesting analogy, the Navy didn't do any "massacring" at My Lai.

Still, in the wake of the now constantly referenced "quagmire" of Vietnam, Hollywood gradually started to back off making war films, at least those that depicted "the Good War," World War II. So as the film industry gave us sinister government agents from our intelligence community committing abominable acts on a helpless citizenry and as stateside military officers became involved in shadowy cover-ups that would have shocked *real* military officers who probably didn't realize that they had the power to do all the things Hollywood said they could, the war film itself became a casualty. This would include the military biography.

Producer and World War II veteran Frank McCarthy gave us a true classic with *Patton*—even though it wasn't what you'd call painstakingly accurate. After struggling for many years to get the project off the boards, he richly deserved his Oscar for Best Picture. (Acknowledging George C. Scott's not showing up to get his Oscar for Best Actor, the producer announced to the audience that he "cheerfully" accepted his own award.) Perhaps McCarthy thought that Oscar lightning would strike twice, so he decided to make another film bio on a hero Army general. Unfortunately, things had changed radically by 1977.

MacArthur was a project McCarthy had started in 1970. However, since the release of the Oscar-winning *Patton*, the American public had now suffered the aftermath of Vietnam, turning their allegiance more to the new no-holds-barred maverick cop films than war films set in a bygone era. Turned down by Fox, McCarthy went to Universal where they agreed to back the film—a big mistake. Not only were Universal's 1970s attempts at film bios or reenactments of 1930s history unintentionally laughable (*Gable and Lombard, The Hindenburg, W.C. Fields and Me*, etc.), but they turned thumbs-down on McCarthy's original plan to shoot on location in Japan and the Philippines. With very few exceptions, it looked like MacArthur would fight World War II and Korea on the Universal backlot.

The film attempts to depict MacArthur's larger-than-life ego and vanity (the film's Harry Truman refers to him as "His Majesty" or "He's probably coming down off the cross..."), so the casting of the always limited Gregory Peck was another mistake. Actors who turned down the chance to play the title role: John Wayne (a better choice), Marlon Brando (horrible choice, and he would have tripled the budget with his infantile, scene-stealing antics) and George C. Scott (his image was now *too* tied in with his portrayal of Patton). The producer's ultimate choice of Peck worked against the film. MacArthur was realistically depicted as a vain and egocentric officer, but Peck's portrayal still seems like an actor in phony makeup and prop corncob pipe playing the part at a costume party. The poor scripting (overseen by McCarthy) didn't help. In fact, one is baffled as to why FDR would give Peck's MacArthur command in the Pacific instead of his Navy rivals, Admirals Nimitz, Halsey and King. After MacArthur's disobedience in Korea, Truman was less tolerant of his "star general," telling writer Merle Miller years later that MacArthur "was always playacting," and that there were times that he felt that he "wasn't right in the head."[3] Yet Peck's performance looks and sounds exactly like what the former president called it, playacting; not a

"I SHALL *NOT* RETURN" (A PROFIT AT THE BOX OFFICE): Gregory Peck as the title role in *MacArthur* (1977), a failure for *Patton* producer Frank McCarthy. Universal's budget cuts, a poor script and Peck's awful performance, essentially killed off any more attempts to film the lives of military heroes.

real performance at all. Peck's "old soldiers never die..." speech seems more like "old actors can't find better roles." MacArthur biographer Robert Sherrod said, "MacArthur was a better actor than Peck."[4]

Taking a cue from the lackluster box office of *MacArthur*, Hollywood basically stayed away from World War II film bios. Frank McCarthy died not long after *MacArthur*'s release. With his death, so too would the World War II film released in the post–Vietnam era. Except for one film, that is. A pretty big one that not only cost millions and was the last of the all-star war film blockbusters, but detailed one of the worst military blunders ever committed by an Allied army during World War II.

It was always the aim of Supreme Commander General Dwight D. Eisenhower that the American and British armies pierce the border of Germany by multiple thrusts consisting of infantry battalions, massive tank deployment and plenty of air support. To Ike, it didn't matter *who* got to Berlin first, just as long as it spelled endgame for the Third Reich. To British Field Marshal General Sir Bernard Montgomery, such a logical plan was utter nonsense; and, to him, typical of the Supreme Commander's faulty planning. It was soon obvious that Montgomery and the British High Command wanted to get to Berlin first. And what was even more important to Montgomery was that *he* be the commander to burst into Berlin and conquer it ahead of his fellow commanders, American *or* British. Thus, with the *Wehrmacht* fleeing back to Germany after being routed on D-Day, Montgomery, the head of the British General Staff, the always obstinate General Sir Alan Brooke, and Lieutenant General Frederick Browning initiated a new plan called Operation Market Garden. According to the Brits, a combination of British and American forces (mostly British, that is) were to take the village of Arnhem in the Netherlands and cross the Rhine and Meuse Rivers. Then, through the liberal use of gliders, paratroopers and ground forces, the British would storm downtown Hitlerland.

General Eisenhower's reply to the arrogant Montgomery was pure non-nonsense "Ike," and necessary to knock the strutting little field marshal down a few pegs:

> What you're proposing is this—if I give you all the supplies you want, you go straight to Berlin—right straight (500 miles) to Berlin? Monty, you're nuts. You can't do it. What the hell? ... If you try a long column like that in a single thrust you'd have to throw off division after division to protect your flanks from attack.

All true; with the Supreme Commander well aware of an already declining flow of supplies from both the American *and* British lines. Also, Ike was reluctant to hand over such an important operation to the self-glorifying little showboat Montgomery. Still, desiring to grab the industrial heartland of the Ruhr—and to keep peace with his sometimes pompous allies—Eisenhower reluctantly approved Market Garden. Most American officers thought the operation was insanity—including, not surprisingly, the usually Montgomery-hating Patton.

And as it turned out, they were right.

Launched on September 17, 1944, after only a few weeks of preparation—instead of several months, like the invasion of Normandy—the mission was doomed to failure. The First Allied Airborne Army was commanded by U.S. Army General Lewis H. Brereton; on the ground, XXX Corps was to advance on Arnhem and link up with the paratroopers. The paratroops were dropped five to eight miles from Nijmegan Bridge where they supposed to land and had to march to their goal. Browning and Brereton did not get along. Supplies weren't arriving. Radios went dead, disrupting communication between all ground forces. And the British ignored vital intelligence from the Dutch Underground. The Americans—as well as a British Army intelligence officer, Major Brian Urquhart—warned the British High Command the danger of ignoring the Dutch, but Montgomery and Browning wouldn't listen. As it turned out, far from being an empty village, Arnhem was heavily occupied by the tanks and infantry of the 9th SS Panzer Division *Hohenstaufen* and the 10th SS Panzer Division *Frundsberg*.

So much for Montgomery's fantasy that the entire German Army was on the run. British soldiers expecting little resistance were stunned to face ruthless SS battalions. Many of the invaders, as well as trapped villagers, were slaughtered. There were over 8000 casualties from the British 1st Airborne Division alone. Quickly scapegoated by Montgomery, Browning and the British High Command was Major-General Stanislaw Sosabowski of the Polish Independent Parachute Brigade and his Free Polish fighters. Browning told Major Urquhart, "I think we might be going a bridge too far." Despite the high Allied casualty rate, and with typical British spin (remember Dunkirk?), Montgomery, Churchill, Brook and the British press lauded Market Garden a great success, totally ignoring the fact that Montgomery's ego trip resulted in the needless loss of men and supplies which *extended* the war by several months, not shortened it

When Richard Attenborough shot *A Bridge Too Far* for six months in mid–1976, it was yet another filmization of a Cornelius Ryan bestseller—Ryan's most famous being *The Longest Day*. It made box office sense in 1962 for Fox to make a movie of *The Longest Day* and lionize the heroes of World War II 17 years after its end; doing it in 1976, while the remains of dead American troops were still trickling out of Vietnam might not have been appropriate. Perhaps taking note of this, Attenborough and screenwriter William Goldman went in a different direction. Fox's *The Longest Day* (which downplayed the horrors of the landings depicted in the Ryan book and other scholars' books on the operation) was about an Allied triumph. *A Bridge Too Far*, despite some scenes with triumphant music on the soundtrack accompanied by the vicarious blowing-away of Germans, focused on a military blunder.

A Bridge Too Far was a good war film, but despite its all-star Longest Day–like cast (with Hollywood leading men Ryan O'Neal and Robert Redford *not* convincing as seasoned officers), the film has dated badly, with readers of the book being the only ones who really understood what was going on. To the general filmgoing audience, Attenborough's epic glorified our side, just like a traditional war movie, but combined it with a post–Vietnam cynicism concerning a military blunder, with Dirk Bogarde's General Browning looking for ways to cover up the fiasco with the British public—which was exactly what happened.

When *The Boys of Company C* was released on February 2, 1978, the film, *far* better than the more famous overblown productions about Vietnam that followed it, became a touchpoint for a whole subgenre of "our boys stuck in the quagmire of Southeast Asia" films. In fact, in its own defiantly non-conventional way, it could also be seen as an anti–anti–Vietnam War film.

And though *Boys of Company C* basically started the soon stereotypical portrayal of American military men as racist, dysfunctional, pot-smoking, drug-dealing neurotics, unlike the films that came after it, its boys were also unapologetically human. It would be awfully hard to like the servicemen later depicted by Coppola,

Cimino, Kubrick and Jane Fonda. Yet audience members had no such problem liking the young Marines of Company C who collectively face an uncaring military bureaucracy, corrupt allies and a psychopathic enemy. The film's tone is set immediately when a gruff little D.I., Sgt. Aquilla, screams at his young charges, "Grab your nuts! Grab your nuts!" In other words, according to Aquilla, a Marine's job is to make sure they still have 'em when they come back. Forgotten today, this post–Vietnam movie image of the foul-talking D.I. would help lay the groundwork for R. Lee Ermey's driven top-kick in *Full Metal Jacket*. (In *Boys in Company C*, Ermey portrays the world-weary and cynical Sgt. Loyce.)

Directed and co-written by veteran helmsman Sidney Furie, *Boys of Company C* is also the first American war film to top-bill an African-American protagonist in uniform since the groundbreaking James Edwards in *Home of the Brave*, as well as the far less controversial Sidney Poitier in *All the Young Men* (billing he had to share with Alan Ladd). Though Sgt. Tyrone Washington (an excellent Stan Shaw) is a drug dealer back in the States, he is respected by Loyce as a man who can instill his own brand of street toughness into his squad of young newbies. Through him, their innate courage and teamwork comes out. Still, there is drug-dealing, racism and other dysfunction. Of course, their superior officers are no better, cold-bloodedly sending these boys out to die to inflate enemy body counts. Needless to say, the Department of Defense did *not* give the film company assistance with the production. Besides drug-dealing (and taking), racism and manufactured victories, there is a derogatory image of our South Vietnamese Army "allies." Unlike the dishonest portrayal of South Vietnamese Army officers in *The Green Berets* as trustworthy allies who believe in teamwork, *The Boys of Company C* shows us a South Vietnamese officer class that is more than willing to deal drugs with peddlers like Sgt. Washington so they can sell them to young Americans back in the States. Towards the end, the disgusted Tyrone finally takes a stand and tells the South Vietnamese Army general, "There are a lot of niggers named Tyrone in the military. You've got the wrong man!" Similarly, ordered to lose football games to the South Vietnamese Army and *not* be sent into combat, Company C rebels and beats the South Vietnamese players soundly.

Like *MASH*, the film climaxes with a football game; only this one is interrupted by enemy attack. After his Vietnamese sweetheart is killed by the Viet Cong, the peace-loving hippie character grabs a Browning, shouts "I'll kill you!" and mows down several of the enemy before getting blown away. In another anti-cliché moment, the writer character who had been taking notes on his experiences (and you'd expect to be the surviving narrator) sacrifices his life by throwing his body on a live grenade.

Had *The Boys of Company C* been a success, anti-war activists like Jane Fonda would surely have howled at the portrayal of the Viet Cong murdering the non-combatant Vietnamese girlfriend. But they showed their displeasure with the war in other ways.

While the war was still going on, Fonda and several of her friends made the nasty *FTA* (for *Free the Army*; or perhaps another F word substituting for Free). A series of badly filmed, unfunny sketches which had originally been a tour of coffee-houses and other such venues near military bases, the film was barely released to theaters.

One of Fonda's collaborators was a feminist writer and activist, Nancy Dowd. Both were members of Fonda's newly formed film company IPC Films, or Indochina Peace Campaign—an interesting name for a company that was going to attack only the *American* side in the conflict. Dowd and Fonda decided to make a film showing wounded veterans from the point of view of their wives and girlfriends. Dowd wrote a screen story called *Buffalo Grass* focusing on hospitalized vets, but Fonda and her more militant collaborators wanted a film directly indicting the American government's Vietnam policy, quite a departure from a realistic story about recuperating veterans who gave so much of themselves in combat. Indeed, with such sensitive subject matter, one wonders why Fonda, of all people, was considered an unbiased authority on a film dealing with the Vietnam War when the actress had her own skeletons to bury on the subject—one memorable one dealing with a North Vietnamese Army anti-aircraft gun.

Unlike USO performers who entertained our boys near the battlefield, Fonda was (as is, to this day) the only famous Hollywood personality giving aid and comfort to an enemy of America during wartime. In July 1972, the actress visited North Vietnam, obviously at the behest of the Communist government, almost certainly with Soviet approval. Her North Vietnamese Army hosts showed her bombed-out hospitals and schools—buildings that had originally had North Vietnam flags flying from them so they would be good targets. The tour was incredibly selective, with her hosts barring the actress from actually meeting Vietnamese civilians under VC rule. (Similarly, playwright Lillian Hellman, in her trips to the USSR, was never allowed to actually see terror-stricken Russian citizens in miserable poverty.) With VC cameras rolling, Fonda was allowed to interview American POWs who spoke well of the North Vietnamese Army, with the actress more than willing to announce that they were treated well. In reality, however, these same POWs, once they were freed, put the lie to their supposedly good treatment, charging that their talks with Fonda were scripted, and that they had to praise their captors under threat of even more torture. Propaganda films showed her posing atop a North Vietnamese Army anti-aircraft gun with smiling Viet Cong applauding in the background. Her broadcasts over Radio Hanoi, ripping American soldiers as murderers and war criminals, were aired between July 14 and 22.

According to Colonel George Day, ranking officer at the North Vietnamese Army's infamous "Hanoi Hilton,"

> It was worse than being manipulated and used. She got into it with all her heart.... She caused the deaths of unknown numbers of Americans by buoying up the enemy's spirits and keeping them in the fight. That was not what you'd expect from Henry Fonda's daughter.[5]

Firmly believing herself to be anti-war—except, apparently, where the North Vietnamese Army was concerned—Fonda had no problem twisting the passions of the day to fit her political agenda. Dowd's original story treatment, soon to be called *Coming Home*, seemed the perfect vehicle for Fonda to bury, once and for all, her controversial visit to North Vietnam. She portrays Sally Hyde, wife of a gung-ho Marine officer, and becomes the lover of a handicapped anti-war veteran and a friend to the vets at the hospital where she was volunteering. In other words, the same woman who had so recently called these same men murderers was now playing their compassionate friend and helper (and in leading man Luke Martin's case, a lover as well).

In Dowd's original story, Sally and her husband live in a trailer park. After "coming home" from the war, he's become a tormented alcoholic; the wife also has an affair with another, more grounded and compassionate veteran. However, Fonda and her collaborators (including formerly blacklisted Party member, Waldo Salt) decided to make the wife one of the upper middle-class—more of an indictment of affluent Americans that way. Also, the tormented husband was now promoted to officer status. Ultimately, the completed film was, for the most part, a critical and box office hit to a nation still angry at our involvement in Vietnam.

But it failed miserably in one of its main goals: to make the American public forever forget that she had given aid and comfort to our North Vietnamese enemy. To many, she will always be Hanoi Jane.

Needless to say, the USMC did *not* provide assistance to the production, despite the fact that many anti-war veterans ended up liking the film. However, even more veterans, those who were proud of their service, disliked the portrayal of themselves as suicidal drug addicts and gun-wielding, wild-eyed maniacs. There is a sympathetic portrayal of the wounded enlisted men in the hospitals, as symbolized by the wheelchair-bound Luke (Jon Voight). However, Bruce Dern (a former B actor at AIP best known in the 1960s for playing psychos) has his Marine officer return from Nam a total nutjob. Again, as in many a left-wing film, the officer class is depicted as being one step away from a straitjacket, with Dern's Captain Hyde doing justice to his namesake: waving loaded rifles, screaming and cursing at the top of his lungs and doing everything but frothing at the mouth. If you will, Hyde can probably be seen as the flip side of Luke's more compassionate Jekyll.

This portrayal of veterans was not going to be accepted by certain segments of

FLAWED HERO: Bruce Dern as the gung-ho, pro-war officer who returns from Vietnam a psychopath in *Coming Home* (1978). The film attacked the government's policies on Vietnam.

the public without complaint. Producer Jerome Hellman got an earful (or rather an eyeful, since it was in a letter) from the Veterans Administration when he sought their help. John Chase, the VA's Chief Medical Director, found that the story

> incorrectly and unfairly portrays veterans as weak and purposeless, with no admirable qualities, embittered against their country, addicted to alcohol and marijuana, and as unbelievably foul-mouthed and devoid of conventional morality in sexual matters.
> There is hardly a scene that does not depict and almost glorify drinking and/or smoking marijuana, drunkenness, drunken driving and other practices that are illegal or are regarded by many veterans and non-veterans as immoral.[6]

Calling the script something that will "exploit men who were severely injured while doing their duty under arms for our country," a VA Information Service Rep, Paul W. Mills, asserted that one paraplegic veteran argued that "(n)ot all paras are drunks, dopers, gamblers."[7]

Ignored by her lunatic husband, Sally has a passionate affair with Luke, which leads to yet *another* scene of Fonda faking an orgasm onscreen (see *Barbarella* and *Klute*). Though Luke seems to be able to please Sally, the scene is an absolute lie since it avoids the uncomfortable fact that the paralyzed-below-the-waist veteran is impotent.

Sally and Luke are put under surveillance by the Man. Just to emphasize what a hottie we're all supposed to think Fonda is, her screenwriters have a racist black FBI agent observing her through a long-distance camera lens, suddenly blurt out, "She's got a nice ass—for a white girl!" For other characters who are supposed to see the aging Fonda as attractive, witness the then-50-year-old actress portraying a 31-year-old virgin in *Old Gringo*.

In the end, after Sally's eyes has been opened by Luke's anti-war activism, Captain Hyde goes to the beach, throws his robe away and walks into the sea, never to return. (He was pro-war, so, in left-wing eyes he *has* to be punished.) And audiences everywhere quickly realized that Fonda and her collaborators stole the far more touching climax to *A Star Is Born*—both the Gaynor and Garland versions! In Dowd's original treatment, the husband more realistically dies while driving drunk.

Hyde's cliché-ridden suicide is also juxtaposed with a Marine captain speaking at a school, and then Luke giving a fiery, tear-streaked rebuttal (that won Voight the Best Actor Oscar). The depictions of these two characters, one pro-military and one anti-war, during their respective speeches, will now revive yet another movie cliché that director Hal Ashby, Fonda *et al.* were foisting on us. Certainly, there is no mistaking the filmmakers' point of view concerning the American military. The Marine giving a gung-ho, patriotic speech is portrayed as smug, humorless, pompous and arrogant. When Luke tears down everything the leatherneck is saying, he scowls and glares at this obviously peacenik interloper. Yet the whole scene, with little change except for time periods, is stolen from the classroom scene in *All Quiet on the Western Front*! Instead of the pro-war teacher exhorting his students to fight for the Kaiser and the Fatherland and getting his spiel shot down by Lew Ayres' bitter young veteran, here we have a Marine officer speaking at schools around the country hoping to increase recruitment—a sometimes thankless job—only to have his sales pitch shot down by a veteran who was now a *peacenik*.

Though the film was a hit, the execution (screenplay, direction and acting) were emblematic of the typical clumsiness and unsubtle propaganda of Fonda's usual film output of the 1970s and '80s (witness everything from *Steelyard Blues* and *The China Syndrome* to *Rollover* and *The Morning After*). Apologizing for "the harm" she caused the veterans—though never apologizing for the act itself; that is, of aiding and abetting an enemy power during wartime—Fonda won the Best Actress Oscar for *Coming Home*. Typically, however, this would include stealing Louise Fletcher's moving acceptance speech when she won as Best Actress for *One Flew Over the Cuckoo's Nest* the year before.

The "guests" at various Hanoi Hiltons around North Vietnam were not so lucky.

The floodgates were now open as Hollywood filmmakers endeavored to depict the Vietnam War at home and "in country."

Francis Ford Coppola conceived the idea of doing a Vietnam film as early as 1975, yet he inevitably focused on a six-year-old script written by John Milius (he began it in 1967 and finished it on December 5, 1969). The conservative screenwriter took Joseph Conrad's rather ponderous *Heart of Darkness* and transferred its messianic lead character (an ex-soldier holding sway over African natives) and made him an ex-colonel holding sway over Cambodians, using his fiefdom as a base of operations to launch attacks on both Americans and Viet Cong.

The character of Kurtz was Conrad's racist fantasy of a charismatic white man easily leading the rather pliable natives (who ordinarily wouldn't have been so easily misled) into carrying out his own agenda. As played by Marlon Brando in Coppola's *Apocalypse Now* (1979), Kurtz is a fat, homily-spouting demagogue who just lumbers in and out of frame in the latter half of the over-long movie. With the casting of the overfed Brando, *no one* was going to believe he was a talented West Pointer who became one of the Army's best officers.

The CIA sends Captain Willard (Martin Sheen) out to terminate the corpulent colonel with extreme prejudice. In other words, Joseph Conrad meets Black Ops. The Department of Defense wasn't buying it. Years later, Major Ray Smith of the Pentagon's film office said, "I read the script and said, 'We can't do this. The Army does not lend officers to

"THE HORROR, THE HORROR" OF BEING OVER-BUDGET: The always eccentric Marlon Brando as the renegade Colonel Kurtz in Francis Ford Coppola's *Apocalypse Now!* (1979).

the CIA to execute or murder other army officers.' And even if we did, we wouldn't help you make it."[8]

Apocalypse Now was over-produced, over-long, badly acted, atrociously directed by a full-of-himself director. (It was assumed Coppola could do no wrong after the *Godfather* movies.) Along with the future release of Michael Cimino's *Heaven's Gate*, it helped put an end to the struggling United Artists. There are reams of material detailing "the horror, the horror" of Coppola's elephantine misfire, from the rampant hedonism and drug-taking of the personnel involved, to the egotistical whims of its director, to the typhoons that occurred during the Philippine location shoot. Then there were dealings with the corrupt government of Philippine President Ferdinand Marcos, whose armed forces charged Coppola's company astronomical fees—much of which Marcos and his generals kept for themselves—for helicopters, military equipment and thousands of Filipino troops to appear as extras in battle scenes. The budget shot up from $12 million to $31.5 million.

Roles were turned down by many male stars of the day: Steve McQueen, Jack Nicholson, Al Pacino, Gene Hackman, etc. The first Captain Willard, Harvey Keitel was fired after a week; replacement Martin Sheen suffered a heart attack. Brando's salary and his time-killing antics sucked up much of the film's budget. The actor spent hours and hours with Coppola discussing his character and doing pointless improvisations while the meter was running; an expensive scene with Christian Marquand as a French planter (shades of *South Pacific*!) was cut; and Coppola could never think of an ending—though his employers at United Artists couldn't think of anything *but*.

Interviewed in the October 1979 issue of *Millimeter*, the director pompously claimed, "My film is not a movie. It's not about Vietnam. It *is* Vietnam."[9]

Well, it wasn't. That is, unless the Vietnam War was a bloated, expensive, overblown and pretentious exercise of artistic expression by a driven and pretentious helmsman. Indeed, the director turned the Vietnam War into a cartoon with live-action characters either shooting at or blowing each other up—Punch and Judy with hand grenades and BARs; napalm in the morning and firefights that end as soon as they start; a phony, disingenuous Vietnam where the armies of Ho Chi Minh are as relevant to the proceedings as a T. Rex in an MGM musical. Coppola didn't have the range or the talent to convey the Vietnam-as-living-dream vision that he was aiming for. (Stanley Kubrick succeeded years later in the final third of *Full Metal Jacket*.) Instead of surreal, Coppola's version of Vietnam was *unreal*. This was definitely highlighted by his rather one-sided portrayal of the American military.

Besides the tormented Willard (whom we first see drowning himself in booze in his room) and the sinister officers of Army G-2 at the beginning of the film, there is Robert Duvall's gung ho Lt. Colonel Killgore, the officer who likes the smell of napalm in the morning. He wears a 19th century cavalry campaign hat, lords it over his men, and basically sets up attacks as excuses for surfing, campfires, barbecues and importing scantily clad dancing girls to entertain his men—kind of an X-rated USO. His men also shoot up villages and kill their inhabitants, including the murder of a woman reaching into a basket, though she's actually reaching for her puppy. When it looks like a wounded woman will slow the troops down, Willard "solves" the problem by blowing her brains out. However, one brainwashed Cong tot is still able to calmly toss a grenade into an Army helicopter, murdering everyone in the vicinity.

Coppola lingered too long with his Vietnam epic; the much better-made *The*

Deer Hunter won the Oscar for Best Picture in 1979 and newcomer Michael Cimino won as Best Director. (The depressed and jealous Coppola served as a presenter!) However, because Cimino depicted the Vietnamese as murderers and exploiters, Jane Fonda confronted him at the Oscars and called him and his film racist. Of course, during her rant, she ignored Viet Cong atrocities and neglected to mention her own little appearance on that anti-aircraft gun. *The Deer Hunter*'s foreign distribution was also predictable: Unlike *Apocalypse Now* and Fonda's *Coming Home*, Cimino's film was *not* seen at the Moscow Film Festival.

Still, to Coppola and his *Apocalypse Now* screenwriters, it was the *Americans* who were going to take the brunt of the audience's contempt. The Navy men going upriver with Willard are a dysfunctional lot as well; more like drug-takers and psychotic losers than seasoned crewmen, with their penchant for panic and hysteria being their most prominent feature. By this time, this was such a common portrayal of the American fighting man by Hollywood filmmakers that one might wonder why these men were ever called heroes.

As we headed towards the 21st century, the American military film entered its predictable stage.

There would still be interference, or at least a little dabbling, by the motion picture sections of various branches of the military; only the tone from the film industry would be one of defiance, not compliments. Soldiers, officers and government figures would more likely be depicted as sinister figures involved in world-shaking cover-ups, sometimes in the name of National Security. There would be no more pro-military works like *Battle Cry* or "military musicals" produced by Warner Brothers.

There were still truly fine films depicting the military experience—even if they were more fantasy than reality (like Kubrick's *Full Metal Jacket*). But there were also far more realistic gems like *Hamburger Hill*. In *Full Metal Jacket*, Kubrick gave us the Vietnam War as dream-like delirium, an approach Coppola failed at attaining in *Apocalypse Now*. With smooth tracking shots through waves of smoke and fog in semi-darkness, with a soundtrack that at times seems to block out normal sounds in favor of droning hums, punctuated by bombs and gunfire, Kubrick gave us a "police action" fought in a land of ghosts. When R. Lee Ermey's psychotic D.I. takes up screen time in the first third of the film, we see the recruits terrorized by a monster who's the stuff of nightmares. As our heroes' platoon is being picked off by a mystery sniper, this attack on the men is far less personal than Sgt. Hartman's destructive insults, but far more permanent. Still, when attacked by the enemy, as in practically every other film made about Vietnam by Hollywood at the time, the troops fumble, panic and scramble about helplessly, sometimes screaming. All this self-defeating behavior could only mean that all of Hartman's harsh discipline amounted to absolutely nothing. Only the macho grunt called Animal Mother is able to liquidate the pajama-clad female VC sniper. The monster of this particular nightmare is destroyed and our heroes triumphant, but Kubrick's ending is ambiguous, because right around the corner there could be other monsters in pajamas (another clue that the final third of the film was like a dream). For all the millions squandered on *Apocalypse Now*, it could never approach Kubrick's nightmarish vision of war—a vision of madness that harkened back to his classic *Paths of Glory*.

In the military-themed films that followed, government conspiracies, sinister officers and the "deep state" became far more commonplace than the old war or

VI. Ceasefire

"LISTEN UP, MAGGOTS!": Ex-Marine war veteran R. Lee Ermey in his signature role as the "hard but fair" Marine Drill Instructor Sgt. Hartman, in Stanley Kubrick's *Full Metal Jacket* (1987).

service films featuring our Armed Forces personnel as heroes. At this point, even if our military wasn't guilty of a blunder, Hollywood would make one up for our usually civilian maverick hero to correct.

How did it get this way? How did the movies go from respect for our Armed Forces personnel to condemnation? Part of it was Vietnam. After the My Lai Massacre and the abuse of the Vietnamese population our soldiers were supposed to protect, Hollywood reflected this new attitude and took steps to demythologize our military. On top of this approach, the country as a whole started to look at *all* previously venerated American institutions as corrupt, especially if said institutions were part of the government; the FBI, the CIA, the president and, of course, the military.

The film divisions of the various branches of the military still work with producers to try to ensure a positive view of the American fighting man or woman, but then *every* institution everywhere wants positive portrayals of their people. It was the job of the military professional dealing with the media to put a positive spin on their activities; and there's nothing wrong with that. It's only when they lie about their blunders, or attempt to bury embarrassing scandals that they stray from their stated goal of reporting the truth to the American people.

However, to say that everything our military has ever done is deceive us and that there were never any American heroes is a lie. If they had not been on the field of battle, or in the air, or at sea, defeating the armies of tyranny, those of us still left alive would probably be speaking German, Japanese or Russian (that is, if you didn't ordinarily speak these languages before). And if our Army of Democracy failed and the forces of totalitarianism reigned, then we would not be allowed to write books like this or any others which would shed light on our mutual histories, warts and all.

And if not for those real-life American heroes who fought and died for us, thousands of others, including Harry and Helen Herzberg, would not have survived.

And though John Ford's *Fort Apache* is set in the late 19th century, the simple words delivered by John Wayne's Kirby Yorke are as true today as ever:

> The faces may change ... the names ... but they're there. They're the regiment. The regular army. Now, and fifty years from now....

Chapter Notes

Chapter I

1. Leslie Midkiff DeBauche, *Reel Patriotism: The Movies and World War I*, XV.
2. Ibid.
3. Mary Raymond Shipman Andrews, *The Three Things*, 1–2.
4. DeBauche, *Reel Patriotism*, 128.
5. Ibid., 131–132.
6. Lea Jacobs, *The Decline of Sentimentality: American Film in the 1920s*, 135.
7. Ibid., 135.
8. Lawrence H. Suid, *Guts and Glory: The Making of the American Military Image in Film*, 30–31.
9. Ibid., 31.
10. Raoul Walsh, *Each Man in His Time*, 185–186.
11. Michael T. Isenberg, *War on Film: The American Cinema and World War I*, 121.
12. Wikipedia, *USS S-4 (SS-109)*; Submarine Force Museum, *The Loss of USS 4*.
13. Ibid.
14. Ibid.
15. Ibid.
16. Wikipedia, *Frank H. Brumby*.
17. Wikipedia, *Tell It to The Marines (1925 film)*.
18. TCM website, *Submarine (1928)*, Articles.
19. Joseph McBride, *Frank Capra: The Catastrophe of Success*, 198.
20. Ibid.
21. Mordaunt Hall, *New York Times*, August 31, 1928.
22. Ibid.
23. "Land," *Variety*, September 5, 1928.
24. Ibid.
25. Ibid.

Chapter II

1. Wikipedia, *The Bonus Army*.
2. Ibid.
3. Edward Ellsberg, *Pigboats*, 1.
4. Mordaunt Hall, *New York Times*, April 26, 1933.
5. Lawrence H. Suid, *Sailing on the Silver Screen: Hollywood and the U.S. Navy*, 24.
6. Ibid.
7. Ibid., 23–24.
8. Ibid., 25.
9. Ibid.
10. Ibid., 24–25.
11. Margaret Herrick Library, *Here Comes the Navy* file, from Joseph I. Breen to Warners (no specific name listed on the memo; August 16, 1934.
12. "F.S.N.," *New York Times*, July 21, 1934.
13. Robert Sklar, *City Boys: Cagney, Bogart, Garfield*, 45.
14. Herrick, letter from Breen to Jack Warner, July 29, 1937, *The Invisible Menace* file.
15. Ibid., August 3, 1937.
16. Ibid., January 18, 1938.
17. Herrick, Letter from Breen to Harry Cohn, February 15, 1935, *Devil's Playground* file.
18. Ibid.
19. Herrick, letter from Breen to Warner, July 21, 1936, *Devil's Playground* file.
20. Suid, *Sailing on the Silver Screen*, 40.
21. Ibid.
22. Ibid.
23. Herrick, Memo from Breen, recommended cuts for distribution to the United Kingdom, March 16, 1937, *Devil's Playground* file.
24. Herrick, letter from Anthony Muto to Fred W. Beetson, October 20, *Devil's Playground* file.
25. Herrick, Letter to Cohn from Admiral William D, Leahy, Undated, *Devil's Playground* file.
26. Herrick, letter from Muto to Beetson, February 24, 1937, *Devil's Playground* file.
27. Herrick, Breen memo to unknown name dealing with cuts to the film for Japanese audiences, November 21, 1939, *Wings of the Navy* file.

Chapter III

1. Herrick, Synopsis from Breen office's C.R. Metzger, March 19, 1941, of *They're in the Navy*.
2. Bob Furmanek and Ron Palumbo, *Abbott and Costello in Hollywood*, interview with Alex Gottlieb, 52.

3. *Ibid.*, 52.
4. Steve Twomey, *Countdown to Pearl Harbor: The Twelve Days to the Attack*, 7: letter from Commander James O. Richardson to CNO Harold Stark, May 13, 1940.
5. Twomey, *Countdown to Pearl Harbor*, 5.
6. *Ibid.*, 8.
7. Scott Eyman, *Print the Legend: The Life and Times of John Ford*, letter from John Ford to General Albert Wedemyer, October 1944, 278.
8. Joseph McBride, *Searching for John Ford: A Life*, 354.
9. *Ibid.*, 353.
10. *Ibid.*, 355.
11. *Ibid.*, 384.
12. James Harris, *Five Came Back: A Story of Hollywood and the Second World War*, 207.
13. McBride, *Searching for John Ford*, 386.
14. Stephen E. Ambrose, *Americans at War*, Page 143.
15. *Ibid.*, 144.
16. Suid, *Guts and Glory*, 69.
17. *Ibid.*, 71; Bosley Crowther, *New York Times*, June 4, 1943; unknown reviewer, *Time*, June 7, 1943.
18. John R. Satterfield, *We Band of Brothers: The Sullivans and World War II*, 148.
19. Bruce Kuklick, *The Fighting Sullivans*, 109–110, letters from Alleta Sullivan to Nell Turner, April 15, November 6, 1943.
20. *Ibid.*, 188; Kuklick, *The Fighting Sullivans: How Hollywood and the Military Make Heroes*, 109.
21. *Ibid.*, 110.
22. *Ibid.*, 109.
23. Bosley Crowther, *New York Times*, February 10, 1944.
24. Kuklick, *The Fighting Sullivans*, 158.
25. Suid, *Guts and Glory*, 92; War Department to Lester Cowan, November 27, 1943.
26. *Ibid.*, 92; Cowan to War Department, June 28, 1944.
27. *Ibid.*
28. Suid, *Guts and Glory*, 93; Cowan to War Department, July 6, 1944.
29. *Ibid.*
30. Suid, *Guts and Glory*, 93; Wellman, William A. *Short Time for Insanity*, Pages 81–82.
31. *Ibid.*
32. Lee Server, *Robert Mitchum: Baby, I Don't Care*, 84.
33. *Ibid.*
34. *Ibid.*, 85.
35. Suid, *Guts and Glory*, 95; Wellman, *Short Time for Insanity*, 83–99.
36. Otto Friedrich, *City of Nets: A Portrait of Hollywood in the 1940s*, 390.
37. Suid, *Guts and Glory*, 94–95.
38. Frank T. Thompson, *William A. Wellman*, 213–214.
39. Wikipedia, *Battle of Monte Cassino*.
40. *Ibid.*
41. *Ibid.*
42. *Ibid.*
43. Andrew Roberts, *Masters and Commanders: How Four Titans Won the War, 1941–1945*, 435.
44. *Ibid.*, 472.
45. *Ibid.*
46. *Ibid.*
47. Wikipedia, *The Battle of Monte Cassino*.
48. Clayton R. Koppes and Gregory D. Black, *Hollywood Goes to War*, 306.
49. *Ibid.*, 307–308.
50. Thompson, *William A. Wellman*, 215.

CHAPTER IV

1. Frank J. McAdams, *The American War Film: History and Hollywood*, 196; James Bradley with Ron Powers, *Flags of Our Fathers*, 321–322.
2. *Ibid.*
3. Suid, *Guts and Glory*, 144.
4. *Ibid.*
5. *Ibid.*
6. James Jones, *From Here to Eternity*, 330.
7. Suid, *Guts and Glory*, 144.
8. *Ibid.*, 145.
9. *Ibid.*
10. *Ibid.*, 144.
11. Wikipedia, *From Here to Eternity the Boo.*
12. Daniel Eagan, *America's Film Legacy: The Authoritative Guide to the Landmark Movies in the National Film Registry*, 472.
13. Unknown reviewer, *Variety*, August 31, 1953.
14. Suid, Sailing on the *Silver Screen: Hollywood and the U.S. Navy*, 120.
15. *Ibid.*
16. *Ibid.*
17. *Ibid.*
18. *Ibid.*
19. *Ibid.*
20. *Ibid.*
21. *Ibid.*
22. *Ibid.*, 122.
23. *Ibid.*
24. Herman Wouk, *The Caine Mutiny Court-Martial*, 126.
25. USC-Warner Archives, memo from Raoul Walsh to Steve Trilling, February 12, 1954, *Battle Cry* file.
26. *Ibid.*, memo from Walsh to Trilling, February 5, 1954.
27. Tab Hunter and Eddie Muller, *Tab Hunter, Confidential: The Making of a Movie Star*, 87.
28. USC-Warner, memo from Walsh to Trilling, February 27, 1954, *Battle Cry* file.
29. *Ibid.*
30. *Ibid.*, memo from Walsh to Jack L. Warner, March 8, 1954.
31. Marilyn Ann Moss, *Raoul Walsh: The True Adventures of Hollywood Legendary Director*, 343.
32. *Ibid.*

33. USC-Warner, letter from Leon Uris to Henry Blanke, October 19, 1953.
34. *Ibid.*, Memo for the Files, December 23, 1953, from "M.V.M." detailing meeting between Warner officials and Geoffrey Shurlock of the PCA.
35. *Ibid.*, letter from Uris to Blanke, October 19, 1953.
36. *Ibid.*, letter from Breen to Hal McCord, July 1, 1954.
37. *Ibid.*, letter from Breen to Warner, February 22, 1954.
38. *Ibid.*
39. *Ibid.*
40. David L. Robb, *Operation Hollywood: How the Pentagon Shapes and Censors the Movies*, 289.
41. *Ibid.*, 292, 296.
42. *Ibid.*, 293.
43. *Ibid.*, 293–294.
44. *Ibid.*, 294.
45. USC-Warner, letter from Walsh to General Lemuel C. Shepherd, December 10, 1954, *Battle Cry* file.
46. Robb, *Operation Hollywood*, 346–347.
47. Douglas Waller, *A Question of Loyalty*, 362.
48. Peter Brunette, ed., *Robert Aldrich: Interviews*, Aldrich interview with Ian Cameron and Mark Shivas, 1963, 26.
49. *Ibid.*, Aldrich Interview with George N. Fenin, 1956.
50. Robb, *Operation Hollywood*, 298.
51. *Ibid.*, January 30, 1956.
52. Robb, *Operation Hollywood*, 298–299.
53. *Ibid.*, 299.
54. *Ibid.*; Aldrich interview with *Variety*, February 24, 1956.
55. Robb, *Operation Hollywood*, 300.
56. IMDB Trivia, *Attack!*
57. Crowther and Bosley, *New York Times*, September 20, 1956.
58. Hunter, *Tab Hunter Confidential*, 134.
59. Wikipedia, *Ribbon Creek Incident*.
60. *Ibid.*
61. *Ibid.*
62. Herrick, Memo for the Files, re: Moore, from "J.A.V." to Jack Webb at Warners, February 8, 1957.
63. Irwin Shaw, *The Young Lions*, 288.
64. *Ibid.*, 289.
65. Suid, *Guts and Glory*, 165.
66. *Ibid.*
67. Kate Buford, *Burt Lancaster: An American Life*, 107; Louella Parsons, *Los Angeles Examiner*, October 12, 1950.
68. TCM Notes, *The Naked and the Dead*.
69. Moss, *Raoul Walsh*, 363.
70. Wikipedia, *The Naked and the Dead*.
71. Norman Mailer, *The Naked and the Dead*, 82–82.
72. Wikipedia, *The Naked and the Dead*.
73. *Ibid.*
74. Jeffrey Meyers, *Gary Cooper: American Hero*, 297.
75. Glendon Swarthout, *They Came to Cordura*, 158.
76. Meyers, *Gary Cooper: American Hero*, 298.
77. *Ibid.*, 297.

CHAPTER V

1. TCM, Articles, *I Aim at the Stars*.
2. Eric Lichtblau, *The Nazis Next Door: How America Became a Safe Haven for Hitler's Men*, 10.
3. *Ibid.*, 94.
4. *Ibid.*, 96.
5. *Ibid.*, 94.
6. Crowther, *New York Times*, October 20, 1960.
7. TCM Articles, *I Aim at the Stars*.
8. Herrick, letter from Shurlock to Walter Mirisch, April 25, 1961, *Town Without Pity* file.
9. *Ibid.*
10. *Ibid.*, undated synopsis from unknown writer.
11. Mick Broderick, *Reconstructing Strangelove: Inside Stanley Kubrick's Nightmare Comedy*, 101.
12. *Ibid.*, 110.
13. Gene Healey, *The Cult of the Presidency: America's Dangerous Devotion to Executive Power*, 96.
14. *Ibid.*
15. Wikipedia, General Edwin Walker.
16. *Ibid.*
17. Broderick, *Reconstructing Strangelove*, 38.
18. Buford, *Burt Lancaster: An American Life*, 228.
19. Herrick, Rod Serling, undated synopsis, *Seven Days in May* file.
20. Kirk Douglas, *The Ragman's Son*, 324.
21. *Ibid.*, 321.
22. *Ibid.*
23. *Ibid.*
24. Arthur Knight, *Saturday Review*, February 14, 1964.
25. Bosley Crowther, *New York Times*, February 20, 1964.
26. Brunette, *Robert Aldrich: Interviews*, Interview by Joel Greenberg, 1968, 50.
27. Crowther, *New York Times*, June 16, 1967.
28. Brunette, *Robert Aldrich: Interviews*, Interview by Harry Ringel, 1974, 83.
29. *Ibid.*
30. Ebert, Roger, *Chicago Tribune*, July 26, 1967.
31. *Hollywood Reporter*, June 16, 1967.
32. *Ibid.*
33. Herrick, Synopsis by unknown writer, read by Maeve Southgate, January 20, 1941.
34. Wikipedia, *Carson McCullers*.
35. Carson McKullers, ed., and Margarita G.

Smith, *The Mortgaged Heart: The Selected Writings of Carson McKullers*, 277.
36. Lawrence Grobel, *The Hustons: The Life and Times of a Hollywood Dynasty*, 578.
37. *Ibid.*, 579.
38. *Ibid.*, 580.
39. *Ibid.*, 583.
40. Roger Ebert, *Chicago Tribune*, October 17, 1967.
41. Gary Carey, *Brando!* 223–224.
42. TCM Articles, *Reflections in a Golden Eye*.
43. Tony Mastroianni, *Cleveland Press*, November 9, 1967.
44. United States Conference of Catholic Bishops, no date.
45. Unknown reviewer, *Time*, October 27, 1967.
46. Unknown reviewer, *Variety*, December 31, 1966.
47. Grobel, *The Hustons*, 583.
48. Randy Roberts and James S. Olson, *John Wayne: American*, 535.
49. *Ibid.*, 540.
50. Michael Wayne, Interview with New York Times, September 27, 1967.
51. Robb, *Operation Hollywood*, 282.
52. *Ibid.*
53. *Ibid.*, 283.
54. *Ibid.*
55. Renata Adler, *New York Times*, June 20, 1968.
56. Unknown reviewer, *Hollywood Reporter*, June 17, 1968.
57. Kevin Hillstrom and Laurie Collier Hillstrom, *The Vietnam Experience*, 143–144.
58. Richard Schickel, *Life*, July 19, 1968.
59. Hillstrom and Hillstrom, *The Vietnam Experience*, 144.
60. Roger Ebert, *Chicago Tribune*, June 26, 1968.
61. A.H. Weiler, *New York Times*, January 3, 1969.
62. Ring Lardner, *I'd Hate Myself in the Morning: A Memoir*, 162.
63. *Ibid.*
64. *Ibid.*, 161–162.
65. Unknown writer, Interview in *New York Times Magazine*, June 20, 1971.
66. Unknown writer, *Hollywood Citizen News*, June 20, 1970.
67. Robert Altman, interview with *Playboy*, August 1975.
68. Roger Ebert, *Chicago Tribune*, January 1, 1970.
69. George C. Scott, interview with *Playboy*, April 1971.
70. Suid, *Guts and Glory*, 261–262.
71. USC-Warner, memo from W.L. Guthrie to Steve Trilling, October 6, 1953, *Patton Story* file.
72. Martin Blumenson, *Patton: The Man Behind the Legend*, 1885–1945, 202.
73. Nicholas Evan Sarantakes, *Making Patton: A Classic War Film's Epic Journey to the Silver Screen*, 16.
74. *Ibid.*, 18.
75. *Ibid.*, 93.
76. Ladislas Farago, *The Last Days of Patton*, 53.
77. *Ibid.*, 54.
78. *Ibid.*, 55.
79. *Ibid.*, 126.
80. *Ibid.*, 160.
81. *Ibid.*, 164.

Chapter VI

1. Suid, *Sailing on the Silver Screen*, 188.
2. Peter Biskind, *Easy Riders, Raging Bulls*, 174.
3. Merle Miller, *Plain Speaking: An Oral Biography of Harry S. Truman*, 315.
4. Robert Sherrod, *Time*, July 4, 1977.
5. Hillstrom and Hillstrom, *The Vietnam Experience*, 75.
6. Herrick, letter from Dr. John T. Chase to Charles P. Mulvehill, Production Manager at United Artists, January 13, 1977, *Coming Home* file.
7. Herrick, letter from Paul W. Mills to Mulvehill, September 22, 1976, *Coming Home* file.
8. Robb, *Operation Hollywood*, 141.
9. Hillstrom and Hillstron, *The Vietnam Experience; Millimeter*, October 1979.

Bibliography

Books

Ambrose, Stephen E. *Americans at War*. Jackson: University Press of Mississippi, 1997.

Belknap, Michal R. *The Vietnam War on Trial: The My Lai Massacre and the Court-Martial of Lieutenant Calley*. Lawrence: University Press of Kansas, 2002.

Bendersky, Joseph W. *The "Jewish Threat:" Anti-Semitic Politics of the U.S. Army*. New York: Basic Books, 2000.

Bennett, David. *A Magnificent Disaster: The Failure of Market Garden, the Arnhem Operation, September 1944*. Drexel Hill, PA: Casemate, 2008.

Beschloss, Michael. *The Conquerors: Roosevelt and Truman and the Destruction of Hitler's Germany, 1941–1945*. New York: Simon & Schuster, 2002.

Biskind, Peter. *Easy Riders, Raging Bulls*. New York: Touchstone, div. of Simon & Schuster, 1998.

Blumenson, Martin. *Patton: The Man Behind the Legend*. New York: William Morrow, 1986.

Brighton, Tony. *Patton, Montgomery, Rommel: Masters of War*. New York: Three Rivers Press, 2008.

Broderick, Mick. *Reconstructing Strangelove: Inside Stanley Kubrick's Nightmare Comedy*. New York: Wallflower Press, 2017.

Buford, Kate. *Burt Lancaster: An American Life*. New York: De Capo Press, 2000.

Carey, Gary. *Brando!* New York: Pocket Books, 1973.

Cawthorne, Nigel. *Turning the Tide: Decisive Battles of the Second World War*. London: Arcturus Publishing, 2002.

Christensen, Terry. *Reel Politics: American Political Movies from Birth of a Nation to Platoon*. Oxford, UK: Basil Blackwell, 1987.

DeBauche, Leslie Midkiff. *Reel Patriotism: The Movies and World War I*. Madison: University of Wisconsin Press, 1997.

Dick, Bernard F. *The Star-Spangled Screen: The American World War II Film*. Lexington: University Press of Kentucky, 1985.

Douglas, Kirk. *The Ragman's Son: An Autobiography*. New York: Pocket Books, 1988.

Eyman, Scott. *John Wayne: The Life and Legend*. New York: Simon & Schuster, 2014.

_____. *Print the Legend: The Life and Times of John Ford*. New York: Simon & Schuster, 1999.

Farago, Ladislas. *The Last Days of Patton*. New York: Berkley Books, 1981.

Fleming, Thomas. *The New Dealers' War: F.D.R. and the War Within World War II*. New York: Basic Books, 2001.

Fursenko, Aleksandr, and Timothy Naftali. *"One Hell of a Gamble": The Secret History of the Cuban Missile Crisis*. New York: W.W. Norton, 1997.

Harris, Mark. *Five Came Back: A Story of Hollywood and the Second World War*. New York: Penguin Press, 2014.

Herzberg, Bob. *The Left Side of the Screen: Communist and Left-Wing Ideology in Hollywood, 1929–2009*. Jefferson, NC: McFarland, 2011.

_____. *The Third Reich on Screen: 1929–2015*. Jefferson, NC: McFarland, 2017.

Hillstrom, Kevin, and Laurie Collier Hillstrom. *The Vietnam Experience*. Westport, CT: Greenwood Publishing, 1998.

Holzer, Henry Mark, and Erika Holzer. *Aid and Comfort: Jane Fonda in Vietnam*. Jefferson, NC: McFarland, 2002.

Hunter, Tab, and Eddie Muller. *Tab Hunter Confidential: The Making of a Movie Star*. Chapel Hill, NC: Algonquin Books, 2005.

Hurley, Alfred F. *Billy Mitchell: Crusader for Air Power*. Bloomington: Indiana University Press, 1964.

Isserman, Maurice, and Michael Kazin. *America Divided: The Civil War of the 1960s*. New York: Oxford University Press, 2000.

Jones, James. *From Here to Eternity*. New York: Charles Scribner & Sons, 1951.

Jordan, Jonathan W. *American Warlords: How Roosevelt's High Command led America to Victory in World War II*. New York: New American Library, 2016.

Knebel, Fletcher, and Charles W. Bailey II. *Seven Days in May*. New York: Harper & Row, 1962.

Koppes, Clayton R., and Gregory D. Black. *Hollywood Goes to War: How Politics, Profits and

Propaganda shaped World War II Movies. New York: The Free Press, 1987.

Kuklick, Bruce. *The Fighting Sullivans: How Hollywood and the Military Makes Heroes*. Lawrence: University Press of Kansas, 2016.

LaGuardia, Robert. *Monty, a Biography of Montgomery Clift*. New York: Avon Books, 1977.

Lichtblau, Eric. *The Nazis Next Door: How America Became a Safe Haven for Hitler's Men*. New York: Houghton, Mifflin, Harcourt, 2014.

Mailer, Norman. *The Naked and the Dead*. New York: Henry Holt, 1948.

Manning, Paul. *Hirohito: The War Years*. New York: Bantam Books, 1986.

McAdams, Frank J. *The American War Film: History and Hollywood*. Los Angeles: Figueroa Press, 2005.

McBride, Joseph. *Searching for John Ford: Life*. New York: Faber & Faber, 2001.

Meacham, Jon. *Franklin and Winston: An Intimate Portrait of an Epic Friendship*. New York: Random House, 2003.

Miller, Eugene L., and Edwin T. Arnold, eds. *Robert Aldrich: Interviews*. Jackson: University Press of Mississippi, 2004.

Miller, Merle. *Plain Speaking: An Oral Biography of Harry S. Truman*. New York: Berkley Books, 1973.

Moskin, J. Robert. *Mr. Truman's War*. New York: Random House, 1996.

Robb, David L. *Operation Hollywood: How the Pentagon Shapes and Censors the Movies*. Amherst, NY: Promethius Books, 2004.

Roberts, Andrew. *Masters and Commanders: How Four Titans Won the War in the West, 1941–1945*. New York: HarperCollins, 2009.

Sarrantakes, Nicholas Evan. *Making Patton: A Classic War Film's Epic Journey to the Silver Screen*. Lawrence: University Press of Kansas, 2012.

Satterfield, John R. *We Band of Brothers: The Sullivans in World War II*. Parkersburg, IA: Mid-Prairie Books, 1995.

Shachtman, Tom. *Terrors and Marvels: How Science and Technology Changed the Character and Outcome of World War II*. New York: HarperCollins, 2002.

Stafford, David. *Roosevelt and Churchill: Men of Secrets*. Woodstock, NY: The Overlook Press, 1999.

Suid Lawrence. *Guts and Glory: The Making of the American Military Image in Film*. Lexington: University Press of Kentucky, 2002.

_____. *Sailing on the Silver Screen: Hollywood and the U.S. Navy*. Annapolis, MD: Naval Institute Press, 1996.

Thompson, Frank T. *William A. Wellman*. Metuchen, NJ: Scarecrow Press, 1983.

Toland, John. *Infamy: Pearl Harbor and Its Aftermath*. New York: Doubleday, 1982.

Twomey, Steve. *Countdown to Pearl Harbor: The Twelve Days to the Attack*. New York: Simon & Schuster, 2016.

Waller, Douglas. *A Question of Loyalty*. New York: HarperCollins, 2004.

Wetta, Frank J., and Martin A. Novelli. *Last Stands from Alamo to Benghazi*. New York: Rutledge, 2017.

INTERNET SOURCES

Internet Broadway Database
Internet Movie Database
www.navalhistory.org
Anatomy of a Tragedy: The Sinking of the S-4
Turner Classic Movies website
www.wikipedia.com
Maxwell Anderson
Lieutenant General Frederick Browning
Admiral Frank H. Brumby
Edward Ellsberg
Laurence Stallings
Ribbon Creek Incident
USS S-4 (SS-109)
USS S-51 (SS-162)
Frank Wead

Index

Abbott, Bud 36, 44, 157
Albert, Eddie 102, 103, 104
Aldrich, Robert 2, 101–102, 103–104, 105, 106, 144, 145, 146
Alexander, Gen. Sir Harold 75
Alexander, Ross 35
All Quiet on the Western Front 9, 104, 175
Altman, Robert 156, 157, 158, 159
Alvin, John 65
Anderson, Maxwell 8
Andrews, Dana 50
Andrews, Mary Raymond Shipman 6–7
Andrews, Robert Hardy 55–56
Apocalypse Now 3, 156, 176–178
Arnaz, Desi 55
Atlas, Leopold 70
Auer, Mischa 37

Back to Bataan 153
Bacon, Lloyd 38, 63, 64–65
Barrett, James Lee 108, 150, 151
Bataan 53–58
Battle Cry (film) 90–95, 114
Battle Cry (novel) 3, 4, 89–90, 94–95
The Battle of Midway 49, 52–53
Battleground 78
Baxter, Anne 65
Beery, Wallace 20
Behind the Door 20
Bellamy, Ralph 98, 99
Best, James 116
The Big Parade 12, 16
Blake, Robert 129
Boardman, Eleanor 17
Bogart, Humphrey 88, 89
Bond, Ward 65
Borgnine, Ernest 82, 143
Bowman, Lee 55
Boyd, William 9
The Boys of Company C 31, 171–172

Bradley, General Omar 162, 163
Brando, Marlon 112–113, 147, 148, 149, 169, 176
Breen, Joseph I. 31, 32, 38, 39, 40, 91, 92
Brent, George 42
A Bridge Too Far 170–171
Bronson, Charles 143, 145
Brooks, Norman 101, 104–105
Brown, Jim 143, 145
Buck Privates 36, 134
Burdick, Eugene 133
Butler, General Smedley 18–19
Byrd, Ralph 49

Cabot, Bruce 151, 153
Cagney, James 13, 32–33, 34, 65, 100
The Caine Mutiny (novel) 1, 85–86, 87, 89
The Caine Mutiny (film) 1, 2, 44, 86–89, 95, 102
Callan, Michael 118
Calley, Lt. John W. 135, 155
Capra, Frank 21, 22
Cassell, Wally 71, 73, 75
Cassevetes, John 143, 145
Castro, Fidel 134
Chaney, Lon, Sr. 17–19
Chodurov, Edward 39, 40
Chodurov, Joseph 39, 40
Churchill, Sir Winston 54, 76, 162, 163, 171
Cimino, Michael 177
Clark, Fred 100
Clark, General Mark 75–76, 77
Clift, Montgomery 3, 84, 111–112, 147
Cloak and Dagger (1945) 51
Cohen, Sammy 13
Cohn, Harry 19–20, 21, 39, 41, 81, 82, 86, 161
Coming Home 156, 173–176
Command Decision 6
Conway, Jack 28, 31

Coolidge, President Calvin 8, 14, 97–98
Cooper, Gary 98, 99, 100, 117–118, 119, 120, 121
Cooper, Merian C. 46
Coppola, Francis Ford 176, 177–178
Costello, Lou 36, 44–45, 157
Court-Martial of Billy Mitchell, The 98–101
Cowan, Lester 68–70, 71
Cromwell, Richard 7, 39
Crossfire 2, 80

Dailey, Dan 13
Daly, James 127, 128
Davenport, Harry 49
December 7th 47–52
The Deer Hunter 177–178
De Havilland, Olivia 42
Del Rio, Dolores 11, 12, 41, 42
Dern, Bruce 174
Devil and the Deep 38
Devil's Playground 40–42, 81–82, 98
The D.I. 18, 108–110
The Dirty Dozen (film) 143–146, 156
The Dirty Dozen (novel) 143–144
Disney, Walt 123–124, 125
Dix, Richard 41
Dmytryk, Edward 2, 80, 85, 86, 89, 101, 111, 112, 153
Dr. Strangelove 133–135, 137–139
Donlevy, Brian 13
Donovan, William "Wild Bill" 48, 50–51
Douglas, Kirk 128, 129, 131, 139–140, 141, 142
Dulles, Allen 124
Dunn, James 77
Duvall, Robert 157, 177

Eadie, Thomas 15, 20
Ebson, Buddy 162
Edison, Thomas A. 7–8

Edwards, James 80, 172
Eisenhower, Gen. Dwight D. 2, 26, 136, 160, 162, 163, 165, 166, 170
Ellsburg, Lt. Commander Edward 27–28, 30
Endore, Guy 70
Engel, Samuel 50, 51
Ermey, R. Lee 79, 92, 107, 172, 178, 179
Evans, Madge 29, 30

Fail-Safe (film) 139
Fail-Safe (novel) 133
Farrow, John 37, 114
Fellig, Arthur (Ascher) "Weegee" 138
The Fighting Sullivans 63–68
Fonda, Jane 171, 172–173, 174, 175, 178
Foran, Dick 35–36, 45, 157
Ford, John 47, 48, 52–53, 55
Forster, Robert 147
Francis, Anne 90, 91–92
Frankenheimer, John 142
Freeman, Mona 90
From Here to Eternity (film) 1, 37, 83–87, 95, 111, 112
From Here to Eternity (novel) 2, 81–84, 85, 89
Full Metal Jacket 79, 92, 172, 178, 179

Gable, Clark 36
Garnett, Tay 55, 56, 57
George, Peter Bryan 132–133, 134, 137, 139
Geray, Steven 102, 104
The Girl He Left Behind 106–107
Gordon, Jean 161, 164–165
Gould, Elliot 156
The Green Berets (book) 108, 150–151
The Green Berets (film) 3, 78, 151–155, 172
Gregory, Paul 114, 115
Griffith, D.W. 12

Haines, William Wister 17, 32
Hamilton, Murray 18, 106–107, 110, 159
Harryhausen, Ray 126–127
Hayden, James, Sr. 159
Hayden, Sterling 135, 137
Hayworth, Rita 118, 119
The Heart Is a Lonely Hunter 146
Hearts of the World 12
Heflen, Van 90, 93, 118
Hell Below 28–32
Hellfighters 150
Here Comes the Navy 32–34

Herzberg, Harry 1, 180
Herzberg, Helen 1, 180
Hirohito, Emperor 44, 47
Hitler, Adolf 74, 125, 126
Holloway, Sterling 29, 31
Holt, Jack 20, 22
Home of the Brave 3, 4, 80, 86, 172
Homma, Gen. Masaharu 55
Hoover, President Herbert 14, 24, 54
Hoover, J. Edgar 51
Huffaker, Clair 150
Hunter, Tab 90, 106–107, 110, 116, 118
Hurley, Patrick J. 24, 25
Hurst, Paul 50
Huston, John 69, 147, 148, 149
Huston, Walter 28, 49
Hutton, Jim 153

I Aim at the Stars 123–128, 138
In the Navy 36, 44–45
The Invisible Menace 37–38

Jaeckel, Richard 102, 104, 129, 143
Janssen, David 106, 151, 152, 153
Johnny Got His Gun (novel) 40
Johnson, President Lyndon B. 123, 137, 142
Johnson, Nunnally 144
Johnson, Van 88
Jones, James 81–82
Jones, L.Q. 90
Jurgens, Kurt 123, 124, 126, 127, 128, 138

Karloff, Boris 37, 38
Kaufmann, Christine 129
Keeler, Ruby 35
Keep 'Em Flying 36
Keith, Brian 147, 149
Keith, Robert 118
Kellerman, Sally 157
Kellogg, Ray 151
Kelly, Paul 6
Kendall, Cy 37–38
Kennedy, George 143
Kennedy, President John F. 123, 136, 139, 140
Kennedy, Senator Robert F. 137, 142
Khrushchev, Nikita 140
Kimmel, Admiral Husband E. 46
Knebel, Fletcher 123, 139–140, 142
Knox, Frank 46, 48
Kramer, Stanley 2, 80, 86–87, 88

Kubrick, Stanley 133, 138–139, 140, 177, 178

Lamarr, Hedy 88
Lancaster, Burt 82, 114, 139, 142
Landsowne, Margaret 97, 99–100
Landsowne, Commander Zachery 97
Lardner, Ring 156, 157, 158
The Last Days of Patton 164–165, 166
The Last Detail 167–168
Laughton, Charles 38, 88, 114, 115
Law, John Phillip 101
Leahy, Admiral William 40
Lehrer, Tom 123
LeMay, Alan 74
LeMay, Gen, Curtis 135–136
Lindsay, Margaret 33
The Longest Day 177
Lopez, Perry 90
The Lost Patrol 55, 56–57
Lowe, Edmond 10, 12
Lowery, Robert 49
Lupton, John 90, 91–92

MacArthur (film) 169–170
MacArthur, General Douglas 25–26, 53–55, 56, 57, 98, 136, 160, 167
MacMurray, Fred 88
Mailer, Norman 3, 81, 114, 115–116
Malden, Karl 163
Malone, Dorothy 90, 91
Manilla Calling 56
March, Frederic 140
Marshall, General George C. 46–47, 54–55, 160, 162
Marvin, Lee 102, 104, 143
MASH (film) 156–159
Massey, Raymond 92, 115
McCall, Mary, Jr. 65–66
McCarthy, Frank 160, 161, 164, 165, 168–169, 170
McDonald, Kenneth 80
McGavin, Darren 98
McGlaglen, Victor 9, 11, 12, 13, 55–56
McHugh, Frank 34
McKee, Raymond 6, 7, 8
McKullers, Carson 146, 147–148, 149
Medina, Captain Ernest 155
Meeker, Ralph 143
Meredith, Burgess 71, 72, 75, 77
Meyer, Russ 143
Millan, Victor 93–94
Miller, David 106

Index

Mitchell, General Billy 95–98, 100–101
Mitchell, Thomas 56, 65
Mitchum, Robert 70, 72, 77, 114
Montgomery, Elizabeth 98, 99–100
Montgomery, Robert 28
Moore, Robin 108, 150–151
Morris, Chester 41
Morris, Wayne 38
Murder in the Fleet 36–37
Murphy, Audie 132

The Naked and the Dead (film) 3, 114–116
The Naked and the Dead (novel) 3, 70, 78, 81, 89, 114–115
Nathanson, Erwin Michael (E.W.) 143
Newman, Paul 90
Nicholson, Jack 167
Nolan, Lloyd 55, 56, 57, 114

Ober, Philip 37
O'Brien, Edmond 141
O'Brien, George 50
O'Brien, Pat 33, 34, 38
Olson, Nancy 90
Operation Eichmann 165
O.S.S. (film) 51
Oswald, Lee Harvey 132, 137
The Ox-Bow Incident (film) 50

Palance, Jack 102, 103, 104
Paris, Jerry 116
Parker, Fess 93, 94
Parker, Jean 37
Parrish, Robert 51, 52
Patton (the film) 162–164, 166
Patton, General George S. 26, 159–160, 161, 162–163, 165, 166
Payne, John 42
Peck, Gregory 169–170
Pershing, General John J. ("Blackjack") 117
Pichel, Irving 50
Pickens, Slim 139
Pigboats 27–28
Pitney, Gene 131
Powell, Dick 35–36
Power, General Thomas S. 136
Preminger, Otto 98
Pyle, Ernie 68, 69, 70, 71

Raintree County (film) 111
Ray, Aldo 90, 115, 152
Reagan, President Ronald 38, 67–68
Reflections in a Golden Eye (film) 147–150

Reflections in a Golden Eye (novel) 146–147
Reinhardt, Gottfried 130, 131, 132
Richardson, Admiral James O. 45–46
Roberts, Stanley 86, 87
Robertson, Cliff 115
Roosevelt, President Franklin D. 25, 44, 46, 47, 48, 52, 55, 58, 96
Rossen, Robert 117–118, 120
Royal, Selena 65
Royce, Lionel 49
Rudley, Herbert 112
Russel, Tony 132
Rutting, Barbara 130, 131
Ryan, Cornelius 171
Ryan, Robert 80, 143

Saint, Eve Marie 164
Sands of Iwo Jima 78–79, 80
Savalas, Telly 143
Schaffner, Franklin 162
Schneer, Charles H. 123, 126–127
Scott, George C. 134, 159, 162, 164, 168, 170
Scott, Kathryn Leigh 164
Sellers, Peter 138
The Sergeant 149–150
Serling, Rod 141
Seven Days in May (film) 3, 4, 139–142
Seven Days in May (novel) 139, 142
Shaw, Irwin 110–111, 112, 113
Shaw, Stan 172
Shipmates Forever 35–36
Short, Lt. General Walter C. 46
Sinatra, Frank 82, 83, 84
Skerritt, Tom 157
Smither, William 102, 103
So Proudly We Hail 56
Southern, Terry 139
Stalin, Joseph 163
Stallings, Laurence W. 8, 9
The Star Spangled Banner (film) 5, 6–7
Stark, Admiral Harold 51–52
Steele, Freddie 73
Steiger, Rod 100, 101, 150
Stimson, Secretary of War Henry 55
Stone, Lewis 35, 36
The Story of G.I. Joe 71–74, 76–77
Strauss, Robert 102
Stuart, Gloria 33
Submarine 19–22, 23, 39, 40
Submarine D-1 38
Sutherland, Donald 143, 156

Sutton, Frank 129
Swarthout, Glendon 116–117, 118, 120

Taradash, Daniel 81–82, 83, 84
Taylor, Elizabeth 111, 147, 148
Taylor, Robert 37, 56, 57
Tell It to the Marines 17–19, 23, 32
They Came to Cordura (film) 117–121
They Came to Cordura (novel) 116–117, 118
They Were Expendable (film) 53, 78
Thomspson, J. Lee 123
Tippit, Police Officer J.D. 132
Toland, Glenn 49
Toomey, Regis 38
Topper, Burt 132
Town Without Pity 3, 128–132
Trumbo, Dalton 39, 40, 41, 98
Tsu, Irene 151

The Unbeliever (film) 3, 6, 7, 79
The Unbeliever (novel) 6
Uris, Leon 89, 93, 94–95

Van Bergen, Ingrid 130
Van Eyck, Peter 102, 104
Vidal, Gore 116
Villa, Pancho 116–117
Voight, Jon 175
Von Braun, Wernher 123–126, 138

Walcott, Gregory 92
Walker, Clint 143
Walker, General Edwin 136–137
Walker, Mayor James 10
Walsh, Raoul 10–12, 13, 89, 90–91, 92, 114, 115, 116
War Is Hell 132
Warner, Jack L. 38, 63, 90, 91, 93, 106, 116, 161
Wayne, John 18, 78–79, 80, 150, 151–152, 153–154, 155, 156, 169, 180
Wead, Frank (Spig) 36, 37
Webb, Jack 18, 108–110
Wellman, William A. 50, 69–70, 73–74, 75, 77, 78
What Price Glory? (film) 3, 9–13, 23, 42, 90
What Price Glory? (play) 3, 9–13
Wheeler, Harvey 133
Whitmore, James 90, 93
Widmark, Richard 89
Willet, Irvin 20, 21
Wilson, Marie 37

Wilson, President Woodrow 50, 67, 117
Wings 69
Wings of the Navy 42–43
Wood, Natalie 106, 107
Woolheim, Louis 9
Wouk, Herman 44, 81, 85–86, 87

Wyman, Jane 37
Wynn, May 90

York, Dick 118
Young, Otis 167
Young, Robert 28
The Young Lions (film) 3, 4, 110, 111–113

The Young Lions (novel) 3, 81, 90, 110–112
Youngston, Robert 139

Zanuck, Darryl F. 63, 65, 67, 90, 161
Zinneman, Fred 84, 85, 113

www.ingramcontent.com/pod-product-compliance
Ingram Content Group UK Ltd.
Pitfield, Milton Keynes, MK11 3LW, UK
UKHW050524150426
5217IPUK00026B/1789